Progress in IS

More information about this series at http://www.springer.com/series/10440

Stefan Beissel

Cybersecurity Investments

Decision Support Under Economic Aspects

Springer

Stefan Beissel
Bergisch Gladbach
Germany

ISSN 2196-8705 ISSN 2196-8713 (electronic)
Progress in IS
ISBN 978-3-319-30458-8 ISBN 978-3-319-30460-1 (eBook)
DOI 10.1007/978-3-319-30460-1

Library of Congress Control Number: 2016932509

Printed on acid-free paper

This Springer imprint is published by SpringerNature
The registered company is Springer International Publishing AG Switzerland

Preface

Today, nearly every company uses the benefits of information technology and the Internet. Therefore, many companies are required to cope with cyberthreats. Only adequate cybersecurity safeguards can protect companies properly. Inadequate safeguards and subsequent breaches or outages can lead to tremendous financial losses and serious reputational damages.

The current big challenge is not the basic decision if a company should invest in safeguards, but, foremost, how much capital it should invest in safeguards. The priority should be to conduct the business safely without impairing the value creation of the company severely. Only the right balance between financial expenditures and risk mitigation helps a company to be solid and competitive in the long term.

In order to identify this balance, it is necessary to apply a multi-disciplinary approach that is located between computer sciences and economics. Only the skillful application and combination of knowledge from both fields can fully support the decision making for the selection of adequate safeguards. On the one hand, the background and provenance of cybersecurity is of great importance. A thorough understanding of information quality and value as well as related cybersecurity principles facilitates the selection and risk-based evaluation of safeguards. On the other hand, the foundations of investment management are essential to develop a reliable monetary assessment of safeguard benefits and costs. Practically proven decision techniques provide the basis for reasonable and transparent choices between multiple safeguards.

This professional book combines well-founded backgrounds on cybersecurity and investment management and, at the same time, delivers practical approaches from the economic point of view. It supports not only interdisciplinary experts but also technical and financial experts to handle cybersecurity investments in order to cope with current cyberthreats. A multi-disciplinary approach facilitates comprehensible decisions before investing in cybersecurity safeguards. Besides, it helps to establish valuable knowledge for the decision-making process in the cybersecurity domain.

Bergisch Gladbach
January 2016

Stefan Beissel

Contents

Chapter 1
Introduction

1.1 Threat Level in Cyberspace

The actual **threat situation** in cyberspace strongly depends on the openness and accessibility of the underlying computer network. Therefore, private company networks could be endangered, but foremost, every system connected to the Internet is threatened by massive attack waves. The Internet is the biggest and most open computer network in the world. Thereby, it is characterized by vast quantities of events caused by criminal and fraudulent activities.

These activities are not only increasing in quantity, but also in quality. They are becoming more and more **sophisticated**. If hackers attack particular companies specifically, they will develop and adjust appropriate threats. They focus on special characteristics of the company, including people, systems and infrastructure components. At first, they gain access to company owned devices and, thereafter, they spread malicious code through all vulnerable systems. The time window between hackers start to access the systems and the system owners recognize the attack is very worrying. In every second until disrupting the attack, hackers can cause severe damages.

The increasing **professionalism** of the hackers is especially remarkable. They belong to an own economic sector, which allows resourceful hackers to earn a substantial amount of money. The criminal scene is highly organized and partially similar to well-organized corporate groups.

Besides, the **tools and techniques** are quickly becoming more comprehensive and are available to an increasing group of people. The access of tools and techniques becomes easier, too. The Internet provides huge resources for hacking attempts and enables individuals to act nearly anonymously. Therefore, the temptation for amateurs to make a step towards criminal or fraudulent activities via the Internet is generally high.

Companies that do not ensure sufficient **protections** against these threats can suffer from compromise, manipulation and corruption of data and systems. Mostly,

S. Beissel, *Cybersecurity Investments*, Progress in IS,
DOI 10.1007/978-3-319-30460-1_1

the consequences are not only a delay of business processes but even expensive rework and reparation.

Besides, the **reputational** aspects usually play an important role. Breaches and outages leave a lasting impression at customers and business partners. This can affect customer retention and sales volumes crucially. Although security within the various Internet possibilities seems to be a matter of course for many people, they often are very touched in case of security incidents. Companies could create the impression that they did not handle customer-related data responsibly. Because customers can also suffer from huge financial damages and inconvenience after being a direct or indirect victim of a security incident, they quickly react very suspicious and often refrain from further businesses with the affected company. Customers know that many attackers focus on theft of financial data or other confidential information. Attackers that gathered this data do not only misuse it themselves, they also trade these data in the underground scene. Many criminals hope for a financial gain by misusing these data.

1.2 New Challenges for Cybersecurity

IT facilitates global businesses, enables market penetration and expansion, enhances resource management and lays the cornerstone for important innovations and new businesses. Especially, the interconnection between devices and systems increases remarkably. Of course, these changes and possibilities create new attack vectors, which can be exploited. New promising IT solutions are normally accompanied by previously unknown **vulnerabilities**. Safeguards must address these attack vectors and vulnerabilities, or else the new IT solution could cause damages that exceed the expected benefits.

New IT solutions and, thereby, new **challenges** for cybersecurity are characterized mostly by the high penetration by the Internet, the increasing integration of IT, a high use of mobile devices, and the demands on availability around the clock, as shown in Fig. 1.1.

- The **penetration by the Internet**—also called the Internet of things—is steadily extending, and even small devices are connected increasingly long. Nowadays, it is normal to use remote home control, e.g. via smartphone. However, the trend goes further and the integration of small-embedded systems into various physical objects is a current issue. Thereby, objects can be controlled and monitored remotely. The conditions of particular objects can be logged and, if needed, they can trigger a workflow. The possibilities go far beyond to those accompanied by the well-known barcodes. For example, automobiles are equipped by sensors that log and process all relevant data about their road behavior. In addition, livestock can be provided with biochip transponders that monitor its health condition. In the enterprise sector, the interconnection through the whole supply chain is continuously extended. Under the collective term

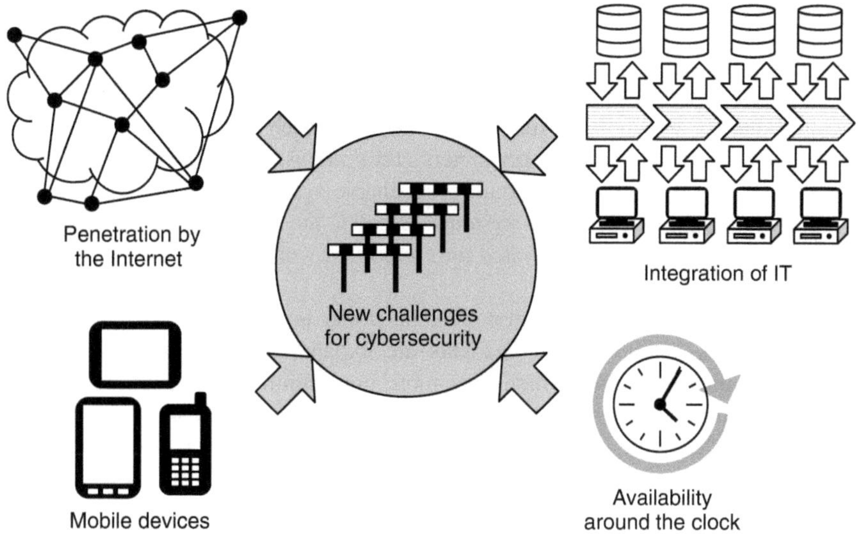

Fig. 1.1 New challenges for cybersecurity

Industry 4.0, every technology and associated progress is understood that facilitates the collection and usage of as much information as possible.

- The increasing complexity related to the **integration of IT** is caused by strong efforts of companies to generate more and more profit by increasing the effectiveness and efficiency of their workflows. The IT provides innovations regularly that can be used to accelerate workflows, enhance quality of products and services, enhance automation or just make the peoples' work easier. A common example is cloud computing, which can facilitate the information processing for companies enormously. By using cloud services, a company can access everything from infrastructure over platforms and applications. Everything required for work can be offered as a service. The staff just need computers with Internet connection.
- The extensive communication over networks is mainly characterized by the persistent popularity of **mobile devices**, e.g. smartphones. In addition, services and products around mobile devices are highly demanded. Today, huge digital markets for mobile apps are settled and they generate a tremendous turnover. The wide distribution and fast-paced market of mobile devices lead to new treats and new security concerns.
- Many private and business people are always online and continuously **available around the clock**. This trend goes hand in hand with the huge distribution of mobile devices. Besides, the boundaries between professional and private life are becoming more and more blurred. In many companies, it became natural to be continuously available, especially for managers.

Just like the importance and possibilities of the Internet is increasing, the attack possibilities and **threats** are growing continuously:

- In result of the penetration of the Internet, the **connection possibilities** of the attackers are expanding. Attackers are able to reach more systems and to get through sensitive company perimeters and systems. If the distribution of safeguards stays put, a bigger amount of reachable systems generally will lead to a bigger amount of vulnerable systems. Besides, the chance to find a vulnerable system that is strongly integrated into important workflows would be far higher than in the past.
- The incessantly communication over networks is also a reason that the connection possibilities of the attackers are expanding. At a given time, more systems are **reachable**, which give more opportunities to hackers to find and exploit vulnerable systems. Furthermore, systems that are always on generally do not have always the attention of the user. It is common that systems are continuously connected to the Internet, but they are unused and unwatched for hours every day. Hackers that exploit such an unwatched system have full control without being disrupted for a long time. This time is crucial because hackers can cause severe damages, and the more time they have available, the more damages can be caused, and the more traces can be erased afterwards.
- One might think that the increasing complexity of IT integration makes life harder for hackers, but the opposite is the case. The complexity makes it more and more difficult for the system owners to manage their systems. The result is an increase of **obsolete and vulnerable systems**. The company staff is often involved in such many activities that the slogan "Never touch a running system." is used still too often. In addition, a high complexity is no obstacle for hackers. Many hackers are very professional and are able to develop sophisticated attacks to most complex systems. This rather leads to the situation that system owners became practically unable to secure complex systems to the smallest detail. This detail can still be a gateway for professional hackers to infiltrate crucial systems and whole company infrastructures.

The field of cybersecurity is strongly influenced by these promising but also dangerous developments around the IT. Even one lonely vulnerable system within a company—the **weakest link**—can cause severe damages like interruption of critical supply systems, huge amounts of fraudulent financial transactions and long-lasting loss of trust and reputation. These damages cause not only financial problems, but also life-threatening situations, e.g. for hospital patients at risk.

Therefore, cybersecurity professionals are continuously required to develop and manage **safeguards** that protect valuable company systems and infrastructure against all kinds of attack. They have to become more nimble in their work and facilitate a more flexible behavior of the company in the case of new vulnerabilities or breaches. Besides, they have to make the company systems intrinsically more secure and increase their resilience against various attacks.

Companies are at risk when safeguards are not consequently implemented. The **quality** of safeguards and all actions affecting the safeguards have to be continually ensured. For example, the best (pattern-based) antivirus software will not operate effectively if no signature updates are delivered. Cybersecurity is not only characterized by higher quantity demands but also higher quality demands.

1.3 Integration of Economic Aspects

Although nearly every company understands the benefits of adequate safeguards, many of them are restrained regarding **budget** approvals and investment decisions. Normally, cybersecurity investments do not improve profits directly. Therefore, their benefits are difficult to demonstrate. The calculation of risks requires knowledge from the probability theory, which is often not easy to understand for people who are not familiar with it. The decision makers within senior management are often focused on investments that generate direct profit. The improvement of the existing value chain or ideas about new promising products, services or sales are preferred in most cases.

In order to protect a company effectively, cybersecurity professionals have to develop an expertise in using **economic indicators**. This expertise will be essential if they try to persuade senior managers. In addition, senior managers have to develop an understanding of economic aspects regarding cybersecurity. By this way, costs and decisions become more transparent.

However, this is not as easy as it sounds. The benefits of safeguards are hard to determine. If no breach occurred in the past, nobody would be able to predict precisely the amount of loss that can be prevented by safeguards in the future. Therefore, **estimations** have to be made that should be as exact as possible. Here, the specifics of the company in focus and its protection needs should be taken into account.

The best way to make reliable estimations is the integration of well-founded **economic indicators**. They facilitate the conviction of senior management and provide transparency even for outside parties. However, most traditional economic indicators cannot directly be used for cybersecurity. That is because safeguards generate no direct profit, but prevent losses that only occur at a specific probability.

To evaluate cybersecurity investments successfully, traditionally economic indicators must be adjusted and technological characteristics must be covered. Furthermore, the indicators must be integrated in a well-founded **decision technique** that considers the special preferences of the decision maker.

1.4 Outlook to the Following Chapters

In the following chapters, the **decision making** for cybersecurity investments is explained. It includes decision techniques, the selection and evaluation of criteria (hereafter called attributes), and the selection and evaluation of safeguards (hereafter called alternatives). Economic indicators are described to facilitate their calculation considering the special conditions of the company in focus and cybersecurity characteristics in general.

At first, the **foundations** of cybersecurity are shown. They enhance the understanding of cybersecurity, especially for managers outside the field. In the following, an overview of common safeguards is given. It helps to lay a ground for the selection of alternatives in the further process. The possible responses to breaches are described in order to enable a thorough understanding of consequences that could have been prevented by safeguards.

Technical details of cybersecurity are not described within this book. Moreover, a solid **understanding** is facilitated without going to much into detail. This suits to common management procedure. Mostly, implementation tasks are delegated to technical experts who are familiar within the field. For this delegation, a solid understanding is more important than knowing specific details.

Next, the chapter five starts, which explains the foundations of **decision making**. Primarily, basic terms and techniques are clarified here. In particular, the simple additive weighting and analytic hierarchy process are described. Besides, decision difficulties that might arise during the decision making process are identified and explained.

The sixth chapter illustrates the decision making process systematically. By considering essential steps, the outcomes of the decision making will be more reliable and solid. The decision making is embedded into a cybersecurity investment **lifecycle**. In addition to finding a proper decision, it covers all important life phases from initiation to termination.

The book is rounded off by a **summary**, which confirms and summarizes material contents of the book. The reader is provided with compressed information about main knowledge gains. Besides, a checklist is provided at the end of the chapter. It includes targeted key phrases that address the core issues of every step of the cybersecurity investment lifecycle. They can be seen as "takeaways" of knowledge after reading through the book or while getting a quick insight.

Chapter 2
Foundations of Cybersecurity

2.1 History

The use of **information systems** and the capabilities of the cyberspace became an integrated part of almost all companies and nearly every individual. Especially remarkable is the fact that the most important part of the cyberspace—the Internet—fundamentally transformed from an exclusive equipment of the government and academic institutions to an essential part of our whole society in less than three decades.

The beginning of the **Internet** is was primarily caused by the Advanced Research Project Agency (ARPA), which is an agency of the U.S. Department of Defense and today called Defense Advanced Research Projects Agency (DARPA). Its intention is to develop emerging technologies for military use. In the year 1969, it created the Advanced Research Projects Agency Network (ARPANET). The goal was to provide a computer network infrastructure that enables various universities to connect to each other and facilitate communication within research activities. It succeeded and the network was joined by more and more nodes over the following years. In 1973, European countries started to join the network, at first United Kingdom and Norway.

In 1981, the basic **protocols**, e.g. IPv4, for the connection and data transmission via the Internet were defined. They are still in use today. Due to the development of the Domain Name System (DNS) in 1984, the usage of human recognizable names for addressing computers within the Internet became possible.

In 1990, ARPANET was dissolved and remaining nodes were connected to the National Science Foundation Network (NSFNET). The NSFNET was created by the National Science Foundation (NSF) in 1979 and was formerly known as Computer Science Network (CSNET). The **commercialization** of the Internet began in 1991 when the NSF modified its acceptable use policy to allow commercial use, which was forbidden before.

S. Beissel, *Cybersecurity Investments*, Progress in IS,
DOI 10.1007/978-3-319-30460-1_2

The Internet had been shaped strongly by the possibilities of content representation to the users. Tim Berners-Lee started in 1989 to develop the Hypertext Markup Language (HTML) that helps to create **webpages** and to make them readable by web browsers. HTML was publically available since 1991. The popularity of the Internet increased highly when the first graphics-capable browser, which was named Mosaic, had been released in 1993.

The intensive integration of interactive content beyond static webpages became widespread in 2004 when the term **Web 2.0** was popularized at the O'Reilly Media Web 2.0 conference. Web 2.0 enhanced the interaction and collaboration between users and made user-generated content popular. The understanding of roles changed, because the internet users were no longer just content viewers, but furthermore, they were creators of their own content.

Currently, one of the biggest trends within the Internet is commonly known as **cloud computing**. Infrastructure, platform and application usage is offered and provided via the Internet to cover exactly the need of the users. They benefit from high flexibility in IT usage, and reduced complexity and costs of IT resources. They do not need to invest in hardware and software anymore. They just have to pay for services. The beginning of cloud computing is difficult to isolate, because even at the beginning of the Internet in 1969, the vision to be interconnected and access resources from everywhere was generally present. Surely, Microsoft, Google and Apple have a big influence by providing reliable and easy consumable services for the public.

Cybersecurity is as old as the cyberspace. Therefore, it is quite as old as the computer. However, real importance of cybersecurity has not been raised until the Internet became open to public access.

The first **cyber threat** was developed in 1989—just before the Internet provided new broad access possibilities beyond universities. The creator of the first cyber threat was Robert Morris, who understood to integrate self-propagating mechanism into the first computer worm. By this threat, highly malicious software vulnerabilities in UNIX systems had been exploited so that these systems became unusable. In result, the first widespread attack had been performed, which impaired the availability of many computers. In the following years, a vast number of viruses and other cyber threats had been developed. The number of threats strongly increased over time. Although the numbers move up and down from year to year, a trend of a general increase in vulnerabilities (Symantec 2015, p. 36) and security breaches (Identity Theft Resource Center 2015) can be seen clearly, as shown in Fig. 2.1.

The **threat landscape**, and the Internet security as a whole, is characterized by constant change. In the recent past, far-reaching vulnerabilities, faster attacks, files held for ransom, and far more malicious code than in previous years have been seen (Symantec 2015, p. 5).

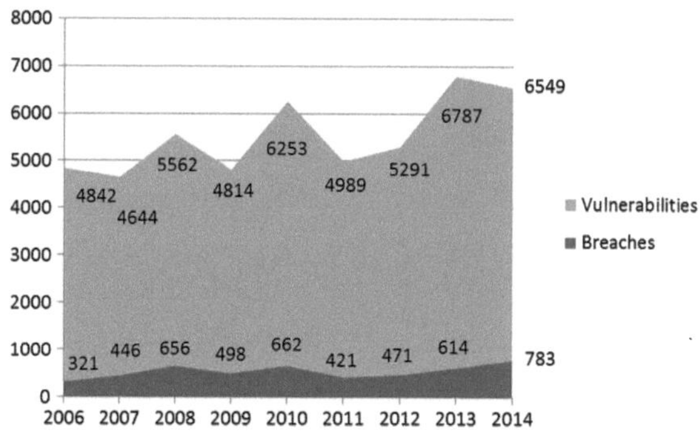

Fig. 2.1 Trend of vulnerabilities and breaches

2.2 Cybersecurity Principles

The **cyberspace** has been formed by the interconnection of information systems to computer networks, like the Internet. It enhances the capabilities of information systems broadly. These networks, especially the Internet, lead to a variety of benefits for company and personal use. Companies can reach an enormous number of potential customers. They can exchange time sensitive information around the globe in seconds. In addition, they can build an own cluster of knowledge, which can be accessed independent from the users' location. They can also participate from existing online communities. Individuals are enjoying the conveniences of the timeliness, transparency and comprehensiveness of information from the cyberspace. They are able to use constantly available shopping opportunities, communication possibilities from everywhere and an extensive knowledgebase.

However, the huge capabilities of the cyberspace are combined with serious **risks** for all connected information systems. Thereby, all information-related values could be at risk and potentially endanger the viability of whole companies, and the financial and personal safety of individuals. These risks are the consequences of countless threats mainly accompanied by the openness of the Internet. Sensitive or classified information could be stolen and misused. For example, competitors could gain advantage from strategic business information or criminals could misuse personal information for the purpose of identity theft or financial fraud. Important and valuable information could be manipulated or damaged. For example, criminals could manipulate the amount of financial transactions or damage files that are essential for business conduction, like customer records. Information systems and, thereby, all stored information could be unavailable because of attacks over the Internet, like a flooding with requests or a harmful infiltration of crucial information systems.

Cybersecurity includes all activities and measures intended to prevent and cover any threats regarding information systems connected to the cyberspace. The prevention of stealing and misusing sensitive or classified information is covered by the principle of confidentiality. The prevention of manipulating or damaging information is covered by the principle of integrity. The prevention of attacks

Fig. 2.2 CIA triad

against the availability of information systems is covered by the principle of availability. These are the three **basic principles** of cybersecurity (see Sect. 2.2.1 for details), which are often described as the CIA triad (see Fig. 2.2), relating to the first letters of these principles.

Furthermore, **extended principles** can be defined that correspond more or less with the above-mentioned basic cybersecurity principles. The extended principles are access control, regularity, legal certainty, authenticity, non-contestability, traceability, non-repudiation, accountability and reliability (see Sect. 2.2.2 for details). It strongly depends on the company which of the extended principles are desirable and sought. For some companies, accountability is very important while, for others, it is of less importance, e.g. because they might have such strict technical controls that performance deviations are prevented or quickly noticed. Some companies could seek obscurity to enhance the protection of their information assets while others could value transparency and pursue security by design.

2.2.1 *Basic Cybersecurity Principles*

2.2.1.1 Confidentiality

Confidentiality means that only authorized individuals or information systems should be able to **access information** that is not intended for the public. This can be achieved by preventing or disturbing activities of unauthorized individuals and systems that aim at the secrecy of private or business information. Attackers try to bypass technical or organizational safeguards in order to unveil information that can be used e.g. for their financial benefit or for harming their competitors. If this bypassing was successful and secret information could be read, the affected information would have been compromised.

Compromise of information and the subsequent misuse can lead to serious damages for the life, health and privacy of individuals as well as the existence of companies. Examples for information influencing the life and health are current medical data, and control data for critical systems. Not only can the data itself be worth to be protected, but also information about the communication process.

Information about which individual transferred or received data from specific sources or sinks can be very sensitive. After compromise, the concerned information could be misused to harm individuals or to disturb life-sustaining systems. Information about the informational self-determination and private interests, e.g. politics and religion, impair the privacy of individuals when compromised. The disclosure of such information could be uncomfortable or even defamatory. A company will be seriously affected, if e.g. secret research results and strategic plans are compromised. This can affect the competitive advantage as well as the financial or reputational situation of the company, possibly leading to bankruptcy.

Common **safeguards** for ensuring confidentiality are access control and encryption. Access control ensures that only authorized persons are allowed to access sensitive data within the company environment. For example, this can be implemented by Microsoft's active directory. However, if data leaves the company, access control will often be more difficult to operate than encryption. Encryption protects data on the hard drive or on the transmission path. The data can only be read by authorized persons that have the decryption key.

2.2.1.2 Integrity

Integrity is a condition, where information and information systems are fully protected against any kind of **manipulation or damage**. Thereby, it can be assured that the information is hundred percent correct. If facts of the real world are reflected by the information, it will have to include the truth without missing essential parts. The information must not be altered in any unintentional or undesirable way, neither by an individual nor by any kind of information system. If alteration of information cannot be excluded, at least, the alteration will have to be discovered and traced reliably. In addition, particular conditions can be essential for the integrity of information. For example, sequences or maximum delay times of transferred data over a network can be important. If the data transfer is not in correct order or if it is delayed too long, the receiver will no longer assume that the integrity of the related information has been met.

In order to ensure the integrity of information fully, both the unintentional and the malicious **type** of data modification must be taken into account. The unintentional part can be the result from technical defects or human errors. The malicious part can be the result from illegal or, at least, unethical attempts of individuals to gain any kind of benefits or to harm their opponents.

Common **safeguards** for protecting data integrity are hashing, and change management. Hashing includes the creation of check sums that can be used to detect if data has been changed. Changes can always be detected because even a small change within a file leads to a different check sum. With hashing, data can be regularly checked regarding intentional or unintentional changes within the company or on the transmission path. Change management is an administrative safeguard that requires all employees to change important data systematically and in a traceable way.

2.2.1.3 Availability

Availability is present if all systems and infrastructure components that are necessary to access and process information are ready for use and if they have sufficient capacity to process all requests quickly enough. The availability is importance because **time** is a valuable resource that can lead to serious benefits or drawbacks in conducting business tasks. Some business processes are time-critical, e.g. because of contractual agreements with customers, or dependencies to other processes. The delay of processes could result in high revenue-losses. External conditions can also lead to time-critical tasks, e.g. the transportation of perishable foodstuffs. The unavailability of crucial information usually delays the affected business processes. For example, a truck driver cannot look into the routing information of his GPS navigation system and has to make a long stop in order to read paper-based maps, and to plan his route manually.

The **capacity** of information systems can also have a serious impact on the availability. An example is a file server that cannot process any write commands because the hard disk storage capacity is completely occupied. Another example is a business application system that cannot be used by more than ten persons at the same time due to license restrictions. In order to protect the availability against capacity problems, all resources required to deliver the needed services must be controlled. In addition, all plans for short, medium and long-term business requirements must be taken into account. For example, a dramatically increase of costumer requests could lead to a high utilization of front-end systems.

Common **indicators** for rating the availability are the downtime und uptime. The downtime indicates how long a system or service was not available, and the uptime indicates how long a system or service has been run without problems or disruptions. Therefore, the availability can be expressed by the ratio of uptime to the sum of uptime and downtime:

$$Availability = \frac{Uptime}{Uptime + Downtime}$$

Another way to calculate the availability is the consideration of time to repair. It is assumed that every failure of a system or service needs to be repaired, and that during the time to repair, the system or service is not usable. The mean time between the occurrences of two sequential failures is called Mean Time Between Failures (MTBF) and the mean time needed to repair a failure is called Mean Time To Repair (MTTR). The availability can be expressed by the ratio of MTBF to the sum of MTBF and MTTR:

$$Availability = \frac{MTBF}{MTBF + MTTR}$$

The scheduled unavailability that is caused by maintenance events is not taken into the account by this formula.

Technical redundancy helps to increase availability rates further. By parallel processing capabilities, the overall availability will only be disrupted if all parallel nodes, e.g. similar servers, are down. The more nodes are present, the higher is the availability:

$$Availability_{overall} = 1 - (1 - Availability_{node})^{number\ of\ nodes}$$

Low availability rates can have a high negative impact on the efficiency of the company's supply chain or on the customer opinion. Availability rates will be of particular importance if the company must meet a service level agreement. If the actual availability rates are below the agreed ones, the company can be obligated to pay penalties.

Common **safeguards** that serve the protection of availability are backups and resilience: Backups ensure that data that has been lost or damaged can be recovered. The more often backups are made, the less data can get lost. Due to the required recovery time, the affected systems are temporarily unavailable. Unavailability can be prevented largely by raising the resilience of a system. Resilience means that a system becomes robust against negative influences. For example, an uninterrupted power supply raises the resilience of a system against power outages. Redundant hardware components, e.g. power supply units and hard drives, raise the resilience of a system against hardware failures.

2.2.2 *Extended Cybersecurity Principles*

2.2.2.1 Access Control

Access control is necessary to control the access to resources, including sensitive information and information systems. The idea is to **restrict access** as much as possible so that unauthorized individuals and potential criminals are not able to misuse access rights that actually would not have been necessary for business operations. The area of access control can be very challenging if a large number of users must be matched to a large number of resources, which also can be affected by continuous changes of the company's environment.

The **stages** of access control mechanisms in sequential order are identification authentication and authorization:

1. The **identification** is used to obtain the identity of a subject, particularly an individual or information system. The identity can be represented by a username or any other kind of unique characteristic.
2. The **authentication** is the process to verify that the given identity is truth. Thereby, the theft and misuse of identity shall be hampered. Common authentication measures are something a person knows, e.g. passwords, and

something a person has, e.g. tokens. Besides of these, something a person is, e.g. fingerprints, is a more secure and sophisticated way of authentication.
3. The **authorization** starts only after the authentication was successful. It matches the subject to the assigned access rights and checks if the desired operation is allowed, and if it does not contradict with the assigned access rights. Only after the successful authorization, the intended operation can be conducted.

The principle of access control itself also has subsequent **principles** that are called least privilege, separation of duties and need to know:

- The principle of **least privilege** means that, per default, nobody should have any access rights. The access rights must be assigned to a user or a user group explicitly.
- The principle of **separation of duties** forbids that a workflow can be fully performed by a single person. By splitting the workflow among multiple users, the risk of fraud and errors can be strongly mitigated.
- The principle of **need to know** requires that all access rights must only be assigned to someone who definitely needs them to perform his or her job.

2.2.2.2 Regularity

The regularity implies **conformity** of IT objects and processes to all required rules, e.g. as stated within laws or contracts. These rules are not only be made by external parties, but also by the company itself. Most companies require their staff to comply with internal guidelines. To fully comply with these rules, the staff has not only "to do the right things", but also "to do the things right". The first means that they have to follow certain processes or to develop certain objects, while the second means that they have to fulfill necessary tasks in the required or approved way.

Which **rules** from external parties have to be taken into account by a company, strongly depends on the location and industry sector of the company and the applicable laws, standards and best practices. For example, the US law includes:

- The **Health Insurance Portability and Accountability Act** (HIPAA) is mandatory for healthcare organizations. It was enacted in 1996, and it is focused on the protection of confidential patient records.
- The **Gramm-Leach-Bliley Act** is mandatory for financial institutions. It was enacted in 1999, and it requires the protection of customer data in the financial sector. Financial institutions must comply with security standards and develop enterprise-wide security policies.
- The **Homeland Security Act** (HSA) contains requirements around security, including information security, and it was enacted in 2002. Among others, it includes the Federal Information Security Management Act (FISMA), which binds federal agencies to secure the information and information systems that support their operations and assets.

Some important **standards** that are related to cybersecurity are:

- The **ISO 27000** series includes several standards relating to IT security. The most important standards in this series are ISO 27001, which contains a process model for an information security management system, and ISO 27002, which was derived in 2005 from the former ISO 17799, and which describes specific control measures for IT security.
- The **Payment Card Industry Data Security Standard** (PCI DSS) is an industry-specific standard for the Payment Card Industry. It aims to improve the security of cardholder data. It includes requirements for data security, and information about related test methods. The PCI DSS will be binding if a company stores, processes or transmits cardholder and authentication data.
- The **National Institute of Standards and Technology** (NIST) provides a resource for various information security standards and guidelines. Among other things, it developed a cybersecurity framework, which utilizes risk management principles and best practices to protect critical infrastructure, and cryptographic standards, which give guidance regarding the usage of algorithms and keys.

Some authors of **best practices** that support cybersecurity are:

- The membership organization **ISACA** has published the framework Control Objectives for Information and Related Technology (COBIT). It is a comprehensive framework to assist companies in achieving sufficient control by the governance and management of IT, including information security.
- The **Center for Internet Security** (CIS) is a non-profit organization that is specialized in IT security recommendations for private and public companies. Very popular are the security benchmarks that are focused on hardening of information systems, e.g. by disabling services, uninstalling software and setting important system parameters.
- In the European area, the **European Network and Information Security Agency** (ENISA) provides best practices around information security, e.g. guidance in cloud computing, incident response and building trust.

2.2.2.3 Legal Certainty

A company will achieve legal certainty if the **rights and obligations** resulting from applicable legal requirements are sufficiently clear, predictable and controllable. Thereby, the legal situation helps to provide an orientation for business actions and a safety in case of legal infringements by others.

For a company, legal certainty is necessary because the **infringement** of binding laws could cause financial and reputational damage. The financial damage can result from compensations for business partners and from penalties from legislative institutions. In addition, fraud by business partners can cause financial damages, especially if they are not held fully accountable. The reputational damage corresponds with a negative impact on the public opinion about the company. The public could avoid businesses with the company, on the one hand, because of ethical reasons, and, on the other hand, because people could assume unreliable work performance.

In order to achieve a sufficient legal certainty, a company should ensure to employ skilled **professionals**, who have solid knowledge in all relevant legal requirements. One option could be to hire a specialized law office. Contracts should be proofed very well regarding any rights and obligations. The work of the employees should be compliant to all relevant legal requirements, and it should be transparent so that this compliance can be proven in case of any dispute. This can be supported by well-trained employees who are supervised or audited sufficiently. Internal policies are an opportunity to restrict the work of the employees in order to ensure that no legal requirements are infringed. A log of all actions by business partners and costumers supports the preservation of evidence in case of fraud or any kind of disputes.

Furthermore, it should be considered that **internationally** operating companies are often faced to new legal situations that are caused by differences in legal requirements from country to country. Besides, to claim the own legal rights could be more or less difficult in other countries.

2.2.2.4 Authenticity

Authenticity means that someone or something has the characteristics of being **genuine and verifiable**. The reason behind authenticity is to get reliable indicators on how much trust should be granted to someone or something.

Authenticity is an important part of access control systems. Only a person or a system with an **identity** that was sufficiently proven should be able to get access to sensitive information and systems. Otherwise, attackers could be able to compromise, manipulate or disturb information and systems.

To prove a person's identity, three **factors** of authentication can generally be used. When two or three factors are combined, it is called two-factor or three-factor authentication. In particular, the three factors of authentication are:

- Something that the user **knows** is a secret information in the user's mind, e.g. a password. The longer and more complicated the information is, the more difficult it is to guess by an attacker. However, long and complicated information is quickly forgotten or written down by the user as a reminder.
- Something that the user **has** is an object owned by the user, e.g. a token. This object cannot be guessed, but there is a risk that it is stolen or lost.
- Something that the user **is** includes any biometric data about a user. Everything that makes a user unique can be used, e.g. a fingerprint, the tone of voice, the handwriting or the inner structure of the eye. This type of authentication can be very reliable, but the user acceptance could be difficult. Some controls like eye scanning can be uncomfortable for the users. Besides, if an attacker seeks to get biometric information by any means, the health and life of the users can be in danger.

In addition to identities, the **truthfulness** of documents, web pages and other kind of data need to be trusted often. Only the processing of trusted data can lead to reliable and sustainable results. For example, a fraudulent payment transaction should not be accepted. Otherwise, it should be challenged after processing so that the received payment can be refunded if possible. By sufficiently ensuring the authenticity of the cardholder, this situation can be avoided. Besides, web pages of companies are sensitive because they often have serious impacts on the costumer opinion and even provide purchasing and payment opportunities. By ensuring the authenticity of web pages, e.g. by digital certificates, the customers can be sure that a web page can be trusted and that it has not been spoofed.

Improper decisions made by authentication mechanisms are called false positives and false negatives:

- **False positives** are positive decisions about something that is actually false; therefore, these decisions should be negative. They are performed e.g. before granting access to a system. The authenticated person or object has not been sufficiently checked by the system. For example, access is achieved with a fake identity or a manipulated object.
- **False negatives** are negative decisions about something that is actually true; therefore, these decisions should be positive. The authenticated person or object is genuine and e.g. it has the right to access a particular system. However, by mistake the authentication was not proven genuine.

Furthermore, false negatives are also known as type one errors, and false positives as type two errors. False positives are generally much more **dangerous** than false negatives. False positives could lead to the situation that an attacker has access to sensitive information, while false negatives cause "only" inconveniences for rightful users.

2.2.2.5 Non-contestability

The term contestability refers to a situation when under legal conditions, particular rights and obligations can be declared **void or voidable**. Void rights and obligations are not valid from the beginning, and voidable ones are valid until they are repudiated or annulated. For example, a declaration of will could be void, if the person was under the influence of alcohol. A contract will be voidable if it is contested in court by one of the parties involved, but stays valid before.

Contestability can lead to the repudiation or annulation of **contracts**, which would be not enforceable anymore. If in consequence, previously legal transactions have to be rolled back, a huge administrative effort for a company can occur. Payments must be refunded and goods must be returned. Especially in case of huge and crucial business transactions, the contestability can cause big uncertainty and even financial damage. The company could already have initiated depending business transactions that are now built on an annulated contract. For example, after a contract with an important supplier has been concluded, multiple contracts with customers could have been followed. After it becomes known that the first contract is voidable and will be annulated, the company could suffer from price calculations that cannot be retained with alternative suppliers. Also resulting from missing supplies, time restrictions from customers could be infringed, which could cause contractually agreed penalties.

Therefore, companies generally try to avoid contestability. Essentially, this can be achieved by supporting the knowledge generation by employees and raising the awareness regarding doubtful situations. Among others, the following **situations** should be particularly taken into account:

- Contracts could be voidable due to a **mistake of fact**. If the performance of a contract is significantly affected by a mistake regarding a fact, the contractual partner will be allowed to repudiate it.
- If the contractual partner is **not physically or mentally able** to fulfill the contract, e.g. due to intoxication, he will have a lack of capacity. That makes a contract voidable.
- **Threat, coercion, undue influence and false statements** also make a contract voidable by the contractual partner, who has been negatively affected by a dubious behavior.
- A contract that has been conducted by a **minor** is voidable and can be repudiated by the minor or a guardian of the minor. The age of majority is reached at the age of 18 years in most states.
- Contracts that involve the contractual partner in **illegal** activities, like prostitution and gambling, are void directly.
- If certain activities are **restrained**, e.g. the right to marry or to work, the contract will also be void.
- A contract that contains clauses against **public policy**—the common sense of the community regarding social and legal situations—is void, too. Among others, the stipulation of unfair disadvantages to other companies, and the custody of a child cannot be contractually defined.

2.2.2.6 Traceability

Generally, traceability can be sought for various reasons. From outside the cybersecurity domain, it is often understood as the possibility to follow someone's conclusions and to **understand** his decision. In addition, traceability can mean that every single step within a chain of activities can be repeated after they have already been performed. In cybersecurity, traceability is focused on logging and monitoring all relevant activities, e.g. administrative activities on sensitive information systems.

In cybersecurity, it is crucial to trace the action of users and administrators. Otherwise, persons cannot be held **accountable** after a breach. This could lead to an unconcerned and possibly fraudulent behavior of employees. In addition, external parties could gain rightful or wrongful access to company owned systems. For example, the technical support of a vendor could use remote access. Without a full trace, nobody could know what exactly has been done by the remote user. Besides, a trace is very useful to support the monitoring of events. Particular events could be connected to user activities that facilitate the early detection and prevention of security breaches.

The **level of detail** that is used to generate traces depends on the preferences and capabilities of the systems' owners. At a less detailed level, only specific events could be logged, especially the ones that could possibly correspond to a security breach. At a more detailed level, all available information about user activities could be logged. Even a full video recording of his desktop can be possible. However, the more information has been logged, the more resources are used for tracing and the more difficult is the processing and monitoring of this information. The company should find the right balance between effort and security.

Although traceability is a security principle, in another context, it can also affect the security level of a company **negatively**. A company normally has a legitimate interest in logging all activities that could affect the security of sensitive information. However, traces that can be accessed by unauthorized persons could be a serious risk. Attackers would be able to analyze the user behavior and violate the privacy of users or the secrecy of sensitive information properties, e.g. the storage location. They could misuse this Meta information and discover additional vulnerabilities. Therefore, every company that generates traces must ensure a secure storage of these traces and enforce a strict policy of need-to-know. Besides, any kind of information regarding user behavior should be obscure because attackers often use this information to prepare a targeted attack.

2.2.2.7 Non-repudiation

Repudiation relates to sending and receiving data. If a person **denies** sending or receiving data and no one can prove otherwise, he will repudiate. The sender could repudiate sending data and the receiver could repudiate receiving data. The reason behind repudiation is mostly that a person does not want to be bound by the consequences of a data transmission, e.g. the approval of a payment transaction.

All measures a company implements to prevent repudiation have the purpose to achieve non-repudiation. Mostly, sufficient **evidence** is collected so that all sending and receiving are completely provable.

Within the private network of a company, non-repudiation is mostly achieved by requiring all users to enter unique **credentials** before using a company owned computer or accessing sensitive information. Thus, strong authentication systems can improve a strong non-repudiation.

One common possibility to achieve non-repudiation via the Internet is the usage of **digital signatures**. The evidence that a certain sender sent the data is generated by verifying his identity. Therefore, the data to be sent is encapsulated within a message that is signed. The signing is done by encrypting the hash value, or digital fingerprint, of the message with the private cryptographic key, which is only known by the sender. The receiver can verify the sender's identity by using the sender's public key for the decryption of the hash value. If the public key fits to the previously used private key, the identity of the sender will be verified. This type of cryptography is called asymmetric. It utilizes two different keys for encryption and decryption. In contrast, both operations are performed with the same key when symmetric cryptography is used.

The evidence that the **receiver** received the data is generated e.g. by a registered e-mail. Registered e-mails require the receiver to confirm his identity before accessing the e-mail, e.g. by entering a secret key.

2.2.2.8 Accountability

Accountability is a similar, but slightly weaker principle than non-repudiation. Since non-repudiation is focused on preventing the repudiation by a sender or receiver of data, it also has to be clear who sent or received the data. The clear **identification** of someone who sent or received data is called accountability.

Accountability can be achieved by the same measures as non-repudiation. The **difference** is primarily that, for accountability, only the identification is needed while, for non-repudiation, also the material evidence is needed that the identification has not been spoofed.

For example, activities executed via a **shared user account** can only be assigned to a particular person if further information is available, e.g. a staffing schedule. If these activities can be assigned to a particular person, this person will be accountable. However, this person can repudiate the activities if the evidence is not material. In contrast, a unique user account that needs biometric authentication would be sufficient to prevent a repudiation by the person.

2.2.2.9 Reliability

Reliability is an attribute of a system, a person, or a process. It defines in which extend pre-defined **rules or requirements** are fulfilled so that the residual risk of violating these rules or requirements can be tolerated by all stakeholders. The pre-defined rules or requirements include mainly cybersecurity requirements, like confidentiality, integrity and availability.

There is a strong connection between **regularity and reliability**. The regularity defines and demands compliance to pre-defined rules. The reliability demands that a violation of these rules has to be so improbable that there is only a small residual risk.

Besides rules, there are requirements, especially of information systems, that affect the **quality**. Software or hardware errors, which lead to outages or damages, must also be minimal. Only after the risk of errors has been mitigated sufficiently, the systems can be called reliable. An indicator for reliable systems regarding errors is e.g. the MTBF, known from the area of availability.

2.3 Protection Level

The **protection level** indicates how well the information and information systems of a company are protected from attacks or disturbances. A protection level that provides a protection of hundred percent can hardly be reached. If it were reached, it would only be of short time due to the fast moving IT environment. Instead of seeking full protection, an appropriate protection level should be seen as sufficient. Costs and benefits of the safeguards should be put in an appropriate **balance**. How a company evaluates the appropriateness of safeguards for themselves depends on the individual preferences of the company. In practice, the company should find a protection level that, on the one hand, excludes unreasonably high risks and, on the other hand, does not require costly safeguards that strongly affect the profit expectations of the company.

The **appropriateness** of safeguards can be defined as their effectivity, suitability, practicality, acceptability and efficiency (Federal Office for Information Security 2008, p. 65):

- **Effectivity**: The safeguards must provide effective protection against the possible threats, i.e. they must fulfil the identified security requirements.
- **Suitability**: It must be actually possible to implement the safeguards in practice, which means they must not impair the organizational procedures or bypass other security safeguards.
- **Practicality**: The safeguards should be easy to understand, easy to apply, and not prone to errors.
- **Acceptance**: All users must be able to use the safeguards (barrier-free), and the safeguards must not discriminate or adversely affect anyone.
- **Efficiency**: With the resources used, the best possible results should be achieved. On the one hand, the safeguards should minimize the risks as much as possible. On the other hand, the cost of implementation should remain in proper proportion to the value of the protected objects.

2.4 Protection Scope

The **protection scope** is determined by identifying the assets that have a specific protection need and all components that are related to these assets. From the **technical** view of cybersecurity, primarily all technical components that store, process, or transmit sensitive information are within the scope:

- While **storing** information, in other words interpretable data, data is technically recorded on a disk. This is done in the form of binary data, which can be converted by systems into program or text data. While program data need to be interpreted by a compatible system, text data can be directly interpreted by humans. Media that store these data can be used either stationary or mobile.

Stationary media are integral parts of systems, like servers, workstations, or network storage. Mobile media, for example CDs, DVDs, tapes and SD cards, can be read by using drives. Other mobile media, for example USB hard drives, USB sticks and FireWire hard drives, can be connected directly to system interfaces. In order to use media storage more efficiently, data are often compressed. Before using compressed data, a performance-intensive decompression must be performed. Therefore, compression is only useful for data that does not have to be directly available.

- The **transfer** of information is performed when data are transferred from one system to another system. For transmission, local area networks (LAN), for example, within a company building, and wide area networks (WAN), such as the Internet, can be used. The infrastructure of local networks can be wired or wireless (WLAN). The protection of confidentiality and integrity of transmitted data plays an important role, in particular for transmissions over the public Internet.
- The **processing** of information includes the transformation of interpreted data into different formats or structures. For example, they can be merged, distributed, enriched, abstracted or otherwise transformed. Processing is often part of a business process or supports it. For example, a merchant, who is active in e-commerce, can process customer data after receiving orders. Among other processing steps, invoicing and shipping are based on these data. The processing can be triggered by a user, who uses an application, or by a time or an event, which triggers a system that begins processing automatically. An example for a time trigger is the start of a certain weekday. An example for an event trigger is the creation of an order by an e-commerce customer.

The technical **components** that should be included in the scope are not only servers and workstations, but also many infrastructure components that are could be overlooked quickly. Examples for these components are:

- Servers that provide network services, like authentication, name resolution or web redirection
- Network segmentation and connection components, like firewalls, routers, switches, hubs and wireless access points
- All applications that are available internally and externally, even if they are hosted by an external service provider
- Other devices that are connected to systems that handle sensitive data, e.g. printers and scanners

In addition, the **organizational** view must be considered. In particular, people that handle sensitive data and processes that use sensitive data must be taken into account while determining the scope.

The correct **determination** of the scope can be very challenging. On the one hand, it should be avoided that relevant components are seen as out-of-scope, although they should not be. These components will probably be not secured sufficiently so that a hacker could easily attack them. On the other hand, it should be avoided that the scope is larger than it has to be. Sophisticated safeguards can be very costly so that components that should be out-of-scope can cause unreasonable costs if they are protected for no purpose. In order to determine the scope as accurate as possible, the following **tasks** should be performed:

1. Sensitive data should be defined so that sensitive data can be clearly distinguished from insensitive data.
2. The existence of sensitive data within the components in the scope should be verified.
3. The nonexistence of sensitive data within the components outside of the scope should be verified. If sensitive data are found outside of the scope, these data will have to be mitigated into the scope or securely deleted.
4. All locations of sensitive data and the related components should be documented, e.g. with a network diagram or an inventory list.

In order to reduce security requirements and testing needs for systems that process data, sensitive environments can be confined. Thereby, they can be isolated from systems with lower security requirements. Consequently, the scope of the sensitive environment has been **reduced**.

The limitation of scope is mainly useful under cost-benefit aspects. To assess the **cost-effectiveness** of the limitation, the investment costs and the operation costs must be compared to the potential savings. The investment costs include the cost of new hardware, software, and installation. In addition, organizational activities, e.g. developing work instructions and guidelines, must be considered. The operation costs include the costs of maintenance and administration of the new infrastructure. Potential savings from the limitation are caused by the fact that, in security design, development, administration and auditing, only systems within the limited scope must be considered. Thus, the effort regarding security can be reduced. In addition, the risk of compromise, manipulation or corruption of sensitive data and the subsequent damages can be reduced by a scope limitation. The administrative effort outside of the secure environment is also reduced because fewer requirements, e.g. regarding hardening, encryption, and logging, need to be implemented on the systems.

While limiting the scope, the potential need for future adjustments, in other words the **scalability**, should also be considered. If business changes and the data to be processed is affected, the company will have to scale the technology that is used to limit the scope. It can be necessary to scale the technology, if an outsourcing of data processing is planned and less sensitive data are processed internally.

Common **techniques** to limit the security scope within environments are tokenization, point-to-point encryption, network segmentation and outsourcing. While the first three techniques are based on technical means to isolate sensitive data, the last one is an organizational matter. In contrast to theses technical means, outsourcing does not reduce the security requirements in general, but rather shifts the duties to another party that has to protect the outsourced environment.

2.4.1 Network Segmentation

Network segmentation is used to **separate** the part of the network, where sensitive data are processed, from the remaining part in order to perform a targeted raise of the protection level. With the network segmentation, the access from insecure network segments to the secure network segment can be limited. Thus, many attack attempts can be blocked. The network segmentation serves to protect the confidentiality, integrity and availability because attack attempts of any kind can be blocked.

The technical **implementation** of the network separation (see Fig. 2.3) can be done with firewalls, routers, or switches with access control lists (ACL). Often, the connected systems are assigned logically to a virtual local area network (VLAN). ACLs can be used here so that the systems in the first segment—an isolated VLAN—cannot communicate with the systems in the second segment.

If network segmentation is implemented with **firewalls**, a standalone firewall will need to be positioned between the secure and the unsecure network environment. Firewalls can filter traffic. Thus, they provide the greatest possible protection in network segmentation. Firewalls and routers can connect network environments with different address ranges or architectures. This will be important if a network environment with a different architecture is present, which is supposed to exchange data with the secure network environment, e.g. for the remote maintenance of systems. **Routers** should be used for network segmentation if the traffic is not required to be filtered, but only to be passed between network environments. **Switches** do not have security features or filter options. If the switch model supports ACLs, it can only be configured with which network environment a system is allowed to communicate. Switches should be used for network segmentation if the network environments use both the same architecture and the same address range.

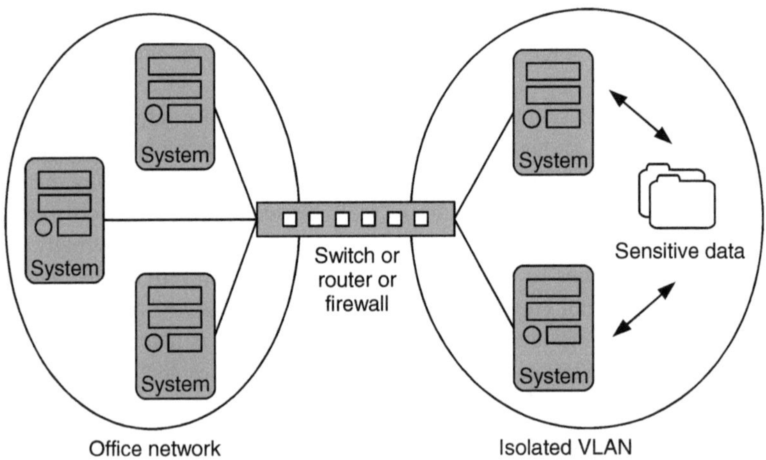

Fig. 2.3 Scope limitation with network segmentation

2.4.2 *Point-to-Point Encryption*

Point-to-point encryption allows **transmitting encrypted data** by encrypting the data at the starting point by the transmitter and decrypting the data at the end by the recipient. Therefore, all intermediate communication points no longer need to be in a secure environment. The point-to-point encryption prevents that tapped data can be read. If an attacker eavesdrops the network traffic, he will not be able to read the collected data. Consequently, it serves to protect the confidentiality.

On the side of the **transmitter**, an encryption component is used and, on the side of the **receiver**, a decryption component is used. These components can be a hardware module or software. Hardware modules are used e.g. in interaction points for card payments. For example, a transaction can be encrypted with this module on a payment terminal and decrypted with software in the secure environment of a payment service provider.

A distinction is made between the **symmetric and asymmetric** encryption technique: In the symmetric technique, the same key is used for encryption and decryption. In the asymmetric technique, data are encrypted with the public key and decrypted with the private key. The symmetric technique is much faster, but the asymmetric technique facilitates greater security because only the recipient is in possession of the decryption key. In practice, the symmetric and the asymmetric encryption technique are often combined (see Fig. 2.4). First, the transmitter sends its symmetric key to the recipient. To prevent that this key is intercepted by an attacker, it is encrypted using the public key of the recipient. Only the recipient is in possession of his private key and therefore only he can decrypt the symmetric key.

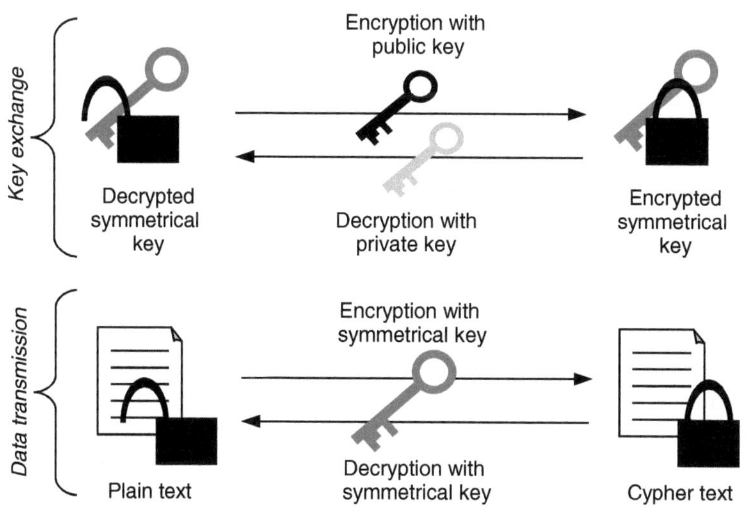

Fig. 2.4 Combined encryption

After both parties are in possession of the symmetric key, the transfer of the data, which is encrypted with the symmetric technique, can be performed.

When using point-to-point encryption, a **key management** must be operated. Thereby, it can be ensured that cryptographic keys are exchanged in case of a compromise or after a defined lifetime. Best Practices for key management have been published by the National Institute of Standards and Technology (NIST) in the Special Publication 800-57 (Barker et al. 2012, p 49 ff.). Each type of key has a certain recommended service lifetime. Private keys that are used to negotiate symmetric keys have a recommended lifetime of one to two years. Symmetric keys should be used for one month to encrypt data and can be used for several years to decrypt data.

2.4.3 Tokenization

Tokenization can be used if no special data contents are required within certain processing steps, but merely the unique **identification** of the data. Tokenization replaces sensitive data with tokens. It transforms sensitive data into anonymous strings—the tokens—that cannot be reconverted into the original data by an algorithm.

By using tokenization, systems that operate with tokens instead of sensitive data can be removed from the **secure network environment**. Tokenization prevents that sensitive data can be found and compromised in areas where only the uniqueness of the data is important. It serves to protect the confidentiality.

Tokens can be designed for single or multiple usage. In the **single usage**, a new token is created for each data value, e.g. a new consecutive number. In the **multiple usage**, always the same token is created for the same data. This usage facilitates cumulative evaluations.

The type of usage must be taken into account when choosing the **generation technique**: Encryption and hashing techniques automatically create the same token for the same data. If numbers are generated as tokens, an additional procedure should be integrated in order to reuse the same token for the same data value. The above-mentioned generation techniques are characterized as follows:

- If **encryption** technologies are used when generating tokens, the sensitive data will be encrypted and the resulting cipher text is used as a token. The possibility that tokens are transferred back to their original form is actually not needed or wanted in tokenization. The encryption key or algorithm could be hacked and, in result, the sensitive data could be compromised by hackers.
- **Hashing** is used to calculate small checksums from large data strings with an algorithm. Hashing is better suited for the generation of the tokens because the tokens cannot be transformed back into sensitive data. Although hashing was originally designed for integrity checks of data, the generated checksums are very suitable to be used as a token. However, the uniqueness of the token might

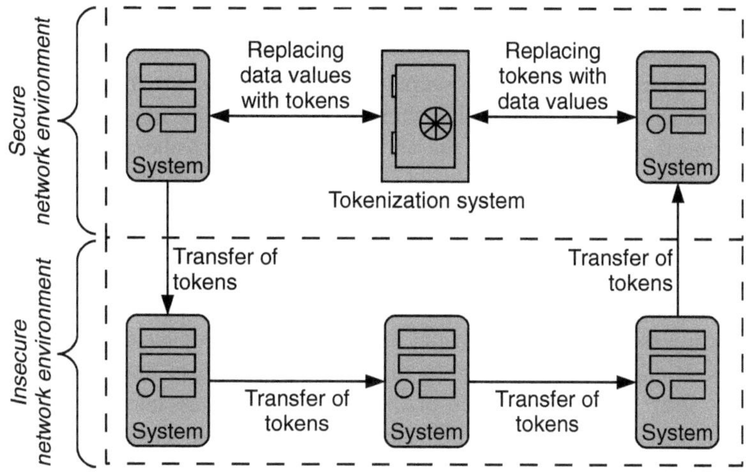

Fig. 2.5 Tokenization system and network environments

not be ensured if a hashing algorithm that is affected by collisions was used. Collisions occur if the same checksum is assigned to different data.

- Tokens can also be generated with **numbers**. Often, a serial number or a random number is used. In principle, any string can be used as a token. It just have to be ensured that it allows a unique identification, includes almost no collisions and cannot be easily converted back to its underlying original data.

Tokens cannot only be generated for individual data values, but also for a **combination** of two or more data values. Optionally, an additional data value (Salt) can be appended to the primary data before generating the token. This makes it more difficult for attackers to guess the original data.

Normally, the original data that is transformed into tokens is retained in its original form, too. The original data are stored in a highly secure environment. If a company wants to know which token represents which original data, an assignment of token to its original data will have to be performed. This is done with a **tokenization system** (see Fig. 2.5). Since the assignment is not possible by using mathematical algorithms alone, the tokenization system must provide association data. Besides the tokenization system, all systems that still process the original sensitive data should be positioned in a secure network environment and should be particularly protected.

2.4.4 Outsourcing

With outsourcing, certain business-related activities can be **transferred** to an external company. This company is contractually bound to perform these activities.

Outsourcing is a safeguard that can be also used to serve other security objectives (see Sect. 3.2.8).

However, in the context of scope limitation, especially those activities are transferred to external parties that include the processing of sensitive data. By transferring these activities and the according data out of the company, the necessary protection level can be reduced strongly. Thereby, activities that are affected by **high security requirements** are outsourced. In this case, it is important to specify the security requirements in the contract and to ensure that the contract is met by the external party. The security requirements should not only be specified in the outsourcing contract, but also related to claims for damages or contractual penalties in case of deviations. If the external party is specialized in high security activities, it can possibly provide a higher protection level than the outsourcing company itself. If several clients of the external party are interested in the protection, independent auditors will be hired to perform an objective audit and to certify compliance.

The outsourcing of activities will not keep the outsourcing company from taking **responsibility** if something goes wrong. The damages might be claimed against the external party, but in the public view, the outsourcing company is the one to blame. In conclusion, the outsourcing company should monitor the outsourced activities continuously. Therefore, the outsourcing company should have a current overview about which activities are outsourced and which are performed in-house. In consequence, the company has always an overview of in-house activities that can be used for planning audits. Auditors that are going to analyze in-house activities can save much effort if they use this overview as a starting point.

With outsourcing, the outsourcing company can optionally **transfer** assets, staff, buildings and existing contractual relationships to the service provider. Thereby, the outsourcing company can benefit from a high flexibility. No costly assets and buildings need to be unused and no staff need to be dismissed. Another advantage in transferring staff is that knowledge remains within the company. Staff can be transferred back to its employer, and, at the end of the outsourcing contract, important specialists will not be lost.

A similar approach to outsourcing is **out-tasking**. Here, specific IT activities are transferred to external parties under the requirement that all the resources and conditions are provided by the service provider. This approach causes high costs. On the one hand, the service provider might need to invest in additional resources. On the other hand, the outsourcing company often has to dismiss employees, which might lead to a loss of specialists and possibly to the payment of compensations.

Another approach is the use of **shared services**. Here, the outsourcing company buys shares from the service provider. The companies share a property and work together. In result, the outsourcing company has comprehensive control options due to its ownership. Shared services are not the ideal option for limiting the scope, because the activities that have been transferred are still performed by a part of the company.

2.5 Stakeholders of Cybersecurity

From the company perspective, stakeholders of cybersecurity are all persons and groups that have an eligible **interest** in the cybersecurity of the company. The term stakeholder can be defined very broadly. It can also include the interest holders that are connected to the company only in an indirect or temporary way, e.g. customers or political interest groups.

The interests of stakeholders can strongly influence the cybersecurity of a company. While some stakeholders, e.g. the members of senior management, have a **direct** impact on cybersecurity decisions, others, e.g. customers, have an influence that is more **indirect**. Customers can affect the sales of a company. Thereby, they can uphold interests in an indirect way.

As shown in Fig. 2.6, the stakeholders with interests in the cybersecurity of a company are mostly:

- **Company owners**, also called shareholders, have a strong interest in the influence of cybersecurity to the company's success. Depending on the company type, the success can be assessed from an economic, idealistic, social or cultural point of view. The economic success of the company can be measured, e.g. with earnings before interest and taxes (EBIT). For economic success, especially the effective management of resources is essential. Therefore, the owners are interested in an appropriate balance of costs and benefits from the cybersecurity safeguards.
- **Executive management** is interested in an optimal implementation of all objectives that have been defined by the company owners. They lead the employees to comply with requirements and to achieve work related targets. Regarding cybersecurity, the executive management gives rough instructions and monitors their detailing and fulfillment.
- **Department management** is responsible for the work of employees within their department. It puts the rough instructions by executive management into concrete terms and incentivizes the employees to meet or implement derived

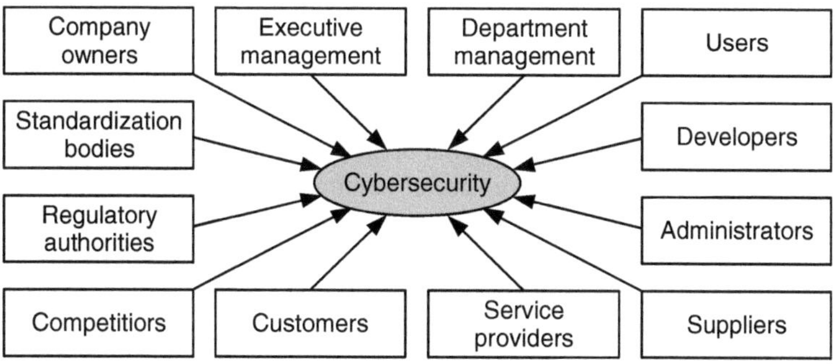

Fig. 2.6 Stakeholders of cybersecurity

objectives for their work. Cybersecurity objectives include e.g. the participation in trainings, the creation of handling instructions for electronic devices, or the secure storage of sensitive files.

- **Users** are interested in the best possible use of their work performance. They can profit from cybersecurity because a secure work environment helps them to concentrate on the work without being distracted, e.g. by outages of systems, or manipulation or comprise of data.
- **Developers** are supposed to consider actual knowledge about vulnerabilities during their coding. The best way to achieve a high protection level is to integrate cybersecurity by design. Already during the early planning phases, cybersecurity should generally be taken into account. Secure software leads to less rework and a tendency to more satisfied users.
- **Administrators** ensure that all systems are reliable and function as supposed. By hardening the systems, administrators make the systems more resilient against external attacks. Cybersecurity is an important way to raise the reliability.
- **Suppliers** deliver goods that are needed by the company to run through the supply chain. Cybersecurity is important to secure any communication between the supplier and the company. Furthermore, a breach could affect the business of the company severely so that the supplier might lose a valuable customer.
- **Service providers** provide various services to the company. Especially if the services are related to data processing, the information systems of the service provider and the company will often be meshed with each other. Therefore, a security breach will probably not only disrupt the processing, but also affect the service provider directly.
- **Customers** are in a business relationship with a company in order to receive a product, which can be a service or good. They are primarily interested in the product, especially in low prices and high quality. If the customers are in a long-term business relationship with a company, e.g. for regular purchases, not only product attributes, but also company attributes, like the cybersecurity protection level, will be of great importance.
- **Competitors** do often have a low interest in the cybersecurity of the company. A low protection level of the company could even lead to a migration of customers to competitors. However, the competitors could also be interested in a mutual improvement of cybersecurity. Because of partially similar processes and systems, a cooperation regarding cybersecurity could be beneficial for both.
- **Regulatory authorities** are mostly government institutions that require companies to adhere certain requirements or specifications. Their primary interest is to protect the public. They give special requirements that protect consumer data and raise the protection levels of companies in general. A well-known example is the Health Insurance Portability and Accountability Act (HIPAA) for the protection of confidential patient records.
- **Standardization bodies** include all companies or organizations that give mandatory or facultative rules for companies in general or for particular sectors. Mandatory rules must be fulfilled by companies and are found e.g. in laws.

Facultative rules can be fulfilled by companies optionally. Companies comply with mandatory rules to prevent the negative consequences, e.g. fines. They comply with facultative rules because they hope for further benefits. A common goal related to facultative rules is the standardization of processes and products. This can lead to a higher efficiency of internal operations, an improved use of resources and a positive public perception. Standardization can also lead to competitive advantage over companies that do not comply with these rules. Various certifications are available in the market. They allow certifying the compliance of facultative rules by an independent third party. A certification is often used as an advertising measure by the marketing department.

Prior to a cybersecurity investment project, there is sometimes uncertainty about the stakeholders, their relationship and their influence. A technique that helps to make this information transparent is the **stakeholder analysis**. It facilitates to distinguish cooperating from competing stakeholders. A targeted addressing of stakeholder interests can stimulate cooperation and prevent resistance. Thereby, key stakeholders can be convinced and—in the best case—encouraged to support the project at senior management level. This often leads to advantages regarding budgeting and prioritization.

The analyst should remind that the stakeholder analysis is characterized by a high **subjectivity**, since both the analyst and the stakeholders are making individual subjective evaluations:

- In order to reduce the subjectivity of the **analyst**, a committee should be set up. In contrast to a single analyst, a committee can find more objective and reasonable evaluations. The committee should consist of a heterogeneous group of people. Only with different perspectives, the widest possible identification and evaluation of stakeholders and their interests can be achieved. In addition, the analysis process should be unified within the committee and should be logged. As a result, the transparency of the evaluation is strongly increased not only within the committee, but also to external parties.
- The **stakeholders** find their own interests mostly in a subjective way. A reduction of this subjectivity cannot be achieved within the stakeholder analysis because the interests are already predefined. However, by using a survey, the interests of stakeholders can be made more transparent so that the understanding will be increased. Thus, at least inter-subjectivity can be achieved.

In order to perform a complete stakeholder analysis the following **six steps** must be completed (Resch 2012, pp. 128 ff.):

1. **Definition of Goal, Scope and Granularity**:
   After the general decision regarding a cybersecurity investment project had been made, further conditions for the stakeholder analysis must be established:
   - The **goal** clarifies why the stakeholder analysis should be performed. For example, it must be determined which addressees shall be identified and

consulted for assistance. Alternatively, the intention of the analysis can be to prevent that any stakeholders block the project.

- The **scope** indicates which perspective will be used for the identification of stakeholders. For example, internal or external stakeholders, managers or employees, and local or international stakeholders could be in focus.
- The **granularity** refers to how much the stakeholders will be abstracted by the analyst. A high level of abstraction summarizes stakeholders to groups, such as companies. A low level of abstraction means that single individuals are considered as stakeholders. In between, there are further levels of abstraction, e.g. departments.

2. **Identification and Selection of Stakeholders**:
The stakeholder role is generally attractive because a company mostly tries to meet stakeholder interests. Therefore, potential stakeholders will endeavor to be included in the group of selected stakeholders. The analyst is affected by a huge amount of work that is caused by not only the analysis itself, but also by the communication with stakeholders. Therefore, only those stakeholders should be selected that have a significant impact on the success of the project. Similar stakeholders can be combined to stakeholder groups.
3. **Prioritization of Stakeholders**:
This step is used to create a ranking regarding the strength of stakeholders' influences. At first, the influence of each stakeholder on the success of the project must be measured. Therefore, attributes can be considered whose values can be arranged on a nominal, ordinal or cardinal scale. Power, authority and involvement are examples for a usage of the ordinal scale. Using weights, the single attribute values can be aggregated to an overall assessment of the stakeholders' influences. It is possible that a stakeholder generally keeps a very important position in the company, e.g. a director, but he has only minor influence on the project.
4. **Identification of Stakeholder Interests**:
The stakeholder interests should be considered in such detail that it is clear if the stakeholders have a positive or negative opinion regarding the project. In some cases, this might overlap with demand management because requirements are also handled there. In contrast to demand management, the level of detail of the stakeholder analysis is rather abstract.
5. **Stakeholder Map**:
The stakeholder map (see Fig. 2.7) visualizes previous findings and provides an overview of priorities, convergences and conflicts of stakeholder interests.
6. **Consideration of Stakeholders' Interests**:
The stakeholders' interests can be considered by adjusting the project or by performing additional measures. Generally, a distinction can be made between three different types of consideration:

   - **Complete satisfaction**: The interests of all selected stakeholders are fully taken into account.

Fig. 2.7 Stakeholder map

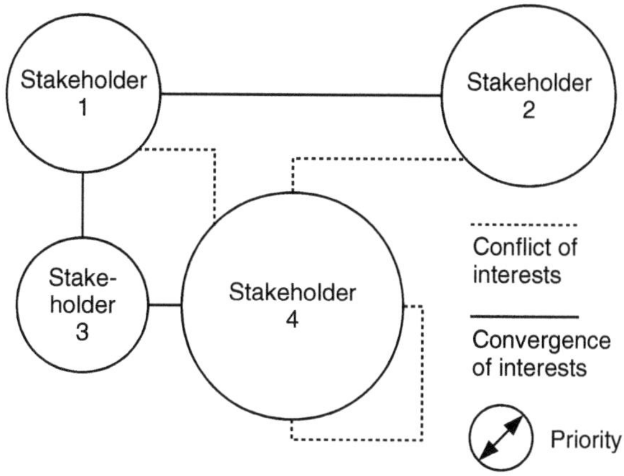

- **Orientation**: The interests of a subset of the selected stakeholders are taken into account. The interests of the other stakeholders will be adjusted accordingly. This can be achieved e.g. by directives that are made by superior stakeholders.
- **Balancing**: Hereby, a compromise between the interests is created. The objective is finding a balance that is accepted by all stakeholders.

The **types of involvement** of stakeholders affect their interests. The identification and understanding of these types help the analyst to improve the quality of the stakeholder analysis and to select the best way of considering the stakeholders' interests. As shown in Fig. 2.8, the types of involvement can be distinguished in six categories, which are known as the **ladder of involvement** (Roper et al. 2006, pp. 75 f.):

- **Ownership**: Stakeholders on this rung of the ladder have assumed responsibility for cybersecurity or a specific security program. They personally identify with it and concentrate in making cybersecurity work. They are willing to devote as much time, attention and resources as needed. Cybersecurity is an integral part of their responsibilities and they are willing to invest in it.
- **Participation**: Stakeholders on this rung believe that cybersecurity and the specific security program make sense. They contribute something worthwhile to

Fig. 2.8 Ladder of involvement

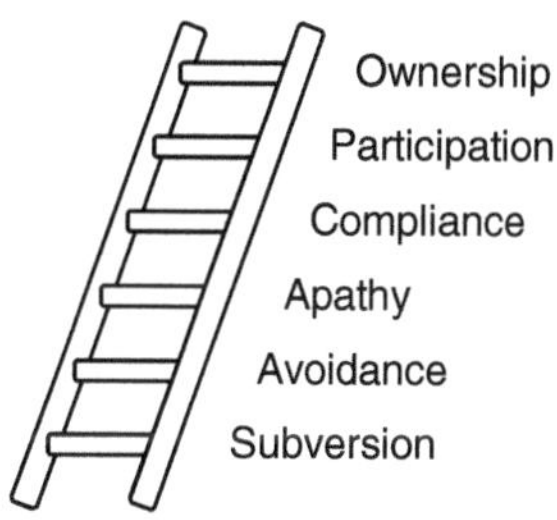

the company. They are willing to cooperate, follow the rules, and even advice in improving cybersecurity.

- **Compliance**: Stakeholders with this attitude will do exactly what they are told to do regarding cybersecurity. They will carefully comply with the rules. If something is not specifically covered by the rules, they will not care in finding a solution or performing any action. If they are criticized, they will get defensive.
- **Apathy**: These stakeholders just do not care about cybersecurity. They might not believe in the existence of the threat or in the appropriateness of the safeguard. They will follow the rules only if they think they will get in trouble if they do not. If they do not think they will get in trouble for wrongdoing, they will not bother with cybersecurity at all.
- **Avoidance**: Stakeholders on this rung view cybersecurity as inherently dangerous. In their eyes, cybersecurity only gets people in trouble. In result, they do everything they can do for not getting involved. If they detect a situation that puts an asset at risk, they will ignore it. They also avoid any contact to the cybersecurity staff.
- **Subversion**: Stakeholders on this rung deliberately and willfully try to make the cybersecurity program break. On the one hand, these stakeholders could just ignore the program, but this would have a negative impact only if the stakeholders participated in cybersecurity tasks directly, e.g. as an administrator. On the other hand, they could also try to influence the program actively. There is even a risk that they act illegally, e.g. by stealing necessary hardware components.

The stakeholders' interests must not necessarily be seen as unchangeable. By moving stakeholders **up the rungs** of the ladder of involvement, the interests could be changed positively. Probably, the strongest influence is firsthand experience. By getting stakeholders involved, they can build new experiences and compare them to their interests repeatedly. In consequence, their interests are likely to change.

Chapter 3
Cybersecurity Safeguards

3.1 Distinction of Cybersecurity Safeguards

Cybersecurity safeguards are all kind of control measures that support the fulfillment of requirements or the achievement of objectives related to cybersecurity. Safeguards can be **functionally** distinguished in administrative and technical safeguards:

- **Administrative** safeguards include all activities that do not necessarily have to be carried out by technical means. Examples are guidelines, trainings, manual controls and planning measures. The effectiveness of these safeguards depends on the awareness and the acceptance of the employees.
- **Technical** safeguards are supported or enabled by technical means, like antivirus software and access control systems. In many cases, the operation of technical safeguards can be automated, e.g. antivirus software can move a malicious program in quarantine or delete it without manual action.

Furthermore, there is the class of **physical** safeguards that are not part of cybersecurity in the narrower sense, but rather part of the more general field of information security (see Fig. 3.1). Physical safeguards are used to protect the physical perimeter and infrastructure of a company. The access by unauthorized persons to sensitive areas shall be prevented. In addition, all events shall be controlled that affect the physical integrity of objects. Physical safeguards are e.g. fences, security guards, security cameras, fire-fighting equipment, uninterruptible power supplies and flood protection mechanisms.

Another way for distinguishing safeguards is the perspective of **time**. As shown in Fig. 3.2, from this perspective, they can be preventive, detective or corrective:

- **Preventive** safeguards become effective before an event occurs. They ensure in advance that an adverse event is prevented or a desired event occurs. Generally, they are the first choice in cybersecurity because negative impacts and resulting damages can be completely avoided.

S. Beissel, *Cybersecurity Investments*, Progress in IS,
DOI 10.1007/978-3-319-30460-1_3

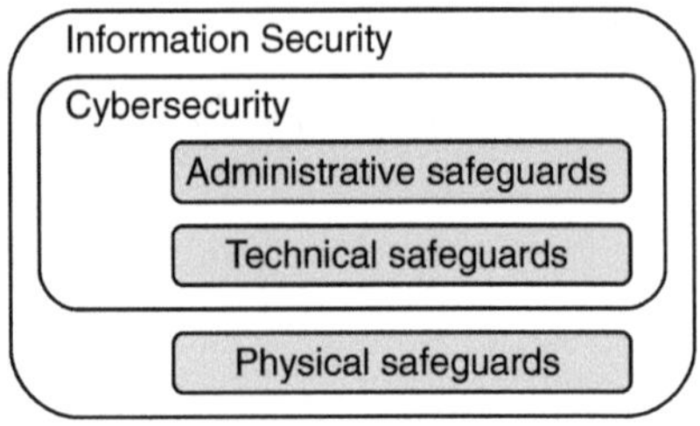

Fig. 3.1 Cybersecurity and information security

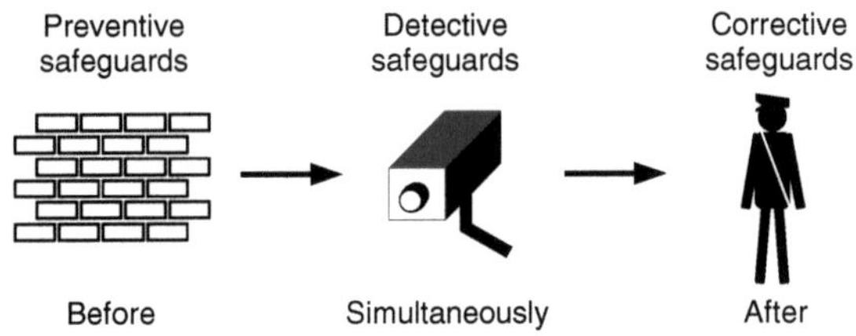

Fig. 3.2 Safeguards from the perspective of time

- **Detective** safeguards become effective while an event occurs. They are focused on the detection of adverse events. They often trigger corrective safeguards.
- **Corrective** safeguards become effective after an event occurs. They are used to correct the negative effects of adverse events.

From the combined perspectives of function and time, six different **safeguard types** can be derived: administrative preventive, administrative detective, administrative corrective, technical preventive, technical detective, and technical corrective. The next chapter describes common safeguards for each of those types. Table 3.1 gives an outlook to this collection of safeguards.

Table 3.1 Common cybersecurity safeguards

Safeguards	Administrative	Technical
Preventive	3.2.1 Policies and Procedures 3.2.2 Need to Know 3.2.3 Separation of Duties 3.2.4 Awareness and Training 3.2.5 Background Checks 3.2.6 Data Classification 3.2.7 Revision Control 3.2.8 Outsourcing	3.2.18 Access Control Systems 3.2.19 Application Control 3.2.20 Network Security 3.2.21 Hardening 3.2.22 Secure Software Development 3.2.23 Encryption 3.2.24 Data Leakage Prevention 3.2.25 Technical Resilience
Detective	3.2.9 Incident Management 3.2.10 Testing 3.2.11 Supervising 3.2.12 Job Rotation and Vacation 3.2.13 Reporting	3.2.26 Malware Protection 3.2.27 Intrusion Detection Systems 3.2.28 File Integrity Monitoring 3.2.29 Audit Trails
Corrective	3.2.14 Business Continuity Management 3.2.15 Software Escrow 3.2.16 Incident Response 3.2.17 Insurances	3.2.30 Patch Management 3.2.31 Disaster Recovery 3.2.32 Backups 3.2.33 Journaling File System

3.2 Common Cybersecurity Safeguards

3.2.1 Policies and Procedures

A **policy** includes statements of expectations that are binding for employees. Normally, it has the objective to guide the behavior and decisions of employees. A security policy is concentrated on all security related guidance that the management of the company wants to give to its employees. This policy encourages a secure and proper use of information technology in the company. Specifically, it binds employees to the adherence of security conditions and to the implementation or support of safeguards.

Standards, like ISO 27000 and PCI DSS, are important **drivers** of the security policy. If the company seeks compliance with a standard, this standard will influence the content of the company policy. Especially, administrative security requirements that must be supported by all employees are described in the policy.

The contents of the policy should be prepared and communicated under consideration of different **audiences** within the company. The security management should address different groups of employees individually. The goal is that all employees know and adhere the security aspects that apply to their workspace. Employees should get exactly the information they really need on a specific topic. They should not be instructed about policies or policy parts that do not apply to their work. For example, employees that do not cooperate with external service providers must not know how those have to be monitored.

It is advantageous to design a policy **hierarchically** with different levels. The higher a level, the more general are the contents and the less frequently they have to be changed. Each level can be addressed by separate documents with different review cycles.

- The **first** level is the highest level. It includes the overall security goals and the security strategy of the company. The management is the primary source for providing the contents. Technical details are not included at this level.
- The **second** level includes basic technical requirements that have been derived from the first level. Different aspects of information security are described without much detail. For example, the general need for antivirus software or encryption can be listed without naming specific products.
- The **third** level is the lowest one. It covers technical details, like configuration parameters for particular security products. Mostly, many very specific documents are used at this level. They have to be changed often and they are used only by a small group of experts. For example, only network administrators use documents that describe the secure configuration of firewalls.

Generally, every policy should address the following **topics**:

- **Objective** of the policy for creating awareness and motivation among the employees regarding the policy

- **Definition** of important terms for creating a common and clear understanding about the terms that are used in the policy
- **Scope** of application for selecting the employee groups or company divisions that are bound to the policy
- **Regulations** that are relevant for the company and influence the contents of the policy, in particular the drivers of the policy
- **Responsibilities** in information security that are assigned to role holders, e.g. for using, implementing or supervising safeguards
- **Contacts** including contact details for feedback and questions about the policy from employees (ideally, a single point of contact)
- **Safeguards** that have to be implemented or supported by employees, e.g. the secure handling of passwords and the responsible usage of company data

The policies have to be **provided** to all relevant employees. Mostly, they are stored on a central file server within the intranet of the company. This ensures that the employees access always the most current versions. Each employee has to confirm the acknowledgment of the policy regularly. Reconfirmation is required after a given time-period, e.g. one year, and after major changes in the policies.

Procedures are strongly related to policies. They implement the general expectations by describing a series of actions that have to be conducted in a certain order and manner. The security management has to establish concrete rules for dealing with relevant security aspects. Employees have to know which actions they have to perform, e.g. for using safeguards or handling information. Examples are security procedures for access control management, and change management:

- In **access control management**, procedures describe how access rights are granted systematically. Access rights are necessary to control which person is authorized to use particular applications or data. Only the persons that have a need to know should be allowed to access those. A relevant procedure can describe which steps have to be performed for granting access rights. In the first step, it has to be checked if duties are clearly assigned to the persons seeking access. Then, the access to systems or applications has to be granted or denied according to the duties. In addition, specific access rights have to be granted, e.g. read or write. Finally, the granted access rights have to be documented. In this way, a transparency is achieved that can be useful to reconstruct certain events or to clean up access rights.
- In **change management**, a systematic procedure is necessary in order to prevent potential errors or vulnerabilities after changes. In addition, a transparency of the implemented changes helps to control the environment and to keep all system as equal as possible. A change management procedure can include the following steps: create a change request, assign responsible persons, assess change, approve change, schedule change, deploy change, assure quality, and close change.

3.2.2 *Need to Know*

The **need to know principle** is closely related to access control. It requires that only these access rights be granted that are based on a specific user need. The user need will be given if the access to an object is necessary for the user to perform his work correctly or to fulfill a specific role. If there is no need to access an object from the business point, the user will not be allowed to access the object, even if he can already access comparable or more sensitive objects.

An appropriate implementation of the need to know principle can be achieved, for example, with the **discretionary access control**. Here, the access rights are granted to user identities or groups. A user with certain access rights is capable of passing access rights to other users. Generally, the owner of an application or system is able to grant access rights for his application or system to other users. Because the owner knows its application or system best, he can adhere strictly to the need to know principle.

Compliance with the need to know principle should be **reviewed** regularly, e.g. once a year. The company should check whether active accounts are still in use and the assignment of rights is all right from the management perspective. Unused accounts should be disabled or deleted and unneeded privileges should be removed.

3.2.3 *Separation of Duties*

The **separation of duties** helps to prevent or, at least, recognize manipulation from a single employee. Due to the division of business processes in tasks that have to be performed by different employees, nobody can disguise manipulation easily. If a single employee were able to perform the work of a complete business process alone, manipulations would remain unnoticed for an indefinite time. There are different **approaches** for implementing the separation of duties:

- The **individual** separation ensures that no single employee is allowed to perform an important action. Instead, two employees must be present while the action is performed. This is also called four eyes principle.
- The **sequential** separation ensures that the result of an already completed task has to be approved before the subsequent task is allowed to start. Often, the employee who completed the task and the employee who approves or denies the further processing use their signature. Therefore, this approach is also called two signatures principle.
- The **spatial** separation requires that sequential steps that belong to a single process have to be performed in different places. For example, a team, group, division or company that is located somewhere else has to be integrated in the completion of the task.

- The **factorial** separation is based on the usage of different factors that are required to complete a task. In other words, different inputs are needed within each task. For example, when granting access rights, the factors can be the employee database, the access control system and the user contact.

Especially dangerous would be a software developer who can change sensitive software and put it in the productive environment by himself. Therefore, the separation of the development and test **environments** from the production environment is essential to prevent the manipulation of productive software.

However, the separation of duties can lead to higher **expenses** in form of work effort and time due to more complex processes with more interfaces. Therefore, not all functions should be affected by separation of duties. Only those functions that have a risk of manipulation should be addressed.

The separation of duties can be **implemented** by choosing a function with a high risk and divide this function into multiple steps. Then, the steps can be separated by the above-mentioned approaches. In result, no single employee should be able to manipulate the entire function on his own.

3.2.4 Awareness and Training

In order to implement cybersecurity efficiently in the whole company, every employee must to know that he is an **important part** of the company's security. Every employee must accept security safeguards and must be willing to support those. This situation can be achieved by creating a high awareness of the employees and by providing adequate trainings.

Awareness means that employees are sensitized regarding cyber threats. They should know which threats might affect their work and the company in general. This helps them to understand and accept implemented safeguards within the company. Without awareness, the employees might try to bypass safeguards if they influence their work. In summary, aware employees understand the need for security; they understand what they are expected to do, and how they have to do it.

Awareness can be achieved by various measures, like posters, flyers, gifts, and live demos. The most important measure is the **training**. It is used to provide knowledge to the employees as needed, and to improve their perception in security-critical situations. The training shall create a competent and responsible behavior of employees.

Especially if cybersecurity safeguards lead to a loss in comfort, the full acceptance and support by the employees will require a long-term change in the behavior. Therefore, a **continuous** awareness program should be established. Already during the start of an employment, awareness measures should be applied. Furthermore, regular events and activities should be carried out to strengthen the awareness steadily. The efficiency of the awareness program can be increased if target groups are differentiated and particular skills and resources are considered.

The **success** of the awareness program of a company can be increased by considering the following success factors:

- The employees should be **addressed** individually. By demonstrating that everybody can influence the security of the company, the employees are incited to develop an understanding about threats that cannot be handled technically, but require manual interaction, like social engineering. The understanding can be further supported by using examples that simplify complex technical circumstances.
- The employees should be **motivated**. Measures that motivate employees are, for example, performance reviews and objectives from the supervisor. He can easily integrate tasks or work results that are relevant to cybersecurity. Especially, employees in leadership positions should be motivated because they often have an exemplary function towards other employees.
- The employees should be **concerned**. By showing how easily hackers can create threats against the company and individuals, the employees are stimulated to care about security. Live demos of hacking tools can be an effective approach. The employees should know about the consequences of their behavior and about the ideal behavior in security-critical situations.
- The employees should be **informed about the benefits**. At first sight, most employees just see the loss in comfort that is caused by safeguards. The benefits that are accompanied by them are mostly not obvious to the employees. Therefore, the benefits from the employee's perspective and the company's perspective should be highlighted. Especially, the protection of identities and finances are personally interesting from the employees' view.
- The employees should be **asked to commend** on cybersecurity safeguards. Criticisms from the employees should be requested and analyzed seriously. Thereby, important indications for improving safeguards can be detected. Besides, some safeguards might be, for a good reason, declared inappropriate or needless. The company could save valuable resources and improve security by considering the comments of the employees.

A good awareness reduces the amount of **human errors** significantly. Some common examples for human errors are:

- An **incorrect use** of information systems can have a negative impact on security if safeguards are bypassed or ignored. For example, information could be compromised because they have not been encrypted correctly. Besides, an incorrect use can lead to the unintentional deletion or manipulation of data. Some examples of incorrect use are the creation of passwords that are easy to guess, the grant of access rights that are not adequately restricted, the use of unprotected media for backups, and the absence of the user from an unlocked workstation.
- A **thoughtless handling** of information can threaten the confidentiality, integrity, and availability of information regardless of the implemented safeguards

within the company. Negligence or recklessness by employees often lead to new threats that could have been easily avoided. For example, employees might write their password on Post-it notes, have confidential phone talks at public locations, not secure their devices while travelling, and dispose confidential paper with regular garbage cans.

- A **lack of acceptance** of safeguards will exist if the employees are not willing to implement, use or support safeguards. Often, this situation is not only caused by an employee exclusively, but rather it is caused by circumstances within the company. These circumstances can be an unfavorable company culture, or missing exemplary employees.

3.2.5 Background Checks

Background checks help to ensure that a newly hired or a promoted employee has a sufficient level of **integrity**. These checks are thorough reviews within the applicable legal boundaries. They help the company to choose a suitable and reliable candidate and minimize the probability of wrong decisions. During background checks, the personal and social environment of the candidate are analyzed. The goal is to detect possible problematic characteristics of the candidate by revealing his lifestyle and leisure-time behavior. For example, a gambling addiction could cause financial conflicts and subsequently fraudulent behavior by an employee. Background checks are based on a thorough **information search**, which include, among other things:

- Internet research
- Verification of certificates and references
- Psychological tests and graphology analysis
- Health checks, alcohol and drug tests
- Credit history
- Criminal record
- Experiences by previous employers

During **interviews**, the company is generally allowed to ask all questions that are based on a legitimate interest regarding an employment relationship.

Besides, employees from **external parties** that work in the company should be checked before they start their work. These employees might need to access data and systems because the company needs project support or cooperation. Possibly, activities have been transferred to external parties with outsourcing. How those employees have to be checked in detail and who has to perform this checks, will be agreed contractually.

3.2.6 Data Classification

A **data classification** is recommended to create transparency about the sensitivity of data. In result, the company knows where sensitive data are processed and stored, and it can apply further safeguards that are highly appropriate and that consider the sensitivity. Thereby, the efficiency of further safeguards can be increased and the business operations can be restricted as little as possible. In contrast, it would be inefficient to protect all data in the same way. The overall protection level would be either too low or too high. In the first situation, highly sensitive data would be not protected sufficiently. In the second situation, the costs and the complexity of operating processes would be far higher than necessary.

The data classification is implemented by assigning all data to appropriate **classes**. Common data classes are:

- **Public**: This is the class with the lowest protection level. It is used for data that are released for general use within and outside the company. Generally, no damages will be caused if they are compromised.
- **Internal**: The data in this class are intended for internal use only. Only minor damages must be expected if internal data are compromised.
- **Confidential**: The data from this class must only be used within a restricted group of people. A careless handling of this data can cause significant damages.
- **Secret**: Secret data is extremely sensitive and restricted to the internal use by a strictly limited group of company members. Often, only trustful people at management level are allowed to access these data. A compromise of this data can cause significant damages to the company and even threaten its economic survival.

It can be difficult to find the **appropriate** class for each type of data. The assignment of data owners can be very helpful in the selection of the classes. Mostly, the data owner is the person who knows the data best and, therefore, can advise in the selection. As a thumb rule, it can be said that the more people are allowed to access the data, the lower—more public—the appropriate class.

The assigned classes can help to identify the **safeguards** that are most appropriate regarding protection levels and costs. The **declassification** is also important. It is necessary when certain data lose their current protection requirements. In this case, they should be classified to a lower class. An obsolete classification can lead to the selection of inappropriate safeguards.

3.2.7 Revision Control

The **revision control** facilitates the identification of changes in documents, software, web pages and other kinds of data. Generally, it includes a version number, a time stamp and the name of the author who changed it. With this information, the validation, comparing and restoring of data is more convenient.

A **version control system** (VCS) is a tool that can manage software versions. Experts in software development are often challenged to store and manage many data, especially different versions of source code. These data can have a fundamental impact on the functionality and security of business operations within the company. Today's software development is characterized by rapid changes caused by functional adjustments or elimination of vulnerabilities. Often, a group of people works in parallel on different changes at the same time. VCS helps to prevent chaotic conditions and ensures that outdated or untested versions are not transferred to the production environment by mistake.

A VCS captures data in its original condition and it logs all subsequent changes of these data, including user name and time stamp. The main **advantages** of a VCS are:

- Old versions are stored in **order** of creation time. They can easily be identified and, in case of any problems, the current data can be reverted to a previous working state.
- All changes are **logged** so that it is transparent who has changed which data at which time. This enables the assignment of accountability in case of errors or fraud.
- The **concurrent** access and change of data by different developers can be handled. Problems caused by duplications or inconsistencies can be avoided.
- Multiple development **branches** of a program can be managed in a structured way. They can be developed simultaneously without negative impacts to each other.

A principle that should be followed during changes in distributed systems and in databases is the **ACID** principle. This acronym refers to four characteristics that ensure the reliability of a system or database during and after a change.

- **Atomicity** means that all sequential operations within a change have to be completed or canceled all together. This must be guaranteed in every situation, e.g. during power outages or software errors.
- **Consistency** means that the system or database must be consistent after the operations within a change were carried out. This requires that the system or database have been consistent before. Consistency can be ensured by adherence to all existing rules, e.g. constraints.
- **Isolation** means that the system or database will not be negatively affected if multiple operations are carried out concurrently. Ideally, uncompleted changes should be irrelevant to other concurrent changes.
- **Durability** means that completed changes must be durable in the system or database. Especially after system failures, the completed changes must not be lost. For example, a transaction log is helpful to reconstruct operations that have been lost after failures or other problems.

3.2.8 Outsourcing

Generally, **outsourcing** is understood as a contractual appointment of an external company to perform business-related activities. The outsourcing contract ensures compliance with specified requirements for the production of goods or the provision of services.

From an economic perspective, the outsourcing of IT activities can be **useful** due to reduction of costs, transfer of risks, increase of liquidity, and improvement of quality. In addition, the company can focus on its core competencies by outsourcing administrative and supportive processes. Normally, a company performs primarily the activities on its own that generate the most value. The company sees them as its core competencies. Other activities that only support core activities or cannot be performed competently in the company are more likely to be outsourced.

The **responsibility** for ensuring the security of outsourced activities cannot be outsourced itself. The companies that outsourced activities can still face reputational damages and legal consequences. Therefore, security requirements should be integrated into the outsourcing contract so that deviations at least lead to contractual penalties.

External companies that take over the outsourced activities can benefit from **synergy** effects while performing similar tasks in a much higher amount. Security and compliance requirements can be standardized and implemented in the same way for many systems in large environments.

Mostly, the **nondisclosure agreement (NDA)** is a highly important part of an outsourcing contract. The engaged company that performs certain services or delivers certain products often has access to confidential information from the outsourcing company. To ensure the confidentiality of such information, a NDA should be created. It helps to ensure the confidentiality of information that must be accessed by external parties. Among other things, it can be used for outsourcing situations. Even during contract negotiations with external parties, a NDA could be necessary. Using a NDA creates a legal liability about the responsible handling of confidential information. Often, penalties are defined, which will be imposed for violations of these agreements, e.g. if a careless handling of confidential information by the external company has been detected.

3.2.9 Incident Management

Incident management aims at the detection of **security incidents**, e.g. attacks, failures and breaches, and at the handling of these incidents by correcting the causes and consequences. Therefore, incident management is not only detective, but also corrective. Incidents are often detected by users or organizations. Therefore, incident management is administrative. In addition, incidents can be detected by a system. Therefore, incident management can be also technical.

For a reliable detection of incidents, a **baseline** must be defined. This baseline describes conditions and indicators that characterize the normal operation of all systems in scope. Only with this information, a deviation from the normal state can be detected clearly. Otherwise, nobody could tell, for example, if a system crash was abnormal or nothing unusual. For the definition of the baseline, the following actions should be performed:

- Documentation of the existing **IT infrastructure**, including the network
- Documentation of the **applications** on the systems in scope
- Determination of the required **protection levels** of data, systems and applications
- Identification of **IT users and administrators**

The **detection** of incidents can be performed by different sources. Mostly, these sources are:

- **Users** detect primarily the incidents that affect their work environment, e.g. system crashes, failures, and viruses.
- **IT employees** might detect not only obvious incidents, but also more hidden irregularities, e.g. during administration or performance analysis.
- **Business partners** might detect abnormalities regarding data transfers via interfaces. Besides, deviations in the provided services might be recognized. Concerns from business partners should be taken serious. They should be transferred directly to responsible experts.
- **Press** reports might address new incidents. When the press finds out about the incident, it might already have affected many individuals. Therefore, a fast and proper response to incidents from press reports is important.
- **Law enforcement agencies** might get insider information from the underground or might coincidently find an evidence about a breach. They cooperate with the affected company to get more evidences and, possibly, help to protect the company against further attacks.
- **Technical solutions** include primarily intrusion detection systems and monitoring systems. Intrusion detection systems are aimed at the identification of potential attacks from the Internet. They are analyzing data that arrives at the network perimeter. Monitoring systems are used to monitor systems regarding anomalies in performance or security. Often, they are connected to other systems via interfaces and they read out system conditions and log data. Technical solutions actually do not belong to administrative safeguards, but rather to technical safeguards.

If the detected incident seems to be very serious, an **incident response team** should be called together. This team is an interdisciplinary group of experts from various departments within the company. In addition, senior management must be represented in order to make the team capable of taking decisions. All members of the team should be experienced and trustworthy. Besides, they should be trained in incident response. The team should be provided with financial and technical resources as needed. Furthermore, they should be allowed to enlarge the team with other experts that are qualified to support handling the particular incident.

After the incident have been detected and a first estimation of the impact has been made to decide if the incident response team has to be called, a thorough **assessment** has to be performed. High impact incidents are assessed by the incident response team, while low impact incidents are assessed by IT staff, e.g. an administrator. During the assessment, the following factors should be considered:

- The affected systems and applications
- Subsequent impacts caused by data transfer over network connections
- Impact to the company and to external parties
- Cause of the incident, e.g. attack, failure or thoughtlessness
- Time and location of the occurrence of the incident, e.g. from log data
- Incident information that has gone public

The next step in incident management is corrective. Here, the **response** by the company is planned and specific corrective actions are prioritized. The priorities are based on the individual situation of the company. This situation is characterized by the needed protection levels of the company and of particular systems, importance of relevant business processes, and internal or external requirements, e.g. laws or standards. The resulting priorities help to distinguish immediate actions from long-term actions. Besides, the resources that are needed to perform the actions have to be considered. High demands in staff, money or other resources mostly have to be approved by upper management.

3.2.10 Testing

Testing is crucial for the security and reliability of applications and systems. Testing can be distinguished in two types: security and functional testing. The difference is that security testing is used to check security requirements and functional testing is used to check functional requirements. Both tests are usually done before the application or system is used within the productive environment. Besides, testing is recommendable after significant changes have been implemented. Security testing should be done regularly because new vulnerabilities might have been found or new attacks might have been developed after the initial testing.

Regular **security testing** includes the search for vulnerabilities and possible attacks. These must be addressed before an attacker tries to exploit the vulnerabilities. Examples for security testing are the search for unauthorized wireless networks as well as internal and external vulnerability scans.

Vulnerabilities can lead to a great threat to the whole IT environment of a company. By exploiting these vulnerabilities, attackers can gain unauthorized access to an application or even break out of this application and attack other applications or systems. Weaknesses are caused often by "dirty" or "faulty" programming. Due to the lack of knowledge or care of the developers, vulnerabilities are often created unintentionally, sometimes even without impairing the functionality of the program. The absent of functional problems makes it difficult for the users to notice a vulnerability.

The examination of the source code with the goal to detect vulnerabilities is called **source code analysis**. Of course, it can only be performed if the source code is fully available. Generally, self-developed applications can be easily analyzed. In contrast, the source code of software developed by third parties is mostly not available to the users. The analysis of the source code should be performed after new developments and significant changes.

Reading and understanding source code is often very challenging. In a manual procedure, there is often a high probability of error. Therefore, specialized **tools** should be taken in consideration. These tools can automatically scan the source code based on algorithms and detect common development errors.

A **vulnerability scan** includes the systematic search for known vulnerabilities. In particular, standard applications, operating systems and network ports are analyzed. It should be performed both from outside and inside the company network. A vulnerability scan is usually performed by automated tools, which match the versions of used applications and operating systems to the latest available versions. Afterwards, they notice the user about possible vulnerabilities of obsolete versions. It should be considered that productive systems can be negatively affected by a vulnerability scan, e.g. due to a high utilization of system resources. The result of a vulnerability scans is a list of identified vulnerabilities, which should be eliminated in the short or medium term, depending on the corresponding risks. For the elimination of high-risk vulnerabilities, a time window of 30 days should not be exceeded. The elimination can be performed by a configuration change, a patch or a workaround. The latter will be the best option if a zero day exploit exists.

Normally, tools for vulnerability scans access a central **database** of known security vulnerabilities. Since new and rarely appearing vulnerabilities are often not fully known, vulnerability scans can never ensure a full detection. In addition, quite unpopular applications, especially self-developed applications, can be affected by unknown vulnerabilities, which cannot not to be found in the database.

Vulnerability scans should be performed **regularly**, e.g. once a quarter, and after a significant change has been implemented in applications, systems or networks.

A **penetration test** complements the vulnerability scan by analyzing to which extent the identified vulnerabilities can be actually exploited. The penetration test should be performed from outside and inside the company network, too. Often specialists are hired who are able to combine manual attacks with automated hacking tools. For example, they can combine information gathered from social media with password cracking tools.

The probability that a penetration test negatively affects productive systems is far higher than in a vulnerability scan. This is because exploiting vulnerabilities often leads to an actual impact. Generally, interference with productive systems can be avoided by using a **non-destructive** penetration test. Hereby, the examination of whether attacks are theoretically possible is sufficient so that the actual execution of the attacks during a penetration test is unnecessary. However, penetration testing should be performed only after receiving the approval from senior or executive management. Unapproved penetration testing might lead to business disruptions and unnecessary alarms, which are sent to emergency teams.

Penetration tests should be performed **regularly**, too. Because of large efforts that are mostly accompanied by penetration tests, a bigger time interval between the tests are understandable, e.g. once a year. In addition, a separate penetration test is recommended after a significant change has been implemented in applications, systems or networks.

A **functional test** of an application or system is used to validate the implementation of functional requirements and to identify possible interdependencies with other applications or systems. This test should be carried out in a separate test environment so that the business operations of the company are protected and negative effects are prevented.

The best **test integration** can be created by developing the test cases and the application or system in parallel. Hereby, the highest possible test coverage can be achieved and as many test cases as possible can be considered. However, a full coverage is practically impossible because the number of test cases would be beyond manageability.

The **test methods** specify how the functionality tests are performed and how the evidence of compliance with functional requirements can be found. The most common test methods are:

- While using **black box testing**, the input and output data of the application or system are examined without knowing the internal processing. Internal errors or missing plausibility checks can only be suspected from indications that are derived from the input and output data.
- **White box testing** requires that the internal processing of the application or system is known. The test is based on a thorough analysis of the internal processes. In contrast to black box testing, the source code is in focus and not the input and output data. The processing will be observed systematically. White-box testing requires the ownership of the source code. Therefore, externally developed applications and systems, e.g. standard third party software, are mostly not suited for white-box testing.

3.2.11 Supervising

Supervising is the **observation** of the behaviors and reactions of individual persons while they are performing their work in the company. Normally, supervising is performed by a person who stands hierarchically above the observed person. The goal is to identify incorrect and malicious actions of the observed person. These actions cannot only be caused intentionally, e.g. when resources are misused, but also unintentionally, e.g. when knowledge is missing. However, supervising can be **problematic** due to the following reasons:

- The observation by the supervisor is highly **subjective**. Therefore, errors in observation could be made. For example, the supervisor might interpret the observed situation in a strongly biased way.
- If people know that they are observed, they usually will **adjust** their own behavior. They stick more to the rules and they do not repeat previously conducted errors or fraud. The supervisor could avoid this effect by masking his intent to observe people, for example by pretending to work on other tasks.

The **intensity** of supervision depends on the type of relation to the observed people and on the reason for the observation:

- **Internal** persons—the employees—cannot be supervised continuously because this would require too much effort. A supervisor usually leads a team or department so that supervising is only one of his various tasks. Besides, the background of internal employees mostly have been already checked so that they own a high trust. In conclusion, the intensity of supervising internal persons is rather low. Often, just short time-periods are used for supervising them. Hereby, samples are created that can be used for getting a general indication about individual behaviors and reactions.
- **External** persons, which are not directly employed by the company, are guests, mechanics, and maintenance staff, among others. These people should be supervised continuously while they are at the company. Thereby, no incorrect or malicious behavior would be possible without an immediate detection. The reason for the high intensity is that these persons, including their integrity, are mostly unknown.
- A **routine** supervision is rather superficial. People are observed with low attention. Especially, internal persons are just supervised temporarily in routine supervisions. The supervisor wants to show presence and raise the awareness at the employees of being supervised.
- If a specific **suspicion** is the reason for a supervision, it will be rather intensive. The supervisor will try to gather as much data as possible. His primary goal will be the identification of sufficient evidence about fraud or errors. If the supervisor is obviously present, finding evidence could be more difficult. Therefore, the supervisor might hide the actual observation, e.g. by using a hidden remote desktop connection.

3.2.12 Job Rotation and Vacation

Job rotation has its origin in the field of labor organization. Originally, it was used to reduce biased stress of workers. By periodic changes within the job requirements, the stress of a worker can be balanced. There are two types of job rotation techniques:

- If the worker exchanges his tasks for other tasks with the same requirement level, it will be called **horizontal** job rotation or job enlargement.
- If the worker exchanges his tasks for other tasks with another requirement level, it will be called **vertical** job rotation or job enrichment.

In addition, job rotation is accompanied by great benefits from the **security** perspective. In order to ensure a continuous operation of the company, normally all jobs must be fulfilled. Therefore, others must substitute persons that change their job. Herein lays the benefit. The other person is automatically analyzing his new work environment and often looks into previous transactions to prepare for the new job. This is a good opportunity to detect errors and malicious behavior from the previous person holding the job. This person is not able to cover up security deviations any more. Besides, collusions get more difficult because of job rotation. If multiple persons conspire to commit fraud, job rotation can interrupt the collaboration of these persons. The person who replaces a conspirer could also detect the fraud and report it to his supervisor or the IT security department.

Another advantage of job rotation is the continuous **availability** of trained workers. In case of an unplanned absence, another person can easily fill in for the absent person. Thereby, the risk of errors due to untrained persons that have to replace someone is reduced.

By using job rotation, it also can be prevented that single persons become **attached** to particular systems too much. If they were attached too much, the system would be prioritized higher than other systems that have a higher benefit to the company. For example, an obsolete operating system could be in use because of a strongly attached administrator. Another operating system would have better support and a more efficient performance, but the administrator avoids it because of his personal preferences.

Mandatory vacation is mostly required due to contractual agreements that address, among other things, the time that has to be spend off work. It is accompanied by the same security benefits as job rotation. A person holding a particular job is forced to go on vacation. This results in substituting this person by another one. The substitution can now easily detect possible errors and malicious behavior. The vacation time should be at least one week so that the work of the absent person can be verified or audited in detail.

3.2.13 Reporting

Reporting is important to support the management in meeting its overall responsibility for cybersecurity. Reports represent fundamental information to the management that can be the basis for subsequent decisions. The more clear and explicit this information describes current cybersecurity facts, the more reasonable and appropriate are the derived decisions by the management.

A report can be **created** regularly or in case of particular events. Common reasons for creating a report in cybersecurity are:

- Regular **status** reports give a valuable indication about the effectiveness of the cybersecurity in the company. Management wants to control and maintain the security process properly. Status reports demonstrate deficiencies that indicate that this process should be improved. For example, a lack in efficiency could be eliminated by hiring more staff, training the actual staff or adjusting particular steps within the process.
- **Audit** results are usually delivered to the management after an auditor has sufficiently checked the protection level and particular safeguards. It includes findings from the auditor that specify insufficient or missing safeguards. Management needs this information to assign resources to the remediation of those findings. Thereby, the protection level of the company can be raised quickly.
- **Breach** reports are focused on security breaches in the company. They describe and summarize information about the source and execution of the breach, its consequences until now, the expected consequences, and, if possible, recommended response actions. In case of a breach, management must act quickly and reasonable. A solid report delivers decision support while selecting an appropriate response and preventing further damages.

In general, a report should be short and clear. Comprehensive technical details are not desired by the management. They should be avoided or placed in the attachment. Among other things, the **content** of a report can include the following points:

- Compliance of the actual safeguards to internal or external requirements
- Effectiveness and deficiencies of existing safeguards
- Results of internal or external audits
- Assessment of the appropriateness of the protection level
- Incidents that have occurred and subsequent damages
- Changes in environmental factors and consequences
- Implementation status of previous management decisions and subsequent successes or failures
- Expenses for cybersecurity in general and for particular safeguards
- Successes in the protection of assets against significant threats
- Comments from customers, business partners, and the public regarding cybersecurity in the company
- Technical trends and innovations in the market

While creating the report, it should be considered how valuable and adequate the particular points are for the reader. In result, the report should be **focused** on the information that has a real benefit for the decision maker. In no case, the report should be overloaded with marginal information.

3.2.14 Business Continuity Management

Business Continuity Management (BCM) is used to ensure the continuity of business operations in case of disruptions and their recovery in case of unavoidable disasters. The goal is to ensure the survival of the company, under consideration of any identified risks. BCM uses knowledge from risk assessments to make critical business processes sufficiently resilient.

An important help is provided by the **business impact analysis**, which is used for evaluation of critical processes and the impact of possible disruptions. It facilitates the definition of maximal accepted downtime and data loss from the perspective of the business departments. The more important the system respectively the business process, the lower are the maximal accepted downtime and data loss. Hereby, importance is not only understood as high influence on the production of goods or generation of services, but also on the adherence to regulations and the protection of people and assets.

However, the company would not be able to protect itself against every possible crisis. Therefore, **documents** must be created that describe the necessary actions during a crisis systematically. In particular, these plans are usually a business continuity directive (BCR), a business continuity plan (BCP) and a disaster recovery plan (DRP). The **BCR** describes all measures that should be implemented and maintained to ensure reliability. It describes the circumstances that characterize a crisis, and a risk-based escalation procedure in case of a disaster. This procedure helps to decide when the BCP or DRP have to be activated. In addition, the responsibilities are listed. The **BCP** describes from an organizational perspective and the **DRP** from a technical perspective what needs to be done in case of a disaster. The separation is necessary because, during some disasters, only one of both plans must be followed. For example, in case of a pandemic, only the BCP must be followed. Both plans can include systematic instructions. The BCP includes e.g. the transfer of personnel to emergency locations, an overall recovery coordination and instructions for handling reputational damage. The DRP includes e.g. the restoring backups or rebuilding systems.

In business continuity management, important plans have to be tested regularly. The **test** verifies that the responsible persons know how and when they have to react during a crisis. It also demonstrates the appropriateness and currency of the plans. Deviations between the plan and actual organizational structures that might be caused by recent changes will be visible after a test. Besides, people that are performing the same actions repeatedly become more familiar with them, and, thereby, these people will cause less errors and delays in an actual crisis.

3.2.15 Software Escrow

Software escrow requires the safekeeping of the original software, the source code and the documentation by a trusted third party. The data are kept safe and will be delivered in certain cases to the user according to a written agreement. Upon delivery, the user might be required to pay the cost of the initial development of the software.

The user can **benefit** from software escrow agreements if the developer of the software terminates its business. In this case, the user has the opportunity to acquire the rights to the source code. Otherwise, the developer could sell the software to anyone else and the user would have to negotiate future usage rights with the new owner.

Software escrow agreements should be created especially with those **developers** who might get out of the business in the short term due to insolvency or other reasons. The bigger the developer and the more popular the software, the less likely is the commitment of the developer to such agreements. For small developers, the software escrow is more common. For example, a disaster recovery plan can be part of an overall business agreement. This plan can define the emergencies that trigger the developers to deliver the source code and documentation to the user. Mostly, an independent third party performs the safekeeping. In addition to an emergency, other triggers for delivery can be agreed, like the violation of certain service level agreements. For example, if the user receives no support any more, he can demand the delivery of the source code so that he can make necessary changes himself.

The software escrow **contract** defines the conditions of the safekeeping and the obligations of the trusted third party. While creating this contract, the following points should be considered:

- The **delivery** of the escrowed material should be clearly defined. It has to be clear how the delivery will be performed in detail.
- The trusted third party must be **trusted** from both the user and the developer. Besides, the actual safekeeping should be adequate. Especially, the data should be protected sufficiently.
- The trusted third party should be competent in **checking** the usefulness of the data, e.g. by compiling source code to a running program.
- The definition of **update cycles** ensures that the data is up-to-date. Changes to the software by the developer should be also transmitted to the data that is kept by the third party.
- The contents of the software escrow contract should not contradict the **terms** of the license agreement.
- The software escrow contract and the license agreement should be conducted at the same **time**. This prevents disadvantages during missing escrow agreements.

3.2.16 *Incident Response*

Incident response is the subsequent step after incident detection, which is also located within the incident management of the company. The primary goal of incident response is a fast **solution** regarding the detected incident. Therefore, similarities to previous incidents and known errors are searched. The knowledge from those could be used to find an appropriate solution. If the actual incident is unknown until now, the incident response will mostly be divided into two steps: At first, a workaround is implemented to prevent further impact of the incident without solving the underlying issue. Next, the actual problem is solved. Finding a final solution can take a long time. These two steps are used because it is more important to limit damages than to understand the source of the incident.

Workarounds aim at the recovery of business processes in the short term. The employees have to continue their work as fast as possible. Workarounds provide an alternative way for achieving the same business outcomes without correcting the actual issue that caused the incident. In result, the incident does not interrupt business processes anymore so that the company can spend more time in finding a long-term solution.

Incidents that have been caused by **intention** might be just observed without responding to them directly. The company might try to catch the attacker in the act. However, during this observation, the attacker could delete or manipulate important data. Therefore, the company has to consider the potential damages over time.

Besides, incidents can be caused by unclear or incorrect security **requirements**. In this case, the requirements have to be corrected. In addition, the requirements can be controlled in another way. For example, if user understanding is a problem, an automatic technical control can be used to replace a previous organizational safeguard. The incident might be enabled by the negligence of particular employees. This should trigger adequate consequences, e.g. disciplinary action.

The correction of **security breaches** should be performed with a fast and systematic procedure. At first, the affected systems have to be taken offline. Every data on the systems that give indication about the cause and details of the breach have to be saved. Log data are mostly a valuable source for this kind of information. Every affected system should be seen as insecure. Therefore, every application and parameter on these systems has to be check regarding manipulation or corruption. If hashing has been used before the breach, check sums before and after the breach can be compared to find irregularities. Alternatively, the whole systems can be restored into a previous secure state or a complete new system installation can be performed. A backup should only be restored if it is safe to say that the breach began after the backup. Infected or manipulated data must not be restored into a productive system. In contrast, backups after the breach might include important information about the course of the breach. However, these backups should only be recovered on an isolated system so that another distribution of malicious code will be prevented.

A **restored system** should not be used without adjustments. On the one hand, an attacker might have gathered confidential information from the system. Especially passwords could have been compromised and should be changed. On the other hand, the vulnerability that has been exploited by an attacker would be addressable again. Secure configurations and available patches should be implemented before activating the system in the productive environment. Furthermore, the restored system should be monitored thoroughly. An attacker might try to cause another breach. The earlier an attack can be detected, the earlier the company can respond to it. Technical safeguards, like incident detection and incident prevention systems, would complement the administrative safeguards perfectly.

The whole incident response procedure should be accompanied by a detailed **documentation**. This documentation gives an overview about the incident, its cause and consequences, and the subsequent measures. It also provides transparency about the details of the incident towards all employees and external parties with a need-to-know. In addition, the documentation delivers valuable knowledge that can be useful in similar situations. Lessons learned can lead to more efficient incident response in the future. Another important aspect of documentation is the prosecution of criminals. Proper documentation can be an important evidence to convict attackers. In order to ensure that the documentation is actually created in a sufficient way, specific requirements regarding its quality and timeframe should be defined, and made binding.

3.2.17 Insurances

Insurances help to cover the **financial consequences** of a security breach. Although most direct costs can be covered with insurances, there are still negative consequences in the long term that cannot be covered. Especially, reputational damages can lead to a negative public opinion for years after the breach. In result, revenues might be affected and well-trained employees might be hard to find. In conclusion, insurances should not be the only safeguard, but they can rather be an additional safeguard to be better prepared for the worst case.

The **selection** of the appropriate insurance should be taken very carefully. Some insurances do not cover damages in the same way like special cyber or Internet insurances. In case of a cyber-attack, the loss of income and the costs of incident management are often unexpected. For example, costs can arise that are caused by public relations, legal advice, forensic investigation and the IT professionals who are required to minimize the impact of the attack. At least half the costs of a cyber-attack are cause by incident management and fees from specialists. It has to be ensured that the insurance will cover these costs. Special consideration should be given to the fact that the actual payment of the damage compensation is mostly performed after the insurance vendor analyzed the situation thoroughly. Possibly, this can take a long time. Therefore, the company has to bridge the resulting gap between the occurrence of the damages and the compensation.

It is very important that the insured company reviews the insurance **contract** thoroughly and only makes accurate statements. If the insurance vendor identifies incorrect statements, it might deny the compensation of damages. Insurance vendors are becoming better informed about cybersecurity. Among other things, they are able to identify insufficient safeguards. They might use this information to deny the coverage of damages at insecure companies. It will be highly problematic if the insured company cannot provide accurate information because it does not know enough about its own safeguards. In this case, an internal analysis of the environment should be performed first.

3.2.18 Access Control Systems

Generally, access control systems can be used to ensure **logical and physical** security. Since cybersecurity is focused on logical security, this will be described here. Logical access control systems help to restrict access as needed. Only those users and systems that have a legitimate interest from the business point of view should be actually able to access an object. Generally, two **types** of access can be distinguished:

- **Operating System Access**: The operating system restricts all resources that are generally provided from the hardware, including all interfaces and connected systems. It does not only abstract the hardware resources, but also controls their usage. The file system is of particular importance. When restricting access within a file system, a user will only be able to access a file if sufficient rights are granted via the file properties. First, parent directories inherit access rights to the file. Next, they can be further adjusted by an authorized user. An example is the New Technology File System (NTFS). It allows the assignment of the following rights:

  - **Full Access**: Users can modify, add, move or delete files, directories and properties. They can also change fixed settings for all files and subdirectories.
  - **Change**: Users can view and modify files and file properties. They can add files to a directory or delete them from it. They can also add or delete file properties.
  - **Read and Execute**: Users can view files, and file properties. They can also execute files and scripts.
  - **Read**: Users can view files and file properties.
  - **Write**: Users can write to a file.

  It should be considered that the access restrictions are closely **related** to the operating system and file system. If files are copied to another file system without access restrictions, e.g. the File Allocation Table (FAT), they will be lost and each user will be able to access the files fully. Besides, a user might bypass the access restriction of files by copying it to a different operating system where he has full administrative rights.

- **Application Access**: Applications enable or support the users to perform business activities related to their job function. To prevent misuse or careless use of the application possibilities, most applications have an integrated access model. The configuration of this access model can be very complex because various requirements can be supported, like different kind of authorizations or multiple controls. On the one hand, the execution of dubious or malicious applications should be prevented. This can be achieved with the help of software for application access control. It uses white lists to allow only the execution of specified applications, or blacklists to allow any application that is not listed. On the other hand, the usage of approved applications should be restricted according to the individual business need of each user.

The reliable **authentication** of the users is essential for a proper access control system. It is necessary to prove the users' identities. As already described in Sect. 2.2.4, the three factors of authentication are something that the user knows, something that the user has and something that the user is. Table 3.2 provides an overview about common authentication methods.

After successful authentication, **authorization** is the next step. It checks whether the authenticated user should be allowed to make a specific access. For this purpose, a lookup within the authorization management has to be performed. Only when the previously assigned rights of the user match the access attempt, the access will be granted.

The **authorization management** is used to control access to applications, systems and data. It grants access to authenticated users in correspondence to the previously defined access options, which are based on the business need. The basic design of an authorization management is strongly determined by the underlying **authorization model**. The most famous authorization models are:

- **Role Based Access Control**: In this model, each user is assigned to a role with appropriate access rights. The creation of roles is based on job descriptions. The idea is that every job description is covered by an adequate role, which enables a user to fulfill this job sufficiently. Roles facilitate an easy handling and administration of access rights within the authorization management.

Table 3.2 Authentication methods

Something that the user knows	Something that the user has	Something that the user is
Password	Chip card	Finger print
Passphrase	Magnetic stripe card	Palm scan
PIN	Digital key	Facial scan
Shared secret (challenge response)	Software certificate	Retina scan
	USB-, NFC- and Bluetooth token	Iris scan
	Smartphone	Signature dynamics
		Voice print

- **Discretionary Access Control**: This model allows the assignment of access rights to individual users or groups directly by users. The owner of an application, a system or data assigns the access rights and, thereby, grants permissions for each user at his own discretion.
- **Mandatory Access Control**: This model is supported by additional rules and attributes. For example, a file can have the attribute "secret". Only if the user has the same attribute, the access will be granted. This model is particularly advantageous if decentralized structures shall be merged. If the same attributes are used, the merger will be trivial, and if different ones are used, similar attributes can easily be linked to each other.

For systems within company networks, there is usually a connection to a **directory service**. This is a central database of all network resources. Users, systems and applications can access the directory service in order to obtain information about resources. Requests are routed by the directory service to the right address. Within the directory service, authentication and authorization are needed. Requests are processed only after successful authentication. Access is granted only after successful authorization. Authentication is required just once before accessing all resources. Therefore, directory services provide a single sign-on. The main advantage is that all access rights are stored centrally and, thus, can be managed centrally. The most common directory services are based on the Lightweight Directory Access Protocol (LDAP), e.g. Microsoft's Active Directory, Novell eDirectory and OpenLDAP.

To protect unattended systems from unauthorized access, a **screen lock** should be used, e.g. a screen saver with password protection. Thereby, the contents are hidden on the screen and the user input is blocked. The unlocking of the screen and the re-activation of the user input should only be possible after the re-authentication of the user. The screen lock should be activated if needed and after a reasonable time of inactivity, e.g. 15 min.

Especially if there is a large number of users, administrators might be challenged by giving all user accounts enough attention. Therefore, an automatic **deactivation or deletion** of user accounts should be performed after a period of inactivity, e.g. after three months. Outdated active accounts can be a major security risk, especially if terminated employees can still access company systems.

3.2.19 Application Control

Application control facilitates the analyzation of applications that are executed by users. Before the application actually starts, it can be decided whether the application is legitimate or illegitimate. This information is used to decide if the application should be allowed or blocked. For this purpose, a previously created whitelist can be used.

The advantage of application control is that not only potentially malicious, but also unwanted applications can be **blocked**. On the one hand, new malware can be blocked before the according signatures have been found by the vendors of anti-virus software. On the other hand, it can be prevented that applications that are irrelevant for business lead to an excessive misuse of resources and time. In addition, the infringement of license agreements can be avoided because the use of insufficiently or unlicensed applications can be prohibited.

Usually, the company allows only the execution of software that is explicitly **validated** for internal use. Mostly, this software is under full administration of the company, which addresses the following topics:

- The company performs comprehensive **tests** of the software regarding its function, security, and interdependencies with other software.
- The most appropriate **security parameters** are identified. Hereby, the right balance between usability and security has to be found.
- The software gets **updates** regularly over the company infrastructure. Functional problems and security vulnerabilities are fixed by these updates.
- The **compatibility** of the software is ensured. By defining an internal standard, it can be guaranteed that employees use the same software. Thus, potential problems in data interchanges are avoided.
- The company usually provides **user support** regarding software use and troubleshooting.
- The **license** situation of the software is clarified so that no software is used illegally.

In the market, a wide range of **software** is available that is specially designated for application control. It is often sold in a suite with antivirus or other security software.

3.2.20 Network Security

Network security is a very comprehensive topic, which can include administrative and technical as well as preventive, detective and corrective safeguards. The technical preventive safeguards are very common in network security. Therefore, this chapter concentrates on widespread safeguards of this type.

The most important task in network security is the **control** of the data transfer. In order to control the data transfer over and within networks, firewalls, routers and switches can be used:

- A **firewall** controls the data transfer from one network to another. It can filter traffic based on network addresses and protocols. Thereby, connection attempts by attackers, who try to compromise, damage or manipulate data, can be blocked. Besides, a firewall can protect an internal network against attackers that flood systems with requests because they want to cause a denial of service.

A firewall can be operated independently as an autonomous system or locally as a software running on a workstation or server. Firewalls can be distinguished in static, stateful and application firewalls:

- **Static firewalls** examine packets to filter the data traffic. Only the header information of a data packet is considered in the filtering decision. Thereby, target and destination address, protocol, and port number are usually taken into account.
- **Stateful firewalls** perform packet inspections by keeping the transmitted data packets that are part of a session. They can decide if new data packets belong to the existing session and if these packets are related to other data packets. Data packets that do not belong to a legitimate session will be blocked.
- **Application firewalls** work on the application layer. They can match the contents of data packets with protocols. If unwanted data is tunneled within a standard protocol, the firewall can detect this. Thus, a traffic control at the application level is possible.

- A **router** forwards data packets between networks. It uses routing tables to store the best possible communication paths between the source and destination addresses. Many router models have built-in security features. Routers enable the connection of network environments with different address ranges or architectures. Thereby, they support, among other things, the remote maintenance of systems from other network environments.
- A **switch** forwards data packets within a network or between network segments. Switches have no particular security features or filter options. However, if the switch model supports access control lists, the connection from systems to network environments can be restricted.

By using firewalls, routers and switches thoughtfully, the network security can be increased significantly. Hereby, the following points should be considered:

- The **perimeter** of the company network that limits the network from the Internet should be controlled by firewalls. They should prevent that attacks are routed into the network and that compromised systems transmit confidential data out of the company network.
- Firewalls should also be used to create a **demilitarized zone** and to secure the connection between the demilitarized zone und the internal network. The demilitarized zone is a subnetwork that includes systems that face to unsecure networks, like webservers that communicate with the Internet.
- Firewalls, routers and switches can also be used to separate the internal network into further **segments**. This can be implemented with virtual local area networks (VLANs). Thereby, systems with different protection levels can be associated to different VLANs.

- Different physical **locations** of the company should be connected under security aspects. Depending on the protection level of the company network and the data transfer, connections to other locations should be secured and encrypted as needed. A virtual private network (VPN) allows the encrypted transfer of data over the Internet. Alternatively, a private connection that is physically separated from the Internet can be used.

3.2.21 Hardening

Hardening concentrates on the security of systems by reducing **attack vectors**. In particular, unnecessary services are disabled, unneeded software is uninstalled and system parameters are configured securely. By hardening a system, the potential targets for attackers can be reduced. The attackers have fewer opportunities to find and exploit vulnerabilities on the system. In addition to the security benefits, the IT system loses **complexity**. Therefore, administration and maintenance costs can be reduced.

Default passwords and other sensitive **settings** that were set by the vendor before delivering the systems to the company are usually publically available. They can easily be misused by attackers. They are available from the Internet or printed manuals, among other sources. After the initial installation of an operating system, many unneeded services might be active. They should be deactivated or secured before using the system productively.

Best practices for hardening include recommendations for securing a system on different levels of abstraction. Some best practices are even tailored to specific systems. They are published by the respective vendors or recognized organizations in the industry, e.g. by

- CIS (Center for Internet Security)
- ISO (International Organization for Standardization)
- SANS (SysAdmin Audit Network Security) Institut
- NIST (National Institute of Standards and Technology)

For example, CIS published benchmarks for multiple operating systems, web browsers, database servers, mobile devices, network devices, and virtualization. The benchmark for **Apple OS X** addresses recommendations in the following topics (CIS 2015, p. 2):

- Install Updates, Patches and Additional Security Software
- System Preferences (Bluetooth, Date and Time, Desktop and Screen Saver, Sharing, Energy Saver, Security and Privacy, iCloud)
- Logging and Auditing (Configure asl.conf)
- Network Configurations
- System Access, Authentication and Authorization (File System Permissions and Access Controls, Password Management)

- User Accounts and Environment (Accounts Preferences Action Items)

A company can create an **individual baseline** for a secure configuration of a system that can be reused for similar systems. After the initial development, this baseline should be reviewed regularly in order to consider changes in requirements and new technical knowledge. The company should plan, document and release changes as part of a change management process.

3.2.22 Secure Software Development

A company can achieve security in software development best by considering security within all phases of the software development **lifecycle**. It should address potential vulnerabilities already within software design. Especially, the software developers should prevent particular vulnerabilities while creating the source code.

The **prevention** of security breaches in the context of software development is far more effective than fixing vulnerabilities that were found by users or attackers after the software had been released. The analysis and elimination of found vulnerabilities are usually associated with a very high workload. Besides, users could already be affected by damages caused by successful exploits. The prevention of vulnerabilities from the beginning can be achieved by a careful and well-thought development. This is the far better choice.

The Open Web Application Security Project (OWASP 2013) provides an overview of the most critical **vulnerabilities**, which should be considered especially while developing web applications. Here, the most critical security risks are:

- Injection
- Broken Authentication and Session Management
- Cross-Site Scripting (XSS)
- Insecure Direct Object References
- Security Misconfiguration
- Sensitive Data Exposure
- Missing Function Level Access Control
- Cross-Site Request Forgery (CSRF)
- Using Known Vulnerable Components
- Unvalidated Redirects and Forwards

Best practices in secure software development provide guidance in implementing security within the software development lifecycle. Common examples are the Software Assurance Maturity Model (SAMM) and the Building Security in Maturity Model (BSIMM):

- **SAMM** (OpenSAMM 2009) contains four business functions at the highest level. They are called Governance, Construction, Verification and Deployment. Each business function includes three security practices, each including two related activities. For each security practice, SAMM defines three maturity levels. The higher the maturity, the more demanding are the objectives to be implemented. Any company that implements security in software development can be categorized with a maturity level.

- **BSIMM** (2012) contains four domains at the highest level. They are called Governance, Intelligence, SSDL Touchpoints and Deployment. Each domain includes three security activities, which are derived from business goals, and categorized to maturity levels. BSIMM identified twelve activities that are commonly found in successful programs and should be considered when starting a secure software development initiative.

3.2.23 Encryption

From the security perspective, confidential data should be stored and transmitted only in an encrypted form. **Encryption** prevents an attacker from eavesdropping and manipulating communication in open networks, like the Internet. In addition, communication via wireless networks, Global System for Mobile Communications (GSM) and General Packet Radio Service (GPRS) should be protected.

The encryption of data **transforms** them into a form—the cipher text—that has no similarity to their original representation form—the plain text. Decryption converts cipher text back to its original form.

In order to encrypt or decrypt data, a digital key and an algorithm are needed. The **encryption techniques** can be distinguished in symmetric and asymmetric ones. The symmetric technique uses the same key to encrypt and decrypt data (see Fig. 3.3).

The asymmetric technique uses a separate key for each step. Generally, the public key is used for encryption and the private key for decryption (see Fig. 3.4).

The **performance** of symmetric encryption techniques is generally higher than that of asymmetric encryption techniques. The symmetric encryption is more than 100 times faster than the asymmetric one. To achieve a comparable security level, the asymmetric keys have to be larger than the symmetric ones. Usually, symmetric keys have a size of 128–256 Bit and asymmetric keys have a size of 1024–4096 Bit.

However, files are not always protected sufficiently just by encrypting them. The **strength** of an algorithm and a key is also very important. If the strength is too

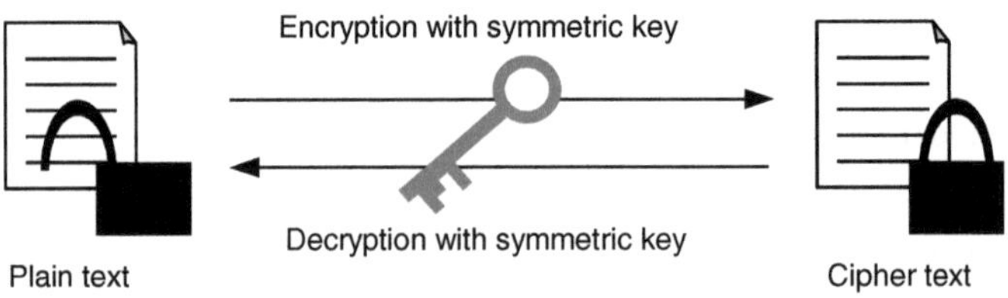

Fig. 3.3 Symmetric encryption

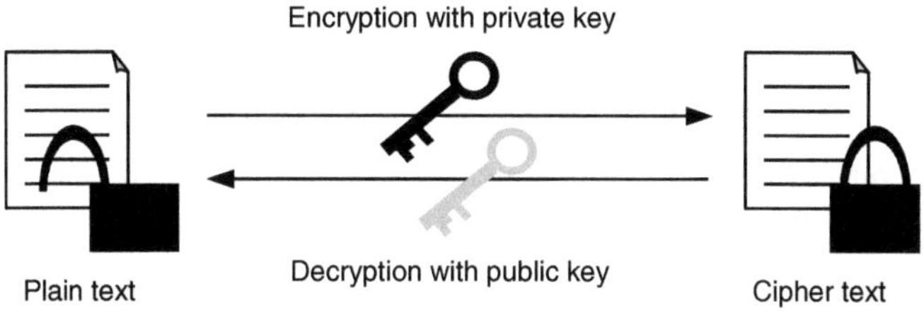

Fig. 3.4 Asymmetric encryption

weak, the encryption can be cracked in a short time and the attacker can easily access the plain text. For strong encryption, the following combinations of algorithm and key can be used: AES (128 bits and higher), TDES (at least three times the key length), RSA (2048 bits and higher), ECC (224 bits and higher), and ElGamal (2048 bits or higher). Further recommendations were published by NIST (Barker et al. 2012).

The keys must always be kept secure. Encryption can only be as secure as the **storage of keys**. Especially if the keys are stored at the same place as the encrypted files, an attacker can easily encrypt the files. Emergency planning must be considered, too. If the keys are lost due to a failure or disaster, even authorized users can no longer read the files.

The **hard disk encryption** provides the encryption of an entire hard disk. Thus, the storage of an entire system can be encrypted. In addition to data partitions, even boot partitions should be encrypted. In contrast to hardware-based encryption solutions, software-based solutions do not encrypt the master boot record of the hard disk. Especially, hard disks of mobile systems, i.e. notebooks and tablets, should be encrypted. Otherwise, an unauthorized person can quickly access the data if the system is stolen or lost.

When using hard disk encryption, a proper **key management** must be implemented. The encryption key must be kept in a safe place so that authentication problems or user termination does not lead to inaccessible data. The disclosure of the encryption key must not be careless. Especially, no person should get the key unauthorized. To secure the restoration of data, a challenge-response method can be used. Hereby, the user and administrator share a secret so that an intercepted communication does not reveal confidential data. At first, the user creates a challenge, which is transferred to the administrator. Then the administrator generates the matching response and transfers it back to the user. He enters the response into the system. Afterwards, he will be allowed to perform a privileged action, e.g. a password reset.

When **transferring data**, symmetric and asymmetric encryption techniques are often combined. At first, the transmitter sends his symmetric key to the recipient. To ensure that this key transfer cannot be intercepted by an attacker, it is encrypted using the public key of the recipient. Only the receiver is in possession of his private key. Therefore, only he can decrypt the transferred symmetric key. Now both parties are in possession of the symmetric key so that the transfer of the symmetrically encrypted data can be performed. There are two encryption methods, which define where the encryption and decryption are performed:

- During **end-to-end** encryption, the encryption of transmitted data is performed on the source system and the decryption on the target system. Hereby, the data is encrypted during the entire transmission path over all networks. There is a high confidentiality protection. However, the transmitted data cannot be scanned for malware or unauthorized transmission of confidential data when reaching the network perimeter. Due to encryption, no anti-malware or other security software can analyze the content.
- During **gateway-to-gateway** encryption, the data is encrypted not until leaving the local network. The data is decrypted already at the entrance to the recipient's network. Since the gateway handles encryption operations, the encryption is transparent for the sender and receiver. There is no need to install encryption software on each system. However, the data transmission within the local network is not encrypted anymore. Thus, it is not protected against compromise.

3.2.24 Data Leakage Prevention

Data leakage prevention (DLP) includes the monitoring of sensitive data while processing, transmitting or storing data. In this context, potential security violations shall be prevented. The purpose is to identify and block the intentional or unintentional disclosure of sensitive information.

This can be achieved by various administrative or technical **safeguards**, which address specific scenarios. For example, policies can include the requirement to encrypt sensitive data that shall be transferred. Web filters can block webpages that provide file hosting services. Firewalls can filter traffic and block unwanted transmissions of data over the Internet. Application-layer firewalls can even detect if an unwanted transmission of sensitive data is hidden in a standard protocol. Intrusion detection systems can detect attacks against systems or networks by analyzing irregularities at the perimeter. After detecting an attack, these systems alarm the relevant security administrators. They are just a detective safeguard, but they are fundamental for triggering subsequent corrective actions by intrusion prevention systems. These systems can react on detected attacks automatically. Attacks are often used as a preliminary stage before data will be compromised. Anti-malware software can protect systems against malicious software that could transmit data without authorization.

However, the best solution would be a single technical safeguard that can be used to control the unwanted leakage of data. **Designated** DLP software is specifically designed for data control. It uses algorithms that are based on predetermined rules. They can identify the actions of users or systems that affect sensitive data and react on them. Among other things, an approval process before sending e-mails with sensitive data can be implemented. Besides, the data transfer via webpages, burning of CDs, and the storage on USB sticks can be checked. Designated DLP software can be implemented in the network or on every host:

- **Network-based** DLP software scans the data traffic in the network in order to identify sensitive data. If the data traffic seems inappropriate under security aspects, the DLP software can report or block it. In order to scan every part of the network and the network perimeter, the DLP software uses multiple agents or sensors. The installation of network-based DLP software is much easier than that of host-based DLP software because the software does not need to be installed on every system in the network. However, network-based DLP software only scans data traffic in the network. Sensitive data that is transferred via other interfaces, e.g. USB, would be undetected.
- **Host-based** DLP software must be installed on every system. Here, it scans all user actions that could lead to a leakage of data. In contrast to the network-based DLP software, the host-based one leads to a high effort in implementation because it must be installed on every system. In big companies, hundreds or thousands of systems could be in scope.

Data classification, as described in Sect. 3.2.6, is an important **requirement** for the implementation of DLP software. If the company does not classify data, the DLP software will have no criteria for checking the data regarding its confidentiality. These criteria must be transformed into rules, which are processed every time when data shall be checked. Not every file must be classified. The rules consider multiple criteria, like storage location or key words in the file, to assign a class during the scan.

After detecting a **violation** of predefined rules, a DLP software can react in different ways. It can display a notification to the user, ask the user for permission, ask the supervisor, block the data transfer, or just log it. A very restrictive configuration could impede normal business operations. Especially in the early period after the DLP implementation, a loose configuration can help to get the acceptance from the users. Displaying notifications is not restrictive, but can raise the awareness of the users significantly.

3.2.25 Technical Resilience

Mostly, the **availability** of systems is of fundamental importance for the business operations of a company. Unavailable systems can interrupt or block business transactions. Performing the operations manually is often very complicated and prone to errors. Unavailability can lead to lost transactions and missed opportunities. This often results in reputational and financial damages.

In order to increase the resilience of systems, whole systems or important components, like storage disks, can be made **redundant**. If a system or component fails, the automatic swap to another one will be crucial for a working redundancy.

The functional data processing should not be affected by the failure. The user should not even notice it.

For example, the storage disk redundancy can be implemented by multiple hard drives that are grouped to a **redundant array of independent disks** (RAID). The hard drives appear as one logical storage area. This can increase the performance and reliability of the hard drives in a cost-effective manner. A RAID can be managed by a separate RAID controller or by the operating system. A RAID controller offers greater reliability because it prevents that the RAID could be damaged by an error of the operating system. The basic RAID techniques are striping, mirroring and parity:

- **Striping** is used to increase the performance. It allows the simultaneous reading and writing with multiple disks.
- **Mirroring** is used to increase the reliability. It allows the mirroring of data to other disks.
- **Parity** is used to increase the reliability at relatively high storage utilization. The data is not mirrored completely. Only parity information is stored across all disks evenly. The parity information is the result of an exclusive OR of the data blocks. In the case that a single hard drive fails, the missing data blocks from this drive can be reconstructed from the parity information.

The RAID levels define which technique will be used. In addition, the **combination** of different techniques is possible. The company can choose the preferred mix of performance and reliability.

3.2.26 Malware Protection

Antimalware and antivirus **software** are important to protect company systems against malicious software—also called malware. Although viruses seem to play the major role for antivirus software, any form of malware, like Trojans and worms, must be handled.

Malware is software that performs actions that are highly unwanted from the user perspective. In particular, sensitive data can be compromised, manipulated or deleted. There are several **sub-types of malware**, which differ in their behavior and the potential subsequent damage:

- **Viruses** become active as soon as they are executed by the user. Often, viruses try to infiltrate other programs and to multiply over other systems.
- **Trojans** become active as soon as they are executed, too. In contrast to viruses, they are hidden in another program. This program seems legit, but performs unwanted activities in the background.
- **Worms** spread independently across networks and become active without user interaction.

- **Time bombs** do not cause immediate damage. Instead, they are triggered after a specific waiting period.
- **Spyware** does not manipulate or corrupt data, but rather violates the confidentiality of data. For example, personal data, like user behavior and web pages history, are transferred to external parties.
- **Grayware** does not cause direct damage, too. However, it also produces no benefit to the user. Often, valuable computing power is utilized by grayware unnecessarily.
- **Rootkits** are a special type of malware that is hidden deep in the operating system and, mostly, difficult to detect. Rootkits are programs that have been developed by attackers specifically to manipulate operating systems. In order to install rootkits, attackers exploit vulnerabilities in operating systems and applications to break through the restricted address space and obtain privileged access rights. There are two types of rootkits:

  - **User-mode** rootkits modify important binaries and programs of the operating system. They are executed in the same part of the operating system as where programs are executed. They try to influence installation processes and modify programming interfaces. Because programs generally run only in a restricted address space of the memory, the rootkit infiltrates this address space even before the programs are fully running.
  - **Kernel-mode** rootkits modify or replace the operating system kernel. By this deep infiltration, they enable attackers to perform unrestricted access to the complete system. They are more complex and harder to detect than user-mode rootkits because they work on a deeper level of the system. Security software that runs on the user level of the system is generally unable to detect these rootkits. In contrast, vendors tend to increase the integrated security measures of operating systems, e.g. by drivers signing. This complicates the execution of kernel-mode rootkits.

Generally, antimalware and antivirus software can use pattern-based and behavior-based **detection mechanisms**:

- The **pattern-based** detection works by matching new patterns, which are delivered within software updates, to potential malware. Thus, a reliable detection will only be possible if actual updates are received by the software.
- The **behavior-based** detection analyzes the software in order to identify unusual behavior, which can indicate the presence of malware. This detection mechanism is generally blurred. It can cause false positives, where clean software was falsely suspected, and false negatives, where existing malware was falsely not detected.

A protection level against malware that reaches **one hundred percent** is very difficult to achieve. This is caused by the situation that pattern-based detection can only identify already known malware and behavior-based detections can only detect malware with unusual behavior. Even the combination of both detection mechanisms does not guarantee a complete protection because both detections have weaknesses. However, they are sufficient for providing a reasonable protection level that protects against the most malware.

Antimalware and antivirus software are not only detective safeguards, but also **corrective** ones. After they detected the malware, they can move it to quarantine and prevent that it causes any damages. They can also remove the malware from the system.

3.2.27 Intrusion Detection Systems

Mostly, cyber-attacks cause irregularities in the **log data** at the company firewall. The regular analysis of this log data in order to detect attacks is the responsibility of the firewall administrator. However, the manual analysis means a huge effort for the administrator. He will probably need days or weeks to detect irregularities. Therefore, a fast response will be nearly impossible.

An **intrusion detection system** (IDS) replaces the manual work with automated mechanisms that can analyze log data directly while it is stored. A fast detection and response will be no problem anymore. Besides, the firewall administrator can focus on other tasks. If the IDS detects a potential attack, it can notify the firewall administrator so that he can react based on his expert decision. Alternatively, the IDS could communicate with an intrusion response or intrusion prevention system that automatically reacts based on predefined rules. An IDS can detect potential attacks with signatures or behaviors:

- **Signatures** help to detect common attacks by comparing a sequence of events with known attacks. If these events are detected within the log data, an attack will be assumed. For example, packets that are send to every TCP Port are probably part of a network scan that might be the first step of a cyber-attack. However, if the expected sequence of events does not match with the actual attack, it can be difficult to detect this attack. The events can be mixed up or performed after different waiting periods or even with different source addresses. In result, signatures can only detect attacks that are already known.
- **Behaviors** of users and systems are observed to build a baseline of normal behavior. Every activity that does not match to the baseline will be seen as a potential attack. For example, a user login outside of normal business hours will be highly suspicious if it has not been logged before. However, it is very challenging to build a reliable baseline. The baseline should cover all regular activity and be representative for the future. On the one hand, the observed behavior for the baseline might not be representative. For example, it can already include undetected attacks or the user behavior can be affected by irregular overtime. One the other hand, the user and system behavior is often characterized by changes. These changes will be seen as attacks, if they do not

match the baseline. This can cause many false alarms and impede normal business operations.

Similar to DLP software, intrusion detection systems can be implemented network-based or host-based. A **network-based** IDS gathers log data from different systems in the network. Comprehensive attacks that affect multiple hosts can be detected fast. However, very complex attacks can be difficult to understand. A **host-based** IDS is integrated in the log file creation at every host. This ensures a high transparency. A host-based IDS can also handle encrypted log data. Regarding the implementation, a host-based IDS is more complicated than a network-based IDS because the required changes in the local log file mechanisms can be challenging.

3.2.28 File Integrity Monitoring

The **integrity** of files is important to ensure that they are in a proper condition. In other words, the files shall be in a condition that is expected and needed for business operations. Among other things, transmission errors, malware, input errors, and attacks can cause a loss of integrity. The consequences can be, for example:

- Data cannot be read.
- Applications cannot be started.
- Tampered information can be processed.
- Encrypted data cannot be decrypted.
- Encryption keys cannot be used.
- Compressed archives cannot be extracted.
- Evidence can be no longer valid.

Tools for file integrity monitoring are helpful to detect manipulation and corruption of sensitive files. They create and monitor **hash values** of important files repeatedly. If a hash value deviates from its predecessor, the tools will alert the staff automatically. Hash values form a digital fingerprint. They are almost unique for each file. If a previously generated hash value differs from an actual hash value that belongs to the same file, there will be a strong indication that the file has been altered with an unauthorized change. Hash values are suitable for file integrity monitoring because they map files of different sizes to a hash value with a fix length. The hash values are quite small, e.g. 256 Bit. They need just a small part of the storage that is used by most files, which often need multiple Megabytes. Therefore, the hash values can be stored repeatedly without using much storage. Good hashing algorithms are resistant to collisions. Without collisions, it can be ruled out that a changed file coincidently leads to the same hash value.

Unauthorized **changes** will be particularly alarming if the affected files contain system parameters or other important data. They should be examined more closely to identify possible manipulations or attacks. Important files should be monitored regularly, at least weekly. In case of unauthorized changes, the relevant staff should be alerted immediately. A fast response is essential for a quick disruption of attacks and a limitation of potential damages.

If changes are **planned**, the integrity should also be considered. The integrity before and after the change can be monitored with the corresponding hash value. However, the integrity during the change might be neglected. During this time, integrity is also important. Updates have to be received from a reliable source in order to prevent manipulation. Adjustments have to be checked by internal quality controls in order to prevent errors and tampering by employees or service providers.

3.2.29 Audit Trails

The read and write access to sensitive data should be logged continuously. The created **log files** include audit trails that can be analyzed to identify security violations and to hold responsible persons accountable. Without logging, many security attacks would be unnoticed. They would not be disrupted and they would not cause consequences for those responsible. Only with a complete and reliable logging, unauthorized access can be identified, events can be reconstructed and persons can be hold responsible:

- The **identification of unauthorized access** by analyzing logs can be performed in real-time or after the event. The higher the protection level, the faster should be the identification. Within logs, indirect references to security breaches can be found, too. For example, an increase in processor utilization can be an indication to a virus. However, excessive reviewing of the logs can lead to a significant workload. As an alternative to a real time analysis, protocols can also be reviewed periodically or on demand.
- The **reconstruction of events** increases transparency about the events that have led to a security breach. The knowledge about these events can help to hold people responsible and it can be used to prevent similar security breaches in the future.
- The **responsibility of persons** can be determined by a very accurate analysis of comprehensive and detailed logs. However, the notice of logging affects the general behavior of people. They will look after their actions more conscientiously if they know that their actions are stored in a log. After a security breach, the log entries are helpful to understand the extent and details of the breach. These findings can be used as a basis for disciplinary or legal actions by the company.

Logging helps to collect **information** about status, errors, alarms and other events or conditions that are necessary for detecting and reconstructing errors or attacks. By applications, especially the following information should be recorded:

- **Exceptions** are unusual program states, like errors, that are logged by the application for further evaluation. The amount of the logged exceptions that are reviewed should be limited. Especially, warnings or plausibility errors that usually can be solved directly by the users should be excluded. Too comprehensive reviews would reduce the efficiency because important log entries would be difficult to distinguish from less important ones.
- **Events** are e.g. the start and stop of the application, incorrect login attempts and the exceedance of threshold limits, like storage limits. They facilitate the detection of irregularities and indicate upcoming problems. A rapid reaction to significant events helps to prevent attacks and business process interruptions.
- **Debug information** should be logged only if needed. They help to find errors in the application and facilitate a thorough analysis. This will be especially helpful if errors occur that cannot be understood directly. Since a continuous logging of debug information generally requires very high storage capacity, this information is usually only logged if necessary.
- **Requests** that are sent by the user, e.g. via HTTP (Hypertext Transfer Protocol) or SQL (Structured Query Language), can give important indications about error conditions and attack attempts that are related to the application.
- **Processes and threads** are used for the technical execution of certain application tasks. Each process uses address spaces and further resources of the system. By dividing a process into threads, parallel processing is possible. Especially in case of negative interdependencies between multiple applications or incompatibilities with the system, the information about processes and threads can be very helpful.

Storing and reviewing protocols can be performed centrally on a dedicated system or locally on a workstation or server where the application is executed. Mostly, **central logging** is preferable because it provides various security-related and functional advantages:

- The **configuration** of the entire logging can be set up and managed in just one place. In comparison to the single configuration of all local systems, the central logging prevents inconsistent local configurations and reduces the related workload.
- All logs can be **centrally filtered** and analyzed. Security problems and attacks on various applications or systems can be easily linked and viewed in a larger context. This accelerates the identification und understanding of problems. Without the right tools, logs are often difficult to understand and evaluate. These tools need to be available only on the central system and not on every local system.
- The **alarming** in case of important events or conditions can also be operated centrally. Notifications can be sent via e-mail or SMS (Short Message Service), without the need for interfaces on all local systems.
- **Attacks** are noticed more likely because it is more difficult for an attacker to cover up his malicious activities. When the logs are sent directly to a central

system, he will have fewer opportunities to manipulate or delete logs, even if he controls the local system.
- The statutory or contractual **retention periods** for data can be better monitored and easily met.

Often, attackers try to cover their tracks. In order to prevent the **manipulation** of logs by attackers, the logs must be stored in a way that they cannot be changed easily. For this purpose, a regular archive can be written on write-once media. Alternatively, a 4-eye procedure for changing logs can be used. In addition, the logging must not be stopped or paused without notice. If logging mechanisms cannot be fully protected, at least, a real-time monitoring of protocol services should be performed.

In practice, the amount of log entries is usually so comprehensive that it cannot be managed within normal reviews. Therefore, **management tools** should be used to filter the logs and extract relevant or suspicious log entries. For this purpose, scripts or dedicated software can be used. Some software even includes a short message service, which can be used to send alerts to relevant security personnel. If a concrete suspicion of a security breach occurs, additional details can be viewed in the logs.

3.2.30 Patch Management

Patches include program code that eliminates vulnerabilities or fixes functional problems within operating systems or applications. If attackers discover a vulnerability, they can exploit it by creating and distributing malware that is targeted on this vulnerability. Once a malware that exploits a new vulnerability is discovered, a zero-day exploit has been found. The term zero-day applies to the time from the discovery of a particular vulnerability until a patch has been created to fix it. From then, the days are counted starting from one. A protection against zero-day exploits can be achieved only with workarounds that mitigate the risk of exploitation. Only when a patch is available and the vulnerability is actually closed, it can be eliminated.

In order to establish a regular search for patches, the company should implement a patch management **process**. All software updates bear the risk that unintentional errors or incompatibilities will be caused. Although software vendors generally assure the quality before patches are released, they still should be tested by the company before implementation so that residual risks are minimized.

After the installation of patches, the functions of the updated systems should be **tested**. In order to protect the productive systems, test systems in a separate test environment are used for this test. Hereby, a selection of common usage scenarios can be simulated on the test systems. The results should be documented and reviewed. Log data are a good source for further checks. If the test does not show irregularities or problems, the patches can be installed on other systems, too.

The company should also provide a **rollback** process. Hereby the systems are set back to a state before the patch installation. Possible problems that were not detected in the test can be handled with the rollback process. Otherwise, problems that cannot be fixed quickly might cause extended impairments of business processes.

A patch management **tool** can facilitate the coordination and implementation of patches significantly. Especially in large and complex environments, a tool can provide an overview about the distribution of various patches. While choosing an appropriate tool for the company, the following attributes should be considered:

- How many different operating systems does the tool support?
- Can the tool receive and analyze additional information about patches, e.g. the priority?
- Can the tool check the integrity of patches so that corrupted patches are not installed?
- Are different distribution modes possible, e.g. a sequential distribution to defined groups?
- Does the tool log the distribution and installation of patches?
- Can the tool control a rollback procedure on updated systems?

3.2.31 Disaster Recovery

Disaster recovery aims at the fastest possible recovery of business operations from the technical view after a disaster occurred. Mostly, hardware that has been damaged or lost must be replaced and data that were stored on this hardware must be restored. Disaster recovery is based on a disaster recovery plan (DRP), which describes what needs to be done from a technical view in order to repair or support interrupted business operations. It supplements the business continuity plan that describes the restoration from an organizational view.

The DRP should include a **schedule** that shows the order of tasks within the restoration process. The recovery of critical systems should be described by a detailed systematic guide that can be followed by any system administrator. The responsibilities in case of a disaster should be clearly defined and communicated. Emergency contacts should be included in the DRP so that important key persons can easily be contacted in the event of an emergency. A clear definition of the situation that shall be understood as a disaster is also of great importance. Otherwise, valuable time can be lost before a disaster is actually recognized. The DRP should be kept secure and in an adequate distance from the company's site.

In order to ensure a quick response in case of a disaster, the DRP should be **available** to all employees who are involved in the recovery process. It should also be regularly reviewed and tested, e.g. once a year. The need for updates can be derived from the review and test results. This is the best way to avoid problems caused by outdated instructions or technical incompatibilities during recovery.

3.2.32 Backups

Backups are copies of relevant data on separate storage media. They are kept ready to restore data as needed and to prevent the loss of data. Backups should be created at regular intervals and before material changes or maintenances will be performed. They should also be checked regularly and be restored at least in samples to ensure their accuracy.

Every file has an archive bit that indicates whether a file has already been backed up. It is set on new and modified files and cleared after backup. Three basic **backup methods** use the archive bit to decide which file has to be copied.

- The **complete** backup saves all data completely to the backup media. All files are backed up regardless of the archive bit. After the backup, the archive bit is cleared. The complete backup is most effective and should be done at least once a week.
- The **incremental** backup saves only the files that were newly created or have been changed since the last full or incremental backup. Only files with a set archive bit are backed up. After the backup, the archive bit is cleared. The incremental backup takes less time than the full backup, but the recovery takes much longer. Incremental backups are suitable between full backups and can be done e.g. once a day.
- The **differential** backup saves only the files that were newly created or have been changed since the last full backup. Files that are already part of an incremental backup are not excluded. Like the incremental backup, all files with a set archive are backed up. In contrast to the incremental backup, the archive bit will not be changed after the backup. Directly after the full backup, the processing time of a differential backup is short. The more files are changed or added after the full backup, the longer will be the processing time. For data restore, the last differential and full backup are required. Using differential backups is a compromise between incremental and full backups.

Multiple backup media should be used so that they can be changed according to a **rotation scheme**. Thereby, the retention period of the backups can be raised and the impact of corrupt backup media can be reduced. Common rotation schemes are:

- **First In, First Out**: For a new backup, the backup medium with the oldest data is used. In this scheme, the daily backups are kept for the longest time. The scheme should be used when backups that are older than one rotation cycle are no longer needed, e.g. because the old data has already been archived.
- **Grandfather-Father-Son**: Here, several rotation cycles are used in parallel, like daily, weekly, monthly and yearly. The backup medium for the daily backups

rotates daily, the medium for weekly backups rotates weekly, etc. In addition, individual media can be kept longer. For example, a monthly backup can be stored on quarterly basis at a remote location.

- **Tower of Hanoi**: This scheme is based on the puzzle game with the same name. Each backup medium corresponds to a disk of the towers. For each motion of a game disk, a backup is saved on the corresponding backup disk. The first medium is used every other day, the second every fourth day, the third every eighth day, etc.

3.2.33 Journaling File System

In a journaling file system, all changes to files are also sent to the **journal** before they are actually executed by the system. This will protect the integrity of the files if the system stops abruptly during file operations, e.g. after a crash or power outage. Every file system uses other operations to carry out changes in the file system. However, the most file systems require that the hard disk will be altered on multiple locations. Files can be partitioned into multiple parts that are not stored together. Besides, the metadata and the actual file data often must both be altered. A disruption of this process can lead to the inconsistency of files. For example, the metadata might describe the storage location wrong if a file is changed without adjusting the metadata. With the help of the journal, file operations that were carried out partially at the time of a system failure can be detected and corrected.

Journals can be distinguished on how extensive the contents of the journal are. In general, there are two **journaling methods**:

- **Block journaling** protects the integrity of the file system and its contents. For this purpose, each block that is going to be written to a file will previously be copied into the journal. Since each write operation is performed twice, there is not only a high level of protection, but also a high resource utilization.
- **Metadata journaling** is focused only on the integrity of the file system. This method has a low resource utilization, but also a lower protection level. A system failure might result in corrupted files that cannot be repaired. If a file has been written, the memory allocation can be restored, but not the actual content of the file. If the system stops during a write operation, the file will remain incomplete.

Chapter 4
Economic Aspects

4.1 Financial Indicators

In general, profit-oriented companies concentrate on performing services or creating goods in order to create a **value**. Thus, they achieve a profitable income. Mostly, the values created are not exchanged against other services or goods, but rather sold for money. In order to measure the value of objects sufficiently, companies are assigning monetary values to all inputs that are necessary for the value creation, like working materials, labor, machinery and other cost incurring factors, and outputs that shall be used to create a profit. Money is a general mean of exchange and a unit for calculation.

Financial indicators are essential to control the value generation. They help to assess actual situations critically and to forecast the expected financial profits and losses. They are also an important part of nearly every economic decision making process. These processes are fundamentally based on attributes that facilitate the evaluation of different alternatives. For this purpose, financial indicators should be considered. They ensure the integration of economic aspects. Among other attributes, financial indicators support the scoring of alternatives. Based on the aggregation of sub scores regarding attributes, overall scores can be calculated for the alternatives and a ranking can be created. The alternative with the highest overall score will be on top of the ranking. Thus, the selection of the best investment can be made.

Cybersecurity investments are a subtype of investments. Therefore, they can be evaluated with financial indicators, too. Financial indicators can be concentrated on cybersecurity by addressing security and risk characteristics. However, the definition of profit must be relaxed. Rather than the profit, the benefit must be considered. The benefit of a cybersecurity investment is not calculated with the expected revenue, but rather with the mitigation of risk, i.e. the decrease of expected losses.

In general, financial indicators are distinguished in **static and dynamic indicators**. Static indicators do not consider the time basis of the calculation. An

S. Beissel, *Cybersecurity Investments*, Progress in IS,
DOI 10.1007/978-3-319-30460-1_4

investment that have to be financed at the beginning would be as preferable as an investment that has to be financed years later. Dynamic indicators consider the time basis by using interests that can be added or subtracted to a payment flow. Generally, the dynamic indicators should be preferred because they give a more specific statement about an investment. Only dynamic indicators take interests and liquidity into account. Interests can significantly increase the overall investment costs. Besides, the company that wants to make the investment might not have sufficient liquidity. The necessity to borrow capital can be seen as very unfavorable, e.g. because of the subsequent dependency to the capital provider. However, static indicators are a reasonable way to evaluate investments, too. If not enough information about the payment flow exits, static indicators will be the best choice. Besides, if the time-period in focus is very short or if the overall costs are very low, static indicators will be sufficient for the decision maker. In these cases, the use of dynamic indicators would only complicate the decision making process.

In order to calculate particular indicators, basic information about the considered cybersecurity investments must be available, like acquisition costs, fixed and variable costs, operating lifetime and liquidation revenue. If some **information is missing** and subsequent indicators cannot be calculated, it must be defined how the specific alternative should be handled within the decision making process. In general, three options can be distinguished here:

- If the decision maker uses the **optimistic** approach, the alternative with the missing value will be evaluated with the same score as the alternative with the most preferable value. The decision maker will choose this approach if he supposes that the alternative has the best characteristic regarding the relevant attribute. Thereby, the decision maker will not rule out the best alternative if he does not know all information about it. In contrast, undesirable alternatives can be overrated. In the worst case, an alternative that is not fully known will be chosen over other alternatives that have better characteristics.
- If the decision maker uses the **pessimistic** approach, the alternative with the missing value will be evaluated with the same score as the alternative with the least preferable value. This approach will lead to the best results if the alternatives with missing values have weak characteristics. The decision maker can be sure that no alternative is overrated. The best alternative is at least as good as he calculated. While implementing and operating the best alternative, no negative surprise should occur. Quite the contrary, alternatives with missing values can lead to positive surprises if the alternative proves more useful than anticipated in the decision process. However, very good alternatives might be overlooked if they are affected by many missing information.
- If the decision maker uses the **mean** approach, the alternative with the missing value will be evaluated with the score that is in the middle between the worst and the best possible value. This approach provides a compromise between the overrating of undesirable alternatives and the underrating of desirable alternatives.

Table 4.1 Approaches for missing information

Approach	Decision risk	Replacement value
Optimistic	Overrating	$1000
Pessimistic	Underrating	$11,000
Mean	Overrating & underrating	$6000

For **example**, the decision maker does not have any information about a particular alternative regarding the attribute "implementation costs". At first, he has to determine the value range for the attribute. The costs are represented by an amount equal to or greater than zero. In order to find the optimistic, pessimistic and mean values, he has to analyze the values of all alternatives from the decision process. When assuming that the best value is $1000 and the worst is $11,000, the different approaches lead to the replacement values that are shown in Table 4.1. These values will be used for every alternative that is affected by missing information regarding implementation costs.

It is not useful to generalize which approach should be preferred. Moreover, the choice should depend on the personal **risk tolerance** of the decision maker and the overall risk tolerance of the company, which sponsors the decision making. However, the pessimistic approach has the lowest risk. The decision maker can be relatively sure that the company will be satisfied with the selected alternative. If the decision process is characterized by many missing information, the best alternative will not be overrated and will probably not lead to negative surprises during or after its implementation.

Financial indicators can be subject to changes that are caused by external or internal factors. For example, an external provider can raise the prices of supplies that are necessary for the implementation of the investment, or the internal scope of information systems can be incremented with additional systems. Financial indicators can give a false sense of control if the decision maker does not consider the **investment risks** that address the possibility of changes. Investment risks are understood as the possibility that the monetary variables are changing in an undesirable way within the investment lifecycle. Among others, the following situations that question the benefit of a cybersecurity investment can occur:

- The **costs** for the safeguard are much higher than expected. For example, many individual changes and error repairs can be necessary. This situation must not be permanently during the whole safeguard usage. It can also be limited to a certain time-period, e.g. the initial phase.
- The company might not be able to **maintain** the safeguard adequately because of missing liquid financial recourses. This can be the result of declining business transactions, e.g. because of new competitors, changed costumer needs or new market regulations. If the company does not generate profit, it will have to use its savings. However, the savings will be spent eventually.
- The safeguard might not be able to **protect** against relevant security breaches as expected. Therefore, subsequent financial losses and penalties can occur. This situation can be caused by incomplete vendor specifications, a misinterpretation of the requirements or a substantial change in cyber-attacks.

4.1.1 Static Indicators

The main characteristic of static indicators is that the time basis of the used calculation values is not taken into account. For example, the advance payment of the acquisition costs will be considered the same as periodic payments over the whole lifetime. In consequence, the results are not very precise and can rather be seen as thumb rules. However, static indicators can be sufficient for simple decisions and decisions with little background information. Before actually calculating static indicators, the underlying time-period must be defined so that the relevant costs and profits can be limited. Often, the time-period is limited to the first year of the investment acquisition.

4.1.1.1 Cost Comparison

The cost comparison facilitates the evaluation of alternatives based on all **costs** that are incurred within a defined time-period, e.g. the first year of operation. Among other things, the costs can include the implementation, operation, maintenance and capital costs (see Sect. 4.4.1 for more details about safeguard costs):

- The **implementation costs** incur when the selected alternative shall be transited into an operational state. Mostly, the required tasks from the implementation phase are collected with a work breakdown structure. For every task, human resources and working materials must be provided. The actual deployment should be performed systematically. The availability and integrity of the existing infrastructure must not be jeopardized. In particular, the tasks from the implementation phase can be, among other things, installation, configuration, integration and validation of a new safeguard.
- The **operation costs** include costs for running, controlling and monitoring of relevant objects, like software, servers and infrastructure, costs for customization and further development, like updates and new releases, administration costs, e.g. for user administration, maintenance costs and training costs.
- The **maintenance costs** are important to ensure a permanent quality level of the investment so that unnoticed errors or obsolete components cannot impede the functional usage of the investment. These costs can also include training costs. They are not only necessary when users have to be trained before a new rollout of software or hardware, but also when new functions are added as part of new releases or updates.
- The **capital costs** include the imputed depreciations, which represent the value impairment after a given time, and imputed interests, which represent the lost interests that would have been gained with the average committed capital.

While the determination of the most costs is quite clear, the capital costs can only be calculated with suitable **formulas**. In the following, general instructions are given about this calculation.

The **imputed depreciations** will arise if the value of an object is impaired. The reasons for depreciations can be manifold and so the calculation approaches. The object can lose its value over time, when work is performed, or when its substance is reduced. The most common depreciation approach is based on the assumption that the object loses its value equally over time. This approach is called linear depreciation. Hereby, the depreciation is calculated by subtracting the liquidation yield from the acquisition costs and dividing this by the lifetime of the investment in years. Thereby, the depreciations are equally partitioned over the expected lifetime of the object. This can be demonstrated with the formula:

$$D = \frac{A_0 - L_n}{n}$$

where:

D depreciation (linear) ($ per year)
A_0 acquisition costs ($)
L_n liquidation yield after n years ($)
n lifetime of the object (years)

The **imputed interests** are calculated on the average committed capital. Generally, it can be assumed that the depreciations are earned by the normal business activities. Therefore, the actual committed capital depends on the depreciation approach (see Fig. 4.1). If the liquidation yield is zero, half of the acquisition costs will be committed in average. If the liquidation yield is bigger than zero, the depreciation will be lower and, consequently, more costs will be committed in average. The liquidation yield is committed fully during the whole lifecycle. The rest of the acquisition costs are committed half in average.

For **example**, a new firewall has been acquired for $2000. It shall be used over a proposed lifetime of three years. The following scenarios are compared: a) after three years, the liquidation yield of the firewall is zero, and b) after three years, the liquidation yield of the firewall is $200. In case a), the average committed capital is calculated by cutting the acquisition costs of $2000 in half. The result is $1000. In case b), the difference of the acquisition costs of $2000 and the liquidation yield of $200, in other words $1800, is cut in half. The result is $900, which has to be added to the liquidation yield of $200. Therefore, the average committed capital is $1100. In summary, the liquidation yield leads to reduced depreciations and subsequently to a higher committed capital.

For calculating the **average committed capital**, the liquidation yield and half of the residual acquisition costs have to be summed. By shifting the variables, the formula can be written as follows:

$$\varnothing C_n = \frac{A_0 - L_n}{2} + L_n = \frac{A_0 - L_n + 2L_n}{2} = \frac{A_0 + L_n}{2}$$

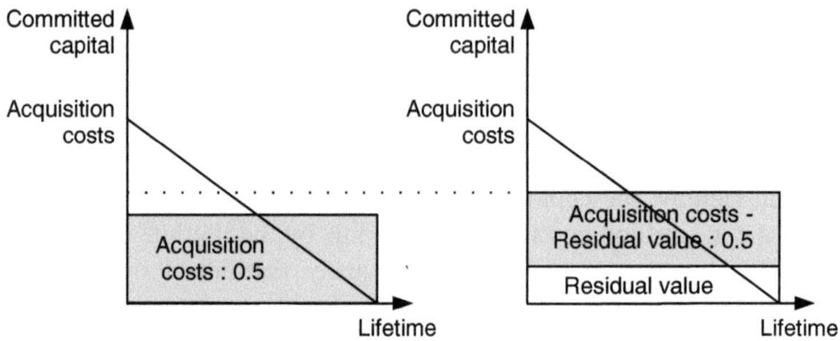

Fig. 4.1 Static acquisition

where:
$\varnothing C_n$ average committed capital over n years ($)
A_0 acquisition costs ($)
L_n liquidation yield ($)

When the average committed capital is known, the **imputed interests** can now be calculated by multiplying the average committed capital by the relevant interest rate:

$$I_n = \varnothing C_n \times i$$

where:
I_n interests over n years ($)
$\varnothing C_n$ average committed capital over n years ($)
i interest rate (%)

In summary, the **total costs** of an alternative can be calculated by creating the sum of all relevant costs. This also includes the capital costs, which consider the imputed depreciations over the given time-period of n years, and the imputed interests, which are caused by the average committed capital.

$$T_n = V_n + n \times D + I_n$$

where:
T_n total costs over n years ($)
V_n various costs for n years ($)
n lifetime of the investment (years)
D depreciation (linear) ($ per year)
I_n interests over n years ($)

In result, the calculated total costs of different cybersecurity investment alternatives can be used for **comparison**. Thereby, an important attribute—the costs—is available that can be helpful for scoring and ranking the considered alternatives.

Although costs are definitely an important attribute, it is not recommended to rely exclusively on it. In particular, the following **restrictions** of the cost comparison should be reminded:

- Only if the **benefits** of the alternatives are the same, the comparison of costs will lead to the best choice. For example, if one antivirus software is half the price of another, but only detects a fraction of current viruses, it will not be a better choice than the other one, which detects 95 % of current viruses.
- Besides, the comparison under the exclusive aspect of costs will only make sense if similar alternatives are compared. Because the underlying **conditions** are not taken into account within the comparison, they should be kept as similar as possible in order to make a reasonable decision. For example, it would be extremely difficult to decide between redundant infrastructure and a backup system because these two alternatives fulfill very different requirements regarding resilience and recovery times.
- Even when assuming that a concentration on the costs aspect is sufficient, the decision maker will only see which alternative would be most favorable. Within the cost comparison, he will not be able to question if the investment generally makes **sense**—even if it is the best one from many considered alternatives. For example, a company can compare proposals from multiple consultants who are asked to create a high protection level on every system in the company. In all proposals, the costs could be higher than the generated business profits. Therefore, even the best alternative would not be reasonable. In contrast, an isolation of sensitive data on a few systems would drastically reduce the scope of the task and, thereby, make the costs more reasonable.
- The **different times** of cost occurrences are not taken into account. However, this is a general point of criticism for static indicators. An alternative that has high acquisition costs and low operation costs, e.g. an integrated automatic monitoring, could be similar to an alternative that has low acquisition costs and high operation costs, e.g. a manual monitoring by administrators. The important difference can be shown with opportunity costs. The capital in the first alternative is committed much earlier and, therefore, cannot be used for other purposes, like other temporal investments. The missed profit from another reasonable purpose is called opportunity costs. In the second alternative, the capital is available longer for company and, therefore, can be used for generating further profits.
- Another problem is the concentration of a specific **time-period**, which represents the whole lifetime of the investment. However, this time-period could include much higher or lower costs than other periods. Therefore, it might not be representative. In consequence, a decision that is based on a "misleading" time-period would not cover enough information for a reasonable decision.

4.1.1.2 Profit Comparison

The **profit comparison** considers not only the costs, but also the benefits of an alternative. Thereby, it eliminates the biggest criticism point of the cost comparison —neglecting the benefits. Therefore, the benefits of the alternatives must not be the same to conduct a reasonable comparison. The profit comparison is focused on the profit gain, in other words the difference of costs and revenues, which are caused by an alternative. The costs can be taken over from the cost comparison calculation. The revenues must be calculated over the same time-period as the costs.

$$P_n = R_n - T_n$$

where:
P_n profit gain over n years ($)
R_n revenue over n years ($)
T_n total costs over n years ($)

The alternative with the highest profit will be the most **favorable**. If the profit of the alternative is higher than zero, the decision maker will also have an indication that it is reasonable from the economic perspective. However, the specific revenue of a cybersecurity investment is generally difficult to measure. Therefore, the risk that is mitigated by the investment must be measured and expressed by a benefit or revenue value.

Although the profit comparison considers the profit gains of the alternatives and, thereby, eliminates one disadvantage, there are still many **restrictions** of the profit comparison:

- Still, the specific underlying **conditions** are not taken into account. The individual preferences of the company that seeks the most suitable cybersecurity investment can be outside of a pure consideration of costs and profits. Since other criteria are influencing the result of the profit comparison, the best alternative under the aspect of profit might not be the alternative that the company really wants and needs. For example, a mobile device management solution that eliminates the most attack vectors will be unfavorable if it requires the use of Android smartphones and the senior management insists on the use of Apple smartphones. Although this case cannot be expressed in profit, it still influences the decision for the best alternative.
- The profit comparison does not take **different times** of cost and profit occurrence into account. As with cost comparison, alternatives might be seen similar, even if high differences in opportunity costs and interests between these alternatives exist.
- The concentration of a specific **time-period** is problematic here, too. The time-period could be characterized by unusual profits or costs and, thereby, it would be hardly representative for the whole lifetime of the investment.

4.1.1.3 Return on Investment

The **return on investment** (*ROI*) is a much better indicator for evaluating an investment than the cost and profit comparison. It allows the comparison of the resources used—the costs—with the resources gained—the profit. In result, the decision maker gets a relative value that puts two single values in relation to each other. Thus, the basic economical principle of using as few resources as possible and gaining as many resources as possible in return can be considered with one indicator. Based on a time-period of one year, the formula for calculating the *ROI* is:

$$ROI = \frac{P_1}{T_1}$$

where:
ROI profitability over one year ($)
P_1 profit gain over one year ($)
T_1 total costs over one year ($)

If the values are related to a time-period of exactly one year, the formula can be used to reveal the annual **interest rate** of the used capital:

$$I_1 = ROI - 1$$

where:
ROI profitability over one year ($)
I_1 interest rate over one year ($)

If the **resulting value** of I_1 is greater than zero, the interests will be positive and a profit will be gained. If the value is lower than zero, the interests will be negative and a loss will be created. A given interest rate can be used as a baseline to decide whether the proposed investment is reasonable in general. It can be derived from a common savings account or other investment alternatives. If the calculated interest rate is below the given one, it will be recommended not to undertake the proposed investment.

The *ROI* has the same **disadvantages** as the profit comparison. It does not take the specific underlying conditions, like individual preferences of the company, into account. It also does not take different times of cost and profit occurrence into account. In addition, the concentration on a specific time-period is problematic here because of potential unusual profits or costs of a given time-period.

In the context of security investments, the *ROI* is often called **return on security investment** (*ROSI*). Technically, it is based on the same calculation. Only the profit gain has to be interpreted from the security view. As described in Sect. 4.5, the security profit is given by the reduction of expected loss. In other words, the difference between the expected loss before the security investment and the expected loss after the security investment represents the profit. The expected loss can be represented by the annualized loss expectancy, which is described in Sect. 4.3.4.1.

4.1.1.4 Static Payback Period

The **static payback period** (*SPP*) represents a time interval in years that has to be expired before the invested capital, which was used for covering the initial costs, has been paid back by the annual returns. In other words, the number of years needed to amortize the initial costs is calculated:

$$n = \frac{T_i}{P_{\varnothing}}$$

where:
n time-period (years)
T_i initial costs of the investment ($)
$P_{\varnothing}$ average annual profit gain ($)

A specific investment will be **favorable** if the calculated time-period is below a given time-period. While choosing between multiple investment alternatives, the one with the lowest time-period will be the best.

Like other static approaches, the missing consideration of the specific time of the occurrence of costs and profits is a big **disadvantage**. For example, one alternative could generate profits after the first three years of its lifetime, while another alternative could generate all of its profits in the first year. If only the average profit is considered, the timely occurrence, which is also an important decision attribute, will be neglected. If the profits are varying strongly from year to year, the *SPP* calculation can be adjusted by subtracting the precise profits for every year, instead of the average profit. In this way, the profits are cumulated until the initial costs have been paid back.

Another disadvantage of the *SPP* is that it gives no indication about the profitability of the investment. An investment with a low amortization time-period can actually have a lower profitability than one with a high time-period. If an investment just has high initial costs but also high annual profits, it will outperform other investments with low initial costs and low profits in the long term.

4.1.2 Dynamic Indicators

The **dynamic indicators** eliminate the biggest drawback of the statistic indicators —the missing consideration of the time perspective. Generally, they take into account different time-periods that can be characterized by different payment flows. In contrast to static indicators that use average values, dynamic indicators use the specific amounts of costs and profits, which are generated during the different time-periods. The most important tool for considering different times is the interest calculation. Based on a given point of time, in other words the calculation point, payment flows are considered plus or minus interests. In this way, all payment flows can be correlated to the calculation point. Thereby, they can be compared without neglecting the time perspective.

As **interests** are the basis for dynamic indicators, they are now described more detailed before explaining the dynamic indicators. Interests can be added or subtracted to a payment flow in order to correlate it to the calculation point. In general, interests have to be added to payments that flow before the calculation point, and interests have to be subtracted from payments that flow after the calculation point. The added interests are commonly called **compounding interests**. They can be added to the payment by multiplying it with the compounding interest factor:

$$c_1 = 1 + i$$

$$c_n = (1+i)^n = c_1^n$$

where:

i interest rate (%)

c_1 compounding interest factor for one year (number)

c_n compounding interest factor for n years (number)

The subtracted interests are called **discounting interests**. They can be subtracted from the payment by multiplying it with the discounting interest factor:

$$d_1 = \frac{1}{1+i}$$

$$d_n = \left(\frac{1}{1+i}\right)^n = d_1^n$$

where:

i interest rate (%)

d_1 discounting interest factor for one year (number)

d_n discounting interest factor for n years (number)

In conclusion, it can be seen that the discounting interest factor is the **reciprocal** value of the compounding interest factor:

$$d_n = \left(\frac{1}{1+i}\right)^n = \frac{1}{(1+i)^n} = \frac{1}{cn}$$

4.1.2.1 Net Present Value

The **net present value** (*NPV*) takes into account the above-described interest factors for making different payment flows comparable. All inflows and outflows are correlated to the calculation point by compounding or discounting the payment values. This makes investments with different inflows and outflows at different times comparable based on a calculation point, which is the present day—as shown by the term "present" in the net present value method.

If a **single investment** is evaluated separately, a *NPV* that is higher than zero will be favorable. If the *NPV* is lower than zero, the investment will cause more costs than profits and it should be rejected. If multiple investments are compared based on their *NPV*, the investment with the highest *NPV* will be the best choice.

The *NPV* is based on the **present day**. Generally, all inflows and outflows regarding a planned investment are in the future. All payments that flow after the calculation point are discounted with the discounting interests. The *NPV* is calculated by summing up all discounted inflows—the profits—and outflows—the investment costs. In addition, the initial investment costs have to be included. They incur in the year zero. Furthermore, the liquidation yields of the investment after the end of the given time-period have to be included. The initial investment costs and the liquidation yield are specifically addressed in the formula:

$$NPV = \sum_{t=1}^{n} (R_t \times d_t - T_t \times d_t) - T_i + L_n \times d_n$$

where:

NPV	net present value of an investment at the present day ($)
R_t	revenue in the year t ($)
d_t	discounting interest factor in the year t (number)
T_t	costs in the year t ($)
T_i	initial costs of the investment ($)
L_n	liquidation yield after n years ($)

Although the *NPV* uses discounting interests to correlate all payment flows to the present day and, thereby, considers time, it is not free from **criticism**:

- The discounting **interest rates** cannot be seen as completely realistic. In particular, the inflows and outflows are discounted with the same interest rate. This does not represent the market in general. Mostly, debit interest rates are higher than credit interest rates. In conclusion, the actual interests during an investment lifecycle can deviate from the calculated interests. Probably, the outflow will be discounted by a higher interest rate than the inflow.

- In the real **market**, the interest rates are changing often. By using the same discounting rate for every time-period, possible changes are not taken into account. In one year, the achievable interest rates might be lower and, in another year, they might be higher.
- Many other **criteria** of the investment might be overlooked by the concentration on payment flows. The company might be also interested in further criteria, like individual preferences or expectations regarding specific investment alternatives. To be precise, the *NPV* alone will only allow a reasonable comparison between multiple investments if they are equal regarding the criteria that are not considered by the *NPV*.

4.1.2.2 Net Future Value

In contrast to the *NPV*, the **net future value** (*NFV*) correlates the payment flows to a future time instead to the present time. This future time is normally the end of an investment lifetime. Inflows and outflows that are correlated to a time later than their occurrence have to be compounded with the compounding interest factor. The initial investment costs have to be compounded over the whole lifetime of the investment and subtracted from the sum of the compounded inflows and outflows. The liquidation yield will be added without interests because it is already correlated to the end of the lifetime. The year zero is the calculation point in the future. The time-periods are counted up from the future to the past. The year one is the time-period of the first year before the calculation point.

$$NFV = \sum_{t=1}^{n} (R_t \times c_t - T_t \times c_t) - T_i \times c_n + L_n$$

where:

NFV net future value of an investment ($)
R_t revenue in the year t ($)
c_t compounding interest factor in the year t (number)
T_t costs in the year t ($)
T_i initial costs of the investment ($)
L_n liquidation yield after n years ($)

The *NFV* is based on similar interest rates as the *NPV*. Therefore, the same **criticism** is applicable for both methods.

4.1.2.3 Equivalent Annual Annuity

The **equivalent annual annuity** (*EAA*) represents the value of an investment in form of an equal value that is applied to every year of the investment lifetime. The average annual profits are confronted to the average annual costs. If the *EAA* is higher than zero, the investment will be reasonable because it generates more profits than costs. If multiple investments are compared, the one with the highest *EAA* will be preferable. The *EAA* also facilitates the comparison of investments with different lifetimes because the *EAA* is related to a time-period of one year. Therefore, it can be compared independently from the investment lifetimes.

The *EAA* is calculated by multiplying the *NPV* by the annuity factor (*ANF*). The *NPV*, which is the value of an investment at the present day, is transformed to a value that is applied equally to every year over the investment lifetime.

$$EAA = NPV \times ANF_{n,i}$$

$$ANF_{n,i} = \frac{(1+i)^n \times i}{(1+i)^n - 1}$$

where:

EAA	equivalent annual annuity of an investment ($)
NPV	net present value of an investment at the present day ($)
$ANF_{n,i}$	annuity factor for a lifetime of n years and an interest rate i (number)
i	interest rate (%)
n	time interval (years)

The *EAA* method will be very helpful if investments with different **lifetimes** have to be compared. In addition, the optimal lifetime of an investment can be determined by using the *EAA* as a variable that shall be maximized.

Because the *EAA* is just another perspective for the *NPV*, the same **criticism** is applicable here. The interest rates cannot be seen as completely realistic, they often change in the real market, and, by the concentration on payment flows, many other criteria might be overlooked, like different investment risks of the investments and the concrete risk appetite of the investor.

4.1.2.4 Internal Rate of Return

The **internal rate of return** (*IRR*) is the interest rate that causes a *NPV* of zero. It represents an average annual yield, which is generated by an investment. Thereby, investments with fluctuating profits and costs can be made comparable.

An investment will be **reasonable** if the *IRR* is equal as or higher than a given interest rate, which, for example, can be derived from the current interest rates for a savings account. In this case, the investment will only be useful if it generates more profit than a savings account. If multiple investment alternatives are compared, the one with the highest *IRR* will be preferable.

The **calculation** cannot be performed by a formula. It has to be done in an iterative way. The basic for this iteration is the formula for the *NPV* calculation that has to be used with different interest rates until the result is zero. The subsequently calculated interest rate is the *IRR*.

$$NPV = \sum_{t=1}^{n} (R_t \times d_t - T_t \times d_t) - T_i + L_n \times d_n = 0$$

$$d_n = \left(\frac{1}{1 + IRR}\right)^n = d_1^n$$

where:

NPV	net present value of an investment at the present day ($)
R_t	revenue in the year t ($)
d_t	discounting interest factor in the year t (number)
T_t	costs in the year t ($)
T_i	initial costs of the investment ($)
L_n	liquidation yield after n years ($)
d_n	discounting interest factor for n years (number)
d_1	discounting interest factor for one year (number)
IRR	internal rate of return (%)

In order to minimize the calculation effort, an **interpolation method** can be performed as follows:

1. At first the *IRR* is estimated in form of an interest rate i_1.
2. The *NPV* is calculated with the interest rate i_1 from step 1. The result is called NPV_1.
3. If $NPV_1 > 0$, another interest rate i_2 will be chosen with $i_2 > i_1$. If $NPV_1 < 0$, another interest rate i_2 is chosen with $i_2 < i_1$.
4. The *NPV* is calculated with the interest rate i_2 from step 3. The result is called NPV_2.
5. A straight-line equation is created with the values of NPV_1, NPV_2, i_1 and i_2. If $i_1 < i_2$, the *IRR* can be interpolated with the first formula. If $i_1 > i_2$, the *IRR* can be interpolated with the second formula.

If $i_1 < i_2$, then:

$$IRR = i_1 + \frac{NPV_1}{NPV_1 - NPV_2} \times (i_2 - i_1)$$

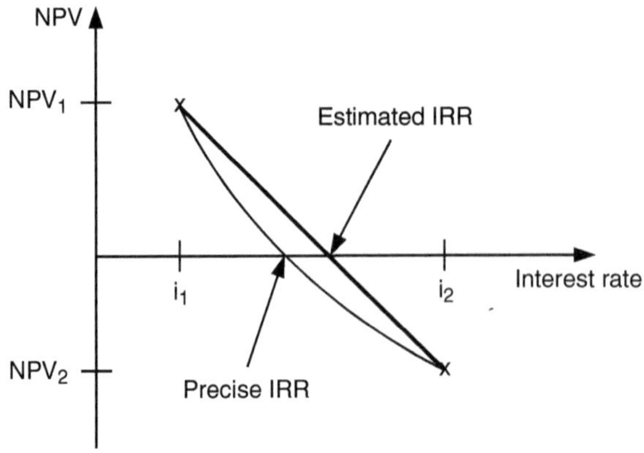

Fig. 4.2 Interpolation of the IRR

If $i_1 > i_2$, then:

$$IRR = i_2 + \frac{NPV_2}{NPV_2 - NPV_1} \times (i_1 - i_2)$$

In reality, the line joining the two points is a curve. However, the interpolation method **approximates** the curve with a straight line. The point at which the straight line crosses the x-axis is the *IRR*. Figure 4.2 illustrates the interpolation of the *IRR* in the case that $i_1 < i_2$.

The **deviation** between the point where the curve crosses the x-axis and the point where the straight line crosses the x-axis is called interpolation error. The closer the interest rates are to each other, the lower is the interpolation error.

The *IRR* is very useful to compare investment alternatives by a single, well understandable percentage value. As a dynamic indicator, it also takes different times of inflows and outflows into account. Because the *IRR* is based on the *NPV*, the **criticism** regarding the interest rates is the same as that for the *NPV*. In addition, the *IRR* has another disadvantage: The size of the investment is not taken into account. For example, an investment where all inflows and outflows are 10 times higher than those of an alternative investment can have exactly the same *IRR*. However, the financial impacts on the company would be quite different.

4.1.2.5 Visualization of Financial Implications

With the **visualization of financial implications** (*VOFI*), all inflows and outflows are recorded over the investment lifetime and interests are calculated like in a bank account. This allows the usage of different interest rates so that a low credit interest rate can be used when the account is on the credit side and a high debit interest rate when the account is on the debit side. Thereby, the interest rates are more realistic and can be oriented on the actual market. The *VOFI* is developed by creating a table

Table 4.2 VOFI table ($)

Time-period	0	1	2
Net cash flows	−24,000	4000	5000
Internal funds			
+Capital contribution	14,000		
−Capital withdrawal			
Instalment loan			
+Borrowing	10,000		
−Redemption		2500	2500
−Debit Interest		1000	750
Financial investment			
−Reinvestment		900	1800
+Disinvestment			
+Credit interest			
Taxes			
−Tax payments		−100	
+Tax refunds			50
Financial balance	0	0	0
Balances			
Debit balance	10,000	7500	5000
Credit balance	0	900	2700
Net balance	−10,000	−6600	−2300

that shows the payments and balances, and even a precise calculation of all interests and taxes.

In the **example** in Table 4.2, various payment flows are shown with a *VOFI*. Here, the following inflows and outflows are listed:

- In the time-period **zero**, the investment had initial costs of $24,000. These costs were covered by a capital contribution of $14,000 and a loan of $10,000.
- In the time-period **one**, the investment led to an income of $4000. The debit balance was reduced by a redemption payment of $2500. A debit interest of $1000 and taxes of $100 were paid. Besides, an additional of $900 had been delivered as a reinvestment. This raised the credit balance.
- In the time-period **two**, the investment led to an income of $5000. Again, the debit balance was reduced by a redemption payment of $2500. A reinvestment of $1800 led to an increase of the credit balance. A debit interest of $750 was paid. A tax refund of $50 had been granted.
- In all time-periods, the **net balance** was calculated by subtracting the debit balance from the credit balance.

Due to the precise calculation of interests and taxes, the *VOFI* is the **most precise** financial indicator. The only **criticism** can be seen in the potentially inaccurate isolation of payment flows that are related to a single investment. Often a company is characterized by various investments and internal and external influences that are more or less strongly related to the payment flows of the company. In consequence, it will often be not clear if the account movements are exclusively related to the investment in focus.

4.2 Asset Appraisement

Assets can be distinguished in current and fixed assets. Current assets are used within the business operations of the company, e.g. raw material. Therefore, the inventory changes continuously. Fixed assets are permanently owned by the company, like an information system. Assets bind capital. The more efficient and effective the assets are acquired and used, the lesser capital is bound. If the assets are related to information, e.g. computers, cybersecurity investments will often be used to protect them. In result of cybersecurity investments, adequate safeguards should be implemented. They can improve the reliability, availability and integrity of assets. This can positively influence the profit generation of the company.

Many cybersecurity safeguards aim at the protection of information and information systems. The first question would be how valuable **information** is. In addition, the business processes that are enabled or supported by this information have a value to the company, too. Information is clearly influencing these processes.

At first, an insight is given into the value of information. This value can be measured indirectly with indicators that only indicate a potential value, and with financial figures that describe the value financially with a specific amount of money. The **measurement** with **indirect** indicators includes qualitative characteristics of information, qualitative improvements of businesses due to information, and particular attributes of information:

- Qualitative **characteristics** of information can be found in the COBIT 5 Information Model (ISACA 2012, p. 82) that describes quality characteristics of information. These features must be met by information in the context of IT in order to be useful for the company. These features include:
  - **Intrinsic quality:** The extent to which data values are in conformance with the actual or true values. Information must be correct and reliable (Accuracy), unbiased, unprejudiced and impartial (Objectivity), regarded as true and credible (Believability), highly regarded in terms of its source or content (Reputation).
  - **Contextual and representational quality:** The extent to which information is applicable to the task of the information user and presented in an intelligible and clear manner, recognizing that information quality depends on the context of use. Information must be applicable and helpful for the task at hand (Relevancy), not missing and of sufficient depth and breadth for the task at hand (Completeness), sufficiently up to date for the task at hand (Currency), appropriate in volume for the task at hand (Appropriate amount

of information), compactly represented (Concise representation), presented in the same format (Consistent representation), in appropriate languages, symbols and units, with clear definitions (Interpretability), easily comprehended (Understandability), easy to manipulate and apply to different tasks (Ease of manipulation).

  - **Security/accessibility quality:** The extent to which information is available or obtainable. Information must be available when required, or easily and quickly retrievable (Availability/timeliness), restricted appropriately to authorized parties (Restricted access).

- Qualitative **improvements** of businesses can be created by information if the information leads to a measureable improvement, which can be seen in e.g. improved key performance indicators (KPIs). If the KPIs do not directly influence the profit, it will not be visible which specific value increase is caused by the information. It will be seen that there is an influence, but it will not be directly quantifiable with an amount of money. For example, if an employee is trained regarding the use of an electronic purchasing system, the availability of work equipment will be strongly increased. Although there is no direct influence on the revenues, it would be safe to say that business processes are positively affected, e.g. by indirectly decreasing the throughput time.
- Particular **attributes** of information can also be interpreted as an indirect influence to its value. Important attributes are the access count and the age. Generally, the more users access the information, the more users can benefit from this information and the more valuable it probably is. However, other conditions should not be ignored, e.g. the type of users accessing the information and the concrete benefits that have been derived from this information. The second mentioned attribute—the age—is important because, today, most information has a short lifecycle. While the newest information can be a crucial competitive advantage, older information becomes obsolete quickly. This does not always apply to all information, but it can be seen in many cases of information distributions.

The measurement methods with **direct** indicators include concrete figures that can be directly interpreted as the value of information or that can be transformed to a specific value. The common methods are focused on replacement costs, revenue changes, and market value:

- The **replacement costs** address the scenario that all information is lost and the company has to replace this information with newly acquired or reconstructed information. These costs include, for example, the development of interview checklists, questionnaires, data analysis, and database design and administration. In this scenario, it is supposed that all information is needed and, consequently, would have to be replaced after a loss. It does not consider the specific benefit that is generated with the information directly or indirectly. Some information might have a high impact on the revenue while other information might not have a benefit at all. Therefore, it will be better if the replacement costs are connected to the considered business impact.

- By looking at the **revenue**, it can be clearly seen how information affects the business. Often, it leads to a raise or reduction of the revenue. For example, a sales team can be monitored before and after using particular information. The difference in the subsequent revenue indicates the information value. Sales can be affected by various influences and market factors, which might even change during the information value measurement. In conclusion, it can be very difficult to isolate business events from all other influences except the information.
- The **market value** of information can also be used to measure the value of company information. The idea is to find out for which price the company information is available in the free market. Alternatively, the price for similar information can be searched in the market. This method might seem to be very objective, but it has some disadvantages, too. On the one hand, the price of information in the market can be very volatile. It depends on the current demands. Therefore, the price can increase or decrease quickly. On the other hand, the market value is often not equal to the value that is assumed from the individual company perspective. Moreover, the company value is affected by various characteristics of the company and its intent to use the information. Among other things, the industry sector can affect the information value. For example, experiences about vendors can be highly valuable in commerce, while they are less interesting in banking. Besides, information that is intended to generate more customer orders can be more valuable than information that is intended to improve the purchase of office equipment.

Besides information, the value of other **assets** can be measured, too. Safeguards can protect these assets directly or indirectly. They prevent tampering, damages, theft and compromise. The compromise is primarily relevant for intangible assets, including information. From the perspective of the **asset type,** the assets can be distinguished in tangible and intangible assets:

- **Tangible** assets have a physical form. They can be further distinguished in short-term and long-term tangible assets:
  - **Short-term** tangible assets are also called the inventory. It includes working materials, raw materials, and finished or unfinished products. These assets are characterized by a short retention period within the company. They are processed and transformed into other assets or they are sold and delivered to other companies or individuals. Due to the high fluctuation of the inventory, its current value is often difficult to measure. For this purpose, the company can use one of various principles, for example LIFO, FIFO or weighted average: With LIFO (Last In—First Out), it is assumed that the consumption of inventory means that the recent inventories are or have been consumed first. This is assumed within measurement, but the physical consumption might be managed differently. With FIFO (First In—First Out), inventory

that has been stored first will be removed first from the storage. With the weighted average, the average cost of an asset over a year is used.

– **Long-term** tangible assets are mainly equipment, land, buildings and plants. The initial cost equals the value at the time of implementation. However, the value is changing over time. The initial cost must be adjusted if the value increases or decreases. For example, this can happen in case of aging, improvements or damages of the asset. Depreciation methods are used to consider the loss in value due to aging. Mostly, it is calculated with a linear method, which assumes the same estimated losses in every year, or with a decreasing method, which assumes higher losses in the earlier years and lower losses in the later years.
– **Intangible** assets are not physical. Examples are trademarks, patents, and the goodwill of the company. Intangible assets can have a crucial impact on revenues and profits. If these assets are generated internally, they will mostly not be measured and reported. In contrast, this is required for externally acquired intangible assets. Information is an intangible asset, too.

The common **measurement methods** of information assets can also be used for other intangible assets and even tangible assets. Generalized measurement methods for any kind of asset can be focused on replacement costs, revenue changes, or market value:

- The **replacement costs** reflect the amount of money that would be required to replace the asset by a new similar one. With the new asset, it must be possible to achieve the same service quality as that of the previous asset. How the asset influences the value generation in the company is irrelevant for determining the replacement costs.
- The **revenue** includes future amounts of values that can be generated by using the asset. Often, the future revenue cannot be determined exactly. Moreover, the revenue can be estimated under the consideration of market expectations. If the decision maker aims at increasing the precision of the estimation, future cash flows must be discounted so that they will be comparable to current cash flows.
- The **market value** is derived from the market transactions that are performed to purchase similar assets. Thereby, the level of similarity must be taken into account. If the same asset is available in the market, the value can be derived more easily than if only a group of other assets is available for providing the needed functionalities. Besides, other factors are relevant, too. For example, the costs of transport or configuration of the new asset should be considered.

The **measurement precision** depends on the preference for quantitative or qualitative determinations.

- The **quantitative** determination of asset values is the preferable way. Hereby, the measurements are performed quantitatively and quite objectively, e.g. with monetary amounts. These amounts are also an important requirement for the quantitative risk assessment because they include enough details for a risk-based decision making from the economic view.

- However, in some situations a quantitative determination will not be possible or will not make sense from the economic view, e.g. if it is much too expensive to gather the needed numbers. In these situations, a **qualitative** determination has to be performed. Here, non-numerical classes are used to express a relative classification of asset values on a scale, e.g. low, middle and high.

Generally, asset values can be measured **independently**, e.g. by considering the replacement costs or the market value of a single asset. However, most assets are needed to provide certain business functions. If an asset is unavailable or faulty, business processes can be impaired or even disrupted. The subsequent losses will not only include the single asset costs, but, moreover, all costs from business problems that are caused by the asset. In conclusion, an asset value should be measured in **dependence** to business processes that are supported or enabled by the asset.

4.3 Risk Evaluation

A special characteristic of cybersecurity investments is that the benefits of the investments are mostly difficult to measure. They primarily protect against negative events, which only occur in a specific probability. In other words, safeguards from cybersecurity investments **mitigate** the risk of a negative event. Therefore, the risk evaluation is also an important part of the cybersecurity investment analysis.

After implementing a safeguard for mitigating the risk, the risk management does not end. On the one hand, the **residual risk** must be handled, e.g. by accepting it. On the other hand, the safeguard must be continuously monitored and maintained so that it will be ensured that it will function properly and can control the risk permanently. In addition, a periodic search for alternative safeguards should be performed. Due to new technical progress or environmental changes, other safeguards can become more cost effective for the company.

4.3.1 Risk Definition

An **IT risk** is derived from the probability and the impact that the business of a company can be affected by, among other things, a compromise, manipulation, damage or malfunction of data and IT systems.

In order to make IT risks generally understood, they should be described with unambiguous and clear business-relevant terms. All stakeholders should be able to understand how IT risks can affect the business performance of the company. Well-known approaches to **associate IT risks to the business** are:

- As described in Sect. 4.2, the **COBIT 5 Information Model** describes quality characteristics of information. Risks arise from the potential failure to fulfil these characteristics. If they are not met, the company can be seriously impaired. Probably, important business tasks will not be performable if fundamental information is unavailable, corrupted or otherwise affected.

- The **Enterprise Risk Management** by COSO (2004, p. 3) includes four business-related objectives that shall be achieved with the support of risk management:
  - **Strategic:** High-level goals, aligned with and supporting the company mission
  - **Operations:** Effective and efficient use of company resources
  - **Reporting:** Reliability of reporting
  - **Compliance:** Compliance with applicable laws and regulations
- The **4A Risk Management Framework** (Westerman and Hunter 2007) is used to describe IT risks as potential unplanned events that threaten four interconnected business goals—the four A's:
  - **Agility:** The ability to change the business while controlling cost and speed
  - **Accuracy:** The ability to provide timely, correct and complete information to meet business needs
  - **Access:** The ability to provide access to information and functionality for the appropriate people, including customers and suppliers
  - **Availability:** The ability to ensure a continuous business operation and information flowing, and to recover after interruptions
- The **Factor Analysis of Information Risk** (FAIR) focuses on asset objects, which can be data, systems or other components that support information-related activities (Jones 2005, p. 15). Risks arise from the potential negative impact on asset objects. In particular, their value, their associated control measures, and related liabilities can be affected.
- The **Balanced Scorecard** (Kaplan and Norton 1992) is a tool that can be used for managing strategies and measuring objectives. IT risks can be derived from the probability that specified objectives cannot be achieved. These objectives belong to four perspectives, as shown in Fig. 4.3:
  - **Finance** objectives are usually focused on increases in profitability, specifically by increasing revenues, costs or profits.
  - **Customer** objectives are related to the competitiveness of the company and the appearance to customers. These objectives can include, among other things, the increase in customer satisfaction and the creation of a unique selling point.
  - **Process** objectives address internal processes. They are optimized regarding their value and impact on the supply chain. Specifically, the efficiency and throughput times of processes can be seen as key issues.
  - **Innovation** objectives facilitate the company's growth with innovations. Innovations can be supported by, among other things, training staff and requesting new product ideas.

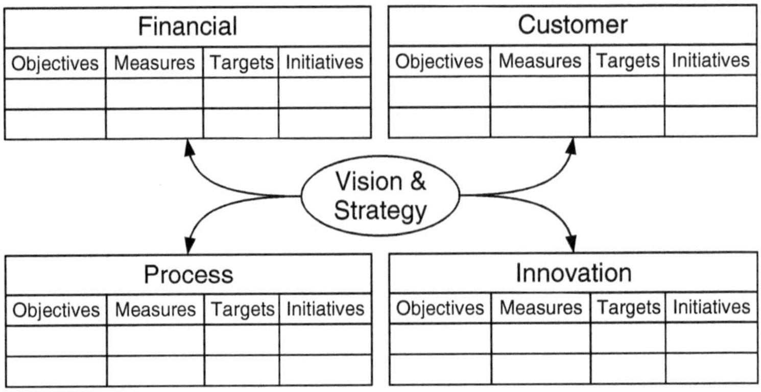

Fig. 4.3 Balanced scorecard

4.3.2 Risk Response

The risk response is focused on the planned actions that shall be performed in the case that specific risks have been identified. The approaches to handle risks can be distinguished to **four types**. On the one hand, a company might prefer a particular type. The selection of a type can be oriented on, among other things, the values of the company. The selected type can be binding for all employees by setting up relevant policies and guidelines. On the other hand, individual risks can fundamentally influence the selection of the type so that it will be difficult to assign a particular type of risk response to the whole company. The four types of risk response include:

- The **mitigation** of risks is the reduction of the probability that an undesirable event occurs or the reduction of the potential damage that can be caused by this event. In the best case, the probability or damage can be reduced to zero. This would result in the elimination of the risk. Normally, safeguards are implemented to mitigate risks as far as possible under consideration of the cost-effectiveness.
- The **transfer** of risks ensures that the potential damages that can be caused by an undesirable event will be taken over by another company. This can be realized by outsourcing tasks that are affected by risks, or by concluding an insurance contract.
- The **acceptance** of risks is based on the decision by senior management not to influence the risk. Generally, this decision is made after a thorough risk analysis. The decision will be seen as reasonable if all available safeguards are affected by a poor cost-effectiveness. In this case, the implementation of a safeguard would result in costs that are higher than the potential damages.
- The **rejection** of risks does not follow a proper analysis. The risks and the underlying probabilities and damages are not considered on purpose. However,

the potential damage can be very high. In conclusion, this approach can endanger the survival of the whole company. Therefore, it is generally inappropriate for a professional risk management.

4.3.3 Risk Management Frameworks

Risk management **frameworks** provide systematic approaches for performing a thorough analysis of threats and subsequent risks. Hereby, risks can be assessed under economic aspects so that the decision making in cybersecurity is supported. The safeguards that are most efficient in mitigating or eliminating the identified risks are most likely to be appropriate for the use in the company.

Generally, a company can also perform a risk analysis without considering any risk management frameworks. However, a **non-standardized** approach has many drawbacks:

- The **transparency** towards outside parties will not be given. External stakeholders cannot see how the risks have been identified and if all the important steps have been really considered. For example, a credit grantor might not be sure that the risk analysis within the company has been successful. The missing transparency makes it also difficult to reconstruct the risk analysis after a breach. Probably, the reason why a specific risk has not been covered sufficiently will be obscure. If there is no comprehensible approach in use, a problem or a guilty employee will be hard to identify.
- The missing **comparableness** of the risk analysis is another drawback. Because of the unique approach, no baseline can be used. Consequently, it cannot be find out if the risk analysis is performed efficiently and in a reasonable time-period. Results from previous risk analysis cannot be compared either.
- Besides, the company will have problems if external **support** or trainings regarding the risk analysis are needed. In this case, no consultant will be available that has knowledge or experience in the company specific, non-standardized risk analysis.

A risk analysis that is based on a **standardized** framework should always be preferred over a non-standardized risk analysis. The reasons for using a risk management framework are primarily the advantages regarding transparency, comparableness and support.

Using a standardized framework is an important step towards a **successful** and reasonable risk analysis. Other success factors are:

- A comprehensive **participation** of responsible individuals should be demanded by management. This ensures that the input is generated by the most appropriate specialists from the company. In result, costs can be reduced and the acceptance among other employees and stakeholders can be raised.

- All **hierarchy** levels of the organization should be involved in the risk analysis. Representatives from the operational staff, department heads and senior management should provide input. If particular levels are not considered, the acceptance and quality of the results will probably be impaired.
- External **support** should be considered if necessary. Especially in the fields of technology, quality management, and project management, a professional support could strongly improve the outcomes of the risk analysis.
- The results of the risk analysis should be used for deriving appropriate **measures**. The knowledge about the status quo should not be satisfactory for the company. Moreover, the company should see the status quo as a starting point for developing appropriate measures and, thereby, improving the protection of the company.
- Cybersecurity should be understood as a continuous **process**. Therefore, risk management is also continuously. Risks are changing over time. New attacks and innovative technologies lead to changes in the risk situation and the protection of the company. In conclusion, a risk analysis should be performed regularly, e.g. once a year. Besides, every crucial change that comes to knowledge of the company, e.g. a new type of malware, should be considered immediately by adjusting or complementing current safeguards.

Common risk management **frameworks** are described in the subchapters 4.3.3.1–4.3.3.8 in alphabetical order. An overview is given by the following bullet points:

- **COBIT:** Risk management is part of the comprehensive COBIT framework for governance of enterprise IT. Risk management can be oriented on the COBIT principles. Therefore, companies can benefit from synergies if they have used COBIT before. The risk assessment is done with qualitative measures. COBIT does not give a strict guideline on how this has to be implemented in detail.
- **CRAMM:** This framework gives guidance on a rigid process for assessing the risks of particular assets. It can be used manually or with software, which lists a huge amount of potential safeguards.
- **FAIR:** It includes a risk management process that is characterized by many quantitative measurements that can be computed mathematically. Besides, this framework is accompanied by a taxonomy of risk terms that strongly facilitate the understanding by involved stakeholders.
- **FRAAP:** In this framework, it is assumed that the available time is strictly limited. Therefore, it is aimed at achieving quick and useful results in a short time-period. It is focused on single assets and it gives guidance on assessing the related risks in hours.
- **OCTAVE:** This framework has been developed in university research. It provides a well-founded process for risk management. Two different versions of this framework (OCTAVE-S and OCTAVE Allegro) give appropriate guidance for small and large companies.
- **RMF:** As official framework from a U.S. government agency, RMF provides a reliable source for risk management guidance. The big advantage of RMF is the

comprehensive documentation in risk management and related fields. In contrast, it can also be a challenge to handle this documentation.
- **RMM:** This framework does not address risk management directly. Moreover, it is used to evaluate the existing enterprise risk management that have been implemented in the company. It can be applied for all risk management frameworks.
- **TARA:** At first, this framework was created and used exclusively by Intel. Over time, it has been recognized by other companies. It gives an interesting view on risk management. Valuable knowledge can be obtained from the aspects of threat agents and their motivation, methods, and objectives. The resulting libraries facilitate the mapping of appropriate safeguards.

It can hardly be generalized which framework will fit best for a particular company. Moreover, the individual goals and objectives of a company should be considered while **selecting a framework**. Some companies require a well-founded and recognized standard—some tend to more innovative approaches. Some appreciate comprehensive documentation—others are focused on a quick applicability without needing to view much documentation. Some want to evaluate the whole information environment—others concentrate on a single asset.

Table 4.3. shows the various **steps** that have to be performed within a risk management process in accordance with the different frameworks. RMM is not comparable to the other frameworks because it is meant exclusively for evaluating a risk management process. Therefore, it is not shown in Table 4.3.

4.3.3.1 COBIT

Control Objectives for Information and Related Technology (COBIT) is a comprehensive framework in the field of governance and management of IT. It also includes a risk management framework. Author of COBIT and the related risk management framework is **ISACA**, which is a nonprofit, global membership association that develops knowledge and practices for information systems.

All the content of COBIT for Risk aims to apply the five general COBIT **principles** to risk (ISACA 2015, S. 13):

1. **Meeting Stakeholder Needs:** Risk optimization is one of the three components of value creation. The other components are benefits realization and resource optimization
2. **Covering the Enterprise End-to-End:** Throughout all phases of risk governance and management, the whole enterprise shall be covered by including everyone and everything, internal and external that is relevant to risk activities.
3. **Applying a Single Integrated Framework:** This framework aligns with all major risk management standards (including ISO 31000, ISO/IEC 27005, and COSO Enterprise Risk Management—Integrated Framework).
4. **Enabling a Holistic Approach:** All interconnected elements required to adequately deliver risk governance and management have to be identified.

Table 4.3 Comparison of process steps in risk management frameworks

#	COBIT	CRAMM	FAIR	FRAAP	OCTAVE-S	OCTAVE Allegro	RMF	TARA*
1.	IT risk identification	Asset identification and valuation	Identify scenario components	Pre-FRAAP	Build asset-based threat profiles	Establish risk measurem. criteria	Categorize information system	Measure current threat agent risks
2.	IT risk assessment	Threat and vuln. assessment	Evaluate loss event frequency	FRAAP session	Identify infrastructure Vuln.	Develop an inf. asset profile	Select security controls	Distinguish threat ag.
3.	Risk response and mitigation	Counterm. selection and recommend.	Evaluate probable loss magnitude	Post-FRAAP	Develop security strategy and plans	Identify inform. asset containers	Implement security controls	Derive primary objectives
4.	Risk and control mon. and reporting		Derive and articulate risk			Identify areas of concern	Assess security controls	Identify methods likely to manifest
5.						Identify threat scenarios	Authorize inform. system	Determine important exposures
6.						Identify risks	Monitor Sec. Con.	Align strategy
7.						Analyze risks		
8.						Select mitigation approach		

*The text in this column has been shortened

5. **Separating Governance From Management:** Good governance ensures that thresholds for the enterprise risk appetite and tolerance are set and that useful, timely and accurate risk information is made available to managers. Good management considers the provided risk information and pursues objectives in ways that align with the enterprise risk appetite and tolerance.

COBIT 5 defines **enablers** as factors that individually and collectively influence whether something will work. In COBIT, risk is examined with regard to these seven categories of enablers. It is described how each enabler contributes to overall risk governance and management. The enablers are organized into seven categories (ISACA 2012, p. 27):

1. **Principles, policies and frameworks** are the vehicle to translate the desired behavior into practical guidance for day-to-day management.
2. **Processes** describe an organized set of practices and activities to achieve certain objectives and produce a set of outputs in support of achieving overall IT-related goals.
3. **Organizational structures** are the key decision making entities in an enterprise.
4. **Culture, ethics and behavior** of individuals and of the enterprise are very often underestimated as a success factor in governance and management activities.
5. **Information** is pervasive throughout any organization and includes all information produced and used by the enterprise. Information is required for keeping the organization running and well governed, but at the operational level, information is very often the key product of the enterprise itself.
6. **Services, infrastructure and applications** include the infrastructure, technology and applications that provide the enterprise with information technology processing and services.
7. **People, skills and competencies** are linked to people and are required for successful completion of all activities and for making correct decisions and taking corrective actions.

The activities in risk management with COBIT are categorized to the following subsequent **steps** (ISACA 2015, pp. 5 ff.):

1. **IT Risk Identification:** This is a goal-driven process that begins with understanding business goals and, then, understanding how IT goals align with and support those business goals. Hereby, a risk is derived from a threat, vulnerability and probability. A threat has an impact to the confidentiality, integrity or availability of the information. A vulnerability is caused by a weakness in design, implementation, operation or internal control of an asset. The probability is a measurement of the likelihood that an event can reach a target. Risk scenarios are used to facilitate the risk identification. An IT risk scenario is a description of an IT-related event that can lead to a loss event that has a business impact, when and if it occurs. Identified risks are entered into a risk register.
2. **IT Risk Assessment:** In this step, a prioritization is created that shows which risk should be given attention first versus which can wait until later. When preparing for the assessment, as much broad-based information about the

enterprise IT systems as reasonably possible shall be gathered. Next, a qualitative analysis, which places significant emphasis on judgement, intuition and experience, shall be performed.
3. **Risk Response and Mitigation:** The goal of risk response is to align risk with the enterprise risk appetite in the most cost-effective manner possible. Therefore, the level of remaining (residual) risk should be within the enterprise risk tolerance. For each risk on the list, an appropriate risk response has to be chosen:

   - Avoid the risk by ending activities that place the enterprise within reach of the associated threat
   - Mitigate the risk by changing affected business processes or implementing new controls
   - Transfer (or share) the risk by outsourcing the process or insuring against the potential cost
   - Accept the risk by acknowledging it and moving on without further action

4. **Risk and Control Monitoring and Reporting:** Risk reporting keeps stakeholders aware of both current risk and any observed risk trends so that business decisions can be made from an informed perspective. Risk monitoring generates the data used in these reports in a manner that is accurate, timely and complete. It follows the goal of ensuring that risk responses put in place by the enterprise continue to maintain risk within tolerable levels.

4.3.3.2 CRAMM

The Central Computer and Telecommunications Agency (CCTA), currently called Office of Government Commerce (OGC), which is part of the **United Kingdom** government has developed the CCTA Risk Analysis and Management Method (CRAMM) in 1985.

The **idea** of CRAMM is to analyze assets and derive risks that shall be mitigated effectively (Marquis 2008). Risks are related to potential damages that can be caused by a failure in confidentiality (unauthorized disclosure), integrity (unauthorized modification or misuse) or availability (destruction or loss). CRAMM is characterized by a **rigid format**. The data collection has to be performed with meetings, interviews, and questionnaires. Identified assets have to belong to one of three categories (data, application/software, physical assets). The impact of the confidentiality, integrity and availability (CIA) of the asset on potential losses has to be considered. The vulnerability has to be measured with an ordinal scale (very high, high, medium, low or very low). The risk has to be expressed also on an ordinal scale (high, medium or low).

The three **steps** of CRAMM, which can be implemented with dedicated software support or manually, are (Marquis 2008):

1. **Asset identification and valuation:** In this step, the assets have to be identified and valued. Under the assumption that the scope has already been determined,

assets within the scope have to be found in the categories data, application/software and physical assets. If a configuration management database (CMDB) is available, it will be a valuable source. Otherwise, the data has to be found with meetings, interviews, and questionnaires. Next, assets have to be valued. With the help of the asset owner, assets can be valued with the impact and cost resulting from a loss of confidentiality, integrity, or availability.

2. **Threat and vulnerability assessment:** With the data from the first step, the CIA risks to assets have to be assessed. Hereby, the vulnerability has to be determined. It indicates how likely potential losses will occur. Among others, support personnel, experts and other personnel can be asked with prepared questionnaires. By multiplying the impact (from step 1) by the vulnerability (from step 2), the actual risk can be calculated.
3. **Countermeasure selection and recommendation:** Here, the data from the previous steps can be used to identify the changes that are required in order to manage the identified CIA risks. Appropriate countermeasures and other ways to mitigate the risks have to be considered and selected. The high-level risks should be managed first. In addition, also quick, easy or cheap fixes to low-level risks should be implemented. Dedicated CRAMM software contains a countermeasure library consisting of over 3000 detailed countermeasures. However, the software is optionally and countermeasures can be found by experienced experts, too.

If CRAMM is performed manually, with pen and paper or office software, the use of **spreadsheets**—as shown in Table 4.4—will be recommended (Marquis

Table 4.4 Example CRAMM Table

Asset: customer addresses Asset owner: Mr. A. Owner						
	Confidentiality: public (0), restricted (1–5), confidential (6–9), secure (10)		**Integrity**: none (0), low (1–3), moderate (4–7), high (8–9), very high (10)		**Availability**: none (0), low (1–3), moderate (4–6), high (7–8), very high (9), mandatory (10)	
Impact:	3		6		7	
Threats:	**Disclosure**	**Loss**	**Input error**	**Hacking**	**Power failure**	**Drive failure**
Vulnerability: none (0), low (1–4), moderate (5–7), high (8–9), very high (10)	8	5	7	6	4	3
Risk: Impact × Vulnerability	24	15	42	36	28	21
Risk Level: Low (1–33), Medium (34–67), High (68–100)	Low	Low	Medium	Medium	Low	Low
Countermeasures:	Password	Encryption	Data validation	Firewall	UPS	RAID

2008). A separate spreadsheet should be drafted for every asset. In the above-mentioned step 1, the asset and the asset owner should be listed. The owner has to choose a value from 0 to 10 for confidentiality, integrity and availability. In step 2, a column for each threat that was identified by the owner has to be created. Next, the vulnerability has to be estimated for each threat. Again, values from 0 to 10 can be used. The risk for each threat is calculated by multiplying the impact by the vulnerability. The risk level can be derived from the resulting risk value. In step 3, the identified countermeasures for each threat of the asset are entered in the bottom line.

Generally, the countermeasures with the following characteristics should be **preferred** during implementation (Marquis 2008):

- Those that address multiple threats concurrently
- Those that can be used to protect assets with high risks
- Those that are applicable for risks where no countermeasures are already in use
- Those that are less expensive in implementation and maintenance
- Those that are more effective at eliminating or mitigating risks
- Those that prevent threats rather than detecting or correcting them
- Those that are quick, easy, and inexpensive in implementation and maintenance

4.3.3.3 FAIR

The Factor Analysis of Information Risk (FAIR) has been developed in order to provide a standard nomenclature in risk management and a primer framework for risk analysis without cover large and complex insights into risk analysis. Moreover, the focus is to provide clear and useful guidance. FAIR provides a risk management **framework** that covers the following subjects (Jones 2005, p. 7):

- A **taxonomy** includes terms and definitions in risk management. Thereby, it provides a foundational understanding of risk.
- A **method** is provided for measuring the values that are used to describe a risk. In detail, various attributes and the impact of the risk are represented, including threat event frequency, vulnerability, and loss.
- A **computational engine** simulates the relationships between the measured attributes. Thereby, a specific risk can be derived.
- A **simulation model** enables building and analyzing risk scenarios of different sizes and complexities. The model allows the application of the taxonomy, measurement method, and computational engine.

In FAIR, a quantitative risk analysis is performed mostly. FAIR uses many **cardinal scales**—specific numbers—and less ordinal scales—like high, medium and low. Losses and probability values are represented with estimations in dollar. This allows a mathematical modeling.

The four main **steps** for managing risks with the FAIR framework are (Jones 2005, appendix A, pp. 1 ff.):

1. **Identify Scenario Components:** In the first step, the asset at risk has to be identified. If a multilevel analysis is performed, additional objects that exist between the primary asset and the threat community will have to be identified, too. Besides, the threat community has to be identified. It describes the origin of the threat. It can be identified as human or malware, and as internal or external. Specific examples for a threat community are the network engineers or cleaning crew.
2. **Evaluate Loss Event Frequency:** In this step, some values have to be estimated. The Threat Event Frequency (TEF) is the probable frequency within a given timeframe that a threat agent will act against an asset. The Threat Capability (Tcap) is the probable level of force that a threat agent is capable of applying against an asset. The Control Strength (CS) is the expected effectiveness of controls over a given timeframe as measured against a baseline level of force. The Vulnerability (Vuln) is the probability that an asset will be unable to resist the actions of a threat agent. It can be derived from the Tcap and CS. The Loss Event Frequency (LEF) is the probable frequency within a given timeframe that a threat agent will inflict harm upon an asset. It can be derived from the TEF and Vuln.
3. **Evaluate Probable Loss Magnitude:** In this step, the losses that can be potentially caused by a risk are estimated. The worst-case loss can be estimated by determining the threat action that would most likely result in a worst-case outcome, estimating the magnitude for each loss form that is associated with that threat action, and summing the loss form magnitudes. The probable loss can be estimated by identifying the most likely threat community actions, evaluating the probable loss magnitude for each loss form that is associated with those threat actions, and summing the loss form magnitudes.
4. **Derive and Articulate Risk:** In this step, a risk is articulated with two key pieces of information: the estimated Loss Event Frequency (LEF) and the estimated Probable Loss Magnitude (PLM). By using a risk matrix, the LEF and PLM lead to a risk level between low and critical.

The **taxonomy** in FAIR provides a structure of many useful terms in risk management. Particularly, the LEF and the PLM are divided in various sub-terms (Jones 2005, pp. 16 ff.). The according branches of the taxonomy are shown in Figs. 4.4 and 4.5.

The terms in the taxonomy branch for **LEF** (see Fig. 4.4) are defined as follows:

- **Loss Event Frequency:** The probable frequency within a given timeframe that a threat agent will inflict harm upon an asset.
- **Threat Event Frequency:** The probable frequency within a given timeframe that a threat agent will act against an asset.
- **Vulnerability:** The probability that an asset will be unable to resist the actions of a threat agent.
- **Contact:** The probable frequency within a given timeframe that a threat agent will encounter an asset.

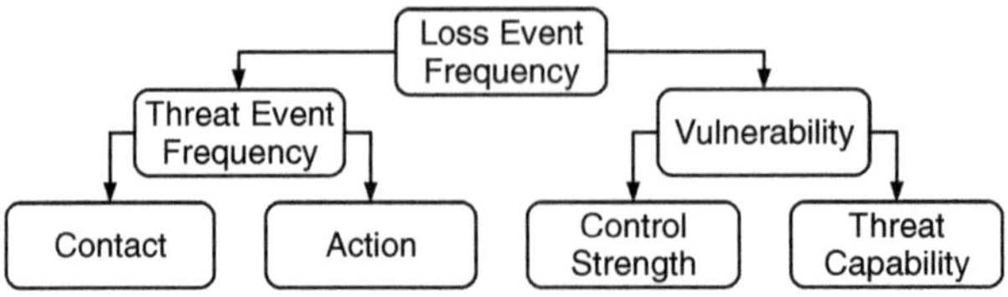

Fig. 4.4 Taxonomy branch for LEF

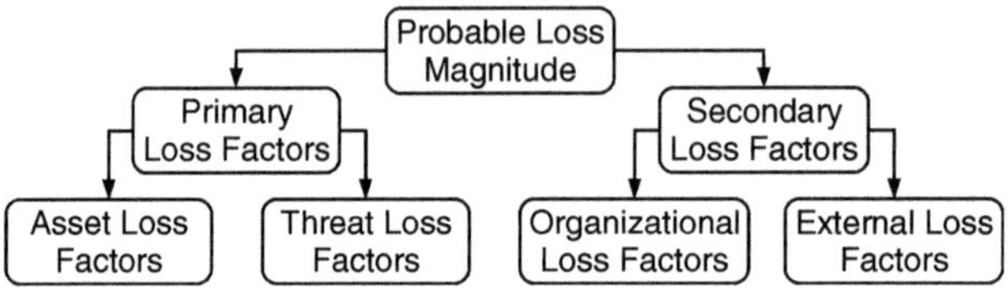

Fig. 4.5 Taxonomy branch for PLM

- **Action:** The probability that a threat agent will act against an asset once contact occurs.
- **Control Strength:** The strength of a control as compared to a baseline measure of force.
- **Threat Capability:** The probable level of force that a threat agent is capable of applying against an asset.

The terms in the taxonomy branch for **PLM** (see Fig. 4.5) address the following information:

- The **Probable Loss Magnitude** is affected by the factors that drive loss magnitude when events occur. In order to make reasoned judgments about the form and magnitude of loss within any given scenario, the loss factors have to be evaluated.
- The **Primary Loss Factors** address the potential losses regarding particular assets—the Asset Loss Factors—and the specific threats that target these assets—the Threat Loss Factors.
- The **Secondary Loss Factors** include organizational and external characteristics of the environment that influence the nature and degree of loss.
- The **Asset Loss Factors** consider in which value, including liability, and volume assets can be lost. The value of an asset depends on the criticality (impact to an organization's productivity), cost (the intrinsic value of the asset) and sensitivity (the harm that can occur from unintended disclosure).
- The **Threat Loss Factors** describe how assets are threatened regarding action (driven primarily by the threat agent's motive, e.g. financial gain, and the nature of the asset), competence (characteristics that enable a threat agent to inflict harm), and whether the threat agent is internal or external to the organization.

- The **Organizational Loss Factors** in FAIR are timing (an event occurring at a certain time might create significantly greater loss than at another time), due diligence (reasonable preventative measures should be in place), response (contain, remediate, recover) and detection (response is predicated on detection).
- The **External Loss Factors** cover four categories: the legal and regulatory landscape (regulations, contract law, and case law), the competitive landscape (competition's ability to take advantage of the situation), the media (affect on how stakeholders, lawyers, and even regulators and competitors view the event), and the external stakeholders (which generally inflict harm by taking their business elsewhere).

4.3.3.4 FRAAP

The Facilitated Risk Analysis and Assessment Process (FRAAP) is a method that is based on a qualitative risk analysis (Peltier 2014. pp. 45 ff.). FRAAP can be applied quickly because it analyses only **one object at a time**, e.g. an information system, an application or a business process. The analysis team is a team of individuals that includes business managers and system users that are familiar with the mission needs of the asset under review, and the infrastructure staff that have a detailed understanding of potential system vulnerabilities and related controls. The FRAAP team shall make conclusions about what threats exist, what their risk levels are and what controls are needed. These conclusions are created within three FRAAP **phases**:

- The **pre-FRAAP** is an introductory meeting that is needed to determine general conditions and to develop a common understanding of the goals. The deliverables of this phase are, for example, the scope, a diagram about the information flow, a member list of the FRAAP team, and definitions of used risk terms.
- The **FRAAP session** includes a brainstorming of the team members in order to identify potential threats that could affect the task mission of the asset under review. Then, the team establishes a risk level for each threat based on the probability of occurrence and the relative impact. In addition, controls have to be identified by the team. The controls that shall reduce the risks are evaluated regarding their cost-effectiveness.
- The **post-FRAAP** includes an analysis of the results and the completion of the management summary report.

After the FRAAP session is completed, the business owner decides which threats have to be assigned to an appropriate control and which threats have to be accepted. Finally, the documents can be **completed** with a specific action plan and the signatures of a participating senior business manager and technical expert.

The phases of FRAAP take only a few hours. The FRAAP session is the longest with about four hours. In conclusion, FRAAP is a very quick method that enables a risk management regarding one particular object in a **short time-period**. FRAAP can be used under the assumptions that time is a critical factor. It can be performed in a short time-period with useful deliverables. However, the more time a company spends to FRAAP, the higher are the levels of comprehensiveness and quality.

FRAAP is primarily driven by the **owner** of an asset. Among other things, he schedules the FRAAP session and invites the team members. However, this requires that asset owners have been clearly identified within the company. Normally, the information security policy of the company is used to describe the circumstances and responsibilities of an asset owner.

4.3.3.5 OCTAVE

The Operationally Critical Threat, Asset and Vulnerability Evaluation (OCTAVE) was developed by the coordination center of the computer emergency response team (CERT/CC) for the **Software Engineering Institute** (SEI). The SEI is a federally funded research and development center at Carnegie Mellon University.

OCTAVE is a framework that facilitates the strategic evaluation and planning of cybersecurity based on a risk analysis. Here, the economic perspective of the risk analysis is in focus. In contrast, the technical perspective is less important in OCTAVE. The implementation of OCTAVE within a company should be managed by a **cross-functional team** that has sufficient knowledge about the business processes and existing security safeguards in the company. This team must get official management approval. The team starts its work by gathering and analyzing all relevant information. Then, the team considers the risks from the economic perspective and develops an according strategy for cybersecurity. OCTAVE requires a high collaboration within and with the risk management team of the company. The experiences and expertise of employees shall be considered. OCTAVE provides a risk management that can be self-directed by the company. An external support will not be necessary, but possibly advantageous, especially if the company does not yet have much experience in risk management. For example, the team could be trained regarding OCTAVE by external trainers. This would lead to a more efficient implementation of OCTAVE.

The first **version** of OCTAVE was developed in 2001 (Alberts and Dorofee 2001). Today, two versions are available: OCTAVE-S (Alberts et al. 2005) addresses the risk management in small companies with a flat hierarchy. OCTAVE Allegro (Caralli et al. 2007) aims at large companies with complex organizational structures.

Three basic steps can be found in the first OCTAVE version. These steps were taken over to the **OCTAVE-S** version. They can be described as follows (Alberts et al. 2005, p. 5 f.):

1. **Build Asset-Based Threat Profiles:** The first step specifies that an evaluation of organizational aspects shall be performed. The analysis team defines the impact evaluation criteria that will be used later to evaluate risks. This team also identifies important organizational assets and evaluates the security current

practice of the organization. Then, the team defines security requirements and defines a threat profile for each critical asset.
2. **Identify Infrastructure Vulnerabilities:** In this step, the analysis team conducts a high-level review of the organization's information system infrastructure. While doing so, it focuses on the extent to which security is considered by maintainers of the infrastructure. The analysis team first analyzes who accesses critical assets and who is responsible for configuring and maintaining them. Then, the team examines the extent to which each responsible party includes security in its information technology practices and processes.
3. **Develop Security Strategy and Plans:** In the third step, the analysis team identifies risks to the organization's critical assets and decides what to do about them. Based on the analyzed information, the team creates a protection strategy for the organization. It also makes mitigation plans to address the risks to the critical assets.

In contrast, **OCTAVE Allegro** provides a more complex approach to consider the complex structures of large companies. Among other things, it is supposed that the company owns a more comprehensive amount of assets, which have to be identified in a more systematic way. OCTAVE Allegro (Caralli et al. 2007, pp. 17 ff.) includes eight steps:

1. **Establish Risk Measurement Criteria:** The first step is needed to establish the organizational drivers that will be used to evaluate the effects of a risk to an organization's mission and business objectives. These drivers are reflected with a set of risk measurement criteria, which include qualitative measures for evaluating the impact of a realized risk. The risk measurement criteria focus on an organizational view and ensure consistency across multiple information assets and operating or department units. In addition, a prioritization of impact areas is also performed in this initial step.
2. **Develop an Information Asset Profile:** This step begins with the process of creating a profile for the assets. A profile describes the unique features, qualities, characteristics, and value of an asset. The profile for each asset is the basis for the identification of threats and risks in the subsequent steps.
3. **Identify Information Asset Containers:** In this step, containers, which describe the places where information assets are stored, transported, and processed, are identified. Information assets can also reside in containers that are not in the direct control of the organization, e.g. in case of outsourcing. By mapping information asset to containers, the boundaries and unique circumstances that must be examined for risk are defined.
4. **Identify Areas of Concern:** In this step, real-world scenarios, which are referred to as areas of concern and which might represent threats and their corresponding undesirable outcomes, are identified. In other words, the scenarios are possible conditions or situations that can threaten an organization's information asset. Primarily, these scenarios shall be captured that come immediately to the minds of the analysis team.

5. **Identify Threat Scenarios:** In the first half of this step, the areas of concern that were captured in the previous step are expanded into threat scenarios that further detail the properties of a threat. In the second half of this step, a broad range of additional threats is considered by examining threat scenarios. The scenarios can be represented visually in a tree structure, which is commonly referred to as a threat tree. A series of threat scenario questionnaires can be used to work through each branch of the threat trees. In the description of threat scenarios, the probability can already be considered. It is represented qualitatively as high, medium, or low, and will be used in later steps.
6. **Identify Risks:** Here, the various consequences of threats are captured. All consequences to an organization from a realized threat are considered as risks, e.g. negative effects on the financial position and reputation of the company.
7. **Analyze Risks:** In this step, a quantitative risk score is computed. It is based on the extent to which the organization can actually be impacted by a relevant threat. Thereby, the impact of the risk, the importance of the impact area, and the probability are taken into account.
8. **Select Mitigation Approach**: In this final step, risks are prioritized based on their relative risk score. The risks that require mitigation can be identified and a mitigation strategy for those risks can be developed. Thereby, the value of the asset, its security requirements, the relevant containers, and the company's unique operating environment are considered.

By **comparing** OCTAVE-S and OCTAVE Allegro, it can be seen that particularly the asset identification and risk analysis are much more comprehensive in OCTAVE Allegro. As shown in Fig. 4.6, the asset identification matches partially to the first step in OCTAVE-S, while three relevant steps can be found in OCTAVE Allegro. The risk analysis matches to step 1 and step 2 in OCTAVE-S, while four relevant steps can be found in OCTAVE Allegro. However, the risk mitigation is covered by one single step in both versions.

4.3.3.6 RMF

The Risk Management Framework (RMF) has been developed by the National Institute of Standards and Technology (NIST). It can be applied to both new and legacy information systems within the context of the life cycle of systems. It includes the following **steps**, which are also called the Security Life Cycle (NIST 2010, pp. 7 f.):

1. **Categorize Information System:** In this step, the information system and the information, which is processed, stored, and transmitted by that system, have to be categorized based on an impact analysis.
2. **Select Security Controls:** Based on the security categorization of the information system, an initial set of baseline security controls has to be selected. Based on an organizational assessment of risk and local conditions, the security control baseline has to be tailored and supplemented as needed.

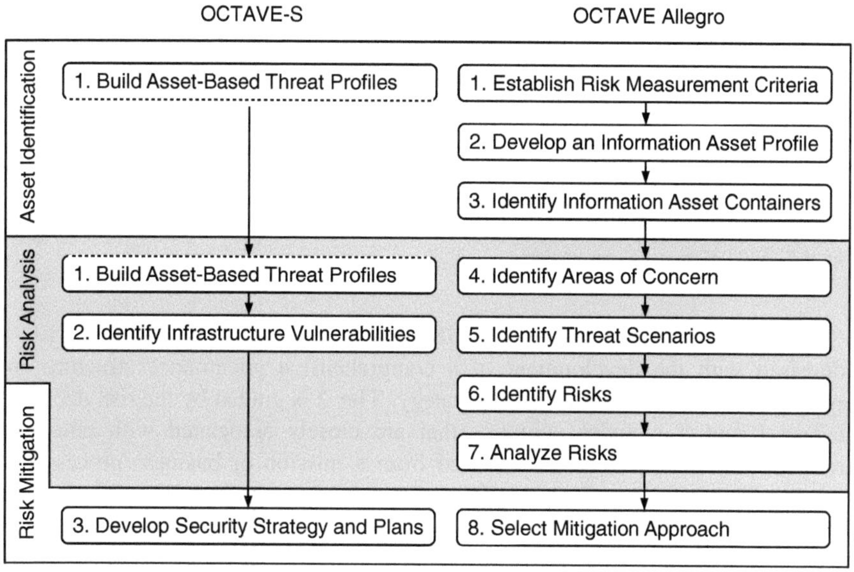

Fig. 4.6 OCTAVE-S and OCTAVE Allegro

3. **Implement Security Controls:** The previously selected security controls have to be implemented. Besides, the deployment of controls within the information system and environment of operation has to be documented.
4. **Assess Security Controls:** After the security controls have been implemented, they have to be assessed with appropriate procedures. The goal is to determine the extent to which the controls are implemented correctly, operating as intended, and producing the desired outcome with respect to meeting the security requirements for the system.
5. **Authorize Information System:** The operation of the information system has to be authorized. This authorization is based upon a determination of the residual risk. Only if the residual risk is acceptable, it should be allowed to operate the system.
6. **Monitor Security Controls:** This step does not end after a given time-period, but rather it has to be performed on an ongoing basis. The selected security controls in the information system have to be assessed regularly. Thereby, the security control effectiveness has to be evaluated. Besides, changes to the system or environment of operation have to be documented, security impact analyses of the associated changes have to be conducted, and the security state of the system has to be reported to appropriate organizational officials.

The NIST distinguishes risk management in three relevant **Risk Management Tiers** (NIST 2010, pp. 5 f.): the organization, mission/business process and information system (see Fig. 4.7).

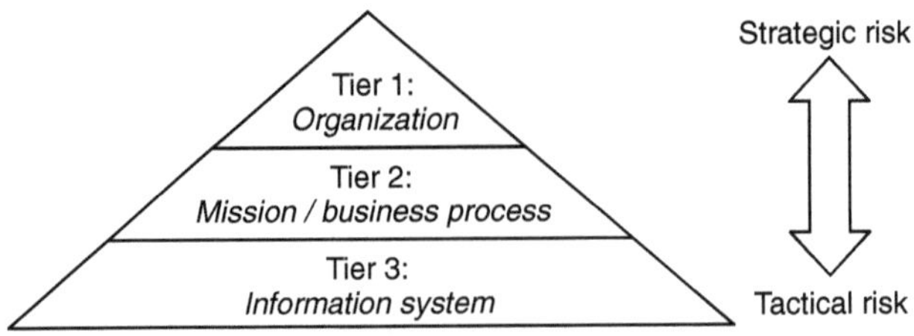

Fig. 4.7 NIST risk management tiers

Tier 1 is oriented on the organizational perspective. In this tier, risk is addressed with the development of a comprehensive governance structure and organization-wide risk management strategy. **Tier 2** is guided by the risk decisions at Tier 1 and it includes activities that are closely associated with enterprise architecture. Thereby, risk is addressed from a mission or business process perspective. **Tier 3** is focused on an information system perspective. The selection and deployment of needed safeguards and countermeasures at the information system level are impacted by the risk decisions at tiers 1 and 2. The RMF operates primarily at tier 3 in the risk management hierarchy, but can also interact with tiers 1 and 2.

The NIST provides not only an isolated risk management framework, but also comprehensive **documentation** to supplement each step in the Security Life Cycle. For example, the step 2, which covers the selection of security controls, is supported by the Special Publication 800-53, which includes more than 400 pages of guidance on this selection. Among other things, it provides a catalog of security controls for organizations and information systems in order to facilitate compliance with applicable federal laws, Executive Orders, directives, policies, regulations, standards, and guidelines.

Given the official role of the NIST as an **agency** of the United States Department of Commerce, the RMF can be expected to be researched and proven thoroughly. Besides, it is probably under continuous maintenance and, therefore, provides a high level of quality and timeliness.

4.3.3.7 RMM

The Risk and Insurance Management Society (RIMS), which is a non-profit membership organization for risk management professionals, has developed the Risk Maturity Model (RMM). This model aims at the development and improvement of existing risk management programs. It can be applied regardless of which risk management standard or framework the company uses. Risk professionals and internal auditors can use the model for **assurance** purposes in order to determine whether the company's risk management program is meeting expectations, and for considering potential recommendations to mature the program (RIMS 2015).

The model is supported by a free assessment tool, which can be used to score an enterprise risk management (ERM) program and receive an immediately available report. In addition, the assessment result serves as a roadmap for improvement.

The assessment of a risk management program is performed by evaluating the program regarding seven **attributes** (RIMS 2006, p. 8). These attributes are understood as core competencies that help to measure how well risk management is embraced by management and ingrained within the organization.

1. **ERM-based approach:** This attribute is used to determine the degree of executive support that exists within the company regarding an ERM-based approach. This goes beyond regulatory compliance across all processes, functions, business lines, roles and geographies. In detail, the degree of integration, communication and coordination of internal audit, information technology, compliance, control, and risk management have to be evaluated.
2. **ERM process management:** This attribute covers the degree of weaving the ERM process into business processes and using ERM process steps to identify, assess, evaluate, mitigate and monitor. In particular, the degree of incorporating qualitative risk management methods that are supported by quantitative methods, analyses, tools and models shall be considered.
3. **Risk appetite management:** Hereby, the degree of understanding the risk-reward tradeoffs within the business shall be considered. It has to be analyzed if accountability exists within leadership and policy to guide decision making and attack gaps between perceived and actual risk. Risk appetite defines the boundary of acceptable risk, and risk tolerance defines the variation of measuring risk appetite that management deems acceptable.
4. **Root cause discipline:** This attribute addresses the degree of discipline applied to measuring a problem's root cause and binding events with their process sources to drive the reduction of uncertainty, collection of information and measurement of the controls' effectiveness. Besides, the degree of risk from people, external environment, systems, processes and relationships is explored.
5. **Uncovering risks:** This attribute covers the degree of quality and penetration coverage of risk assessment activities in documenting risks and opportunities. In addition, the degree of collecting knowledge from employee expertise, databases and other electronic files (such as Microsoft Word, Excel, etc.) to uncover dependencies and correlation across the enterprise has to be considered.
6. **Performance management:** This attribute aims at evaluating the degree of executing vision and strategy, working from financial, customer, business process and learning and growth perspectives, such as Kaplan's balanced scorecard or similar approaches. The degree of exposure to uncertainty, or potential deviations from plans or expectations is also relevant.
7. **Business resiliency and sustainability:** This attribute helps to evaluate the extent to which the ERM process's sustainability aspects are integrated into operational planning. This includes evaluating how planning supports resiliency and value. The degree of ownership and planning beyond recovering technology platforms is covered by this attribute, too. Examples include vendor and

Table 4.5 Key Drivers in the RMM (RIMS 2006, p. 9)

Attributes:	Key Drivers: Degree of …
1. ERM-based approach	• Support from senior management, Chief Risk Officer • Business process definition determining risk ownership • Assimilation into support area and front-office activities • Far-sighted orientation toward risk management • Risk culture's accountability, communication and pervasiveness
2. ERM process management	• Each ERM Process step (see definition) • ERM Process's repeatability and scalability • ERM Process oversight including roles and responsibilities • Risk management reporting • Qualitative and quantitative measurement
3. Risk appetite management	• Risk-reward tradeoffs • Risk-reward-based resource allocation • Analysis as risk portfolio collections to balance risk positions
4. Root cause discipline	• Classification to manage risk and performance indicators • Flexibility to collect risk and opportunity information • Understanding dependencies and consequences • Consideration of people, relationships, external, process and systems views
5. Uncovering risks	• Risk ownership by business areas • Formalization of risk indicators and measures • Reporting on follow-up activities • Transforming potentially adverse events into opportunities
6. Performance management	• ERM information integrated within planning • Communication of goals and measures • Examination of financial, customer, business process and learning • ERM process goals and activities
7. Business resiliency and sustainability	• Integration of ERM within operational planning • Understanding of consequences of action or inaction • Planning based on scenario analysis

distribution dependencies, supply chain disruptions, dramatic market pricing changes, cash flow volatility, business liquidity, etc.

The RMM includes five **maturity levels** for each attribute with diminishing maturity from level 5 to level 1. Key drivers (Table 4.5) are used to detail the evaluation attributes and identify the appropriate maturity level.

A maturity level is determined for each attribute. The **overall ERM maturity** is determined by the weakest link. In Fig. 4.8, an ERM profile is visualized that has an overall ERM maturity of level 2 (Initial).

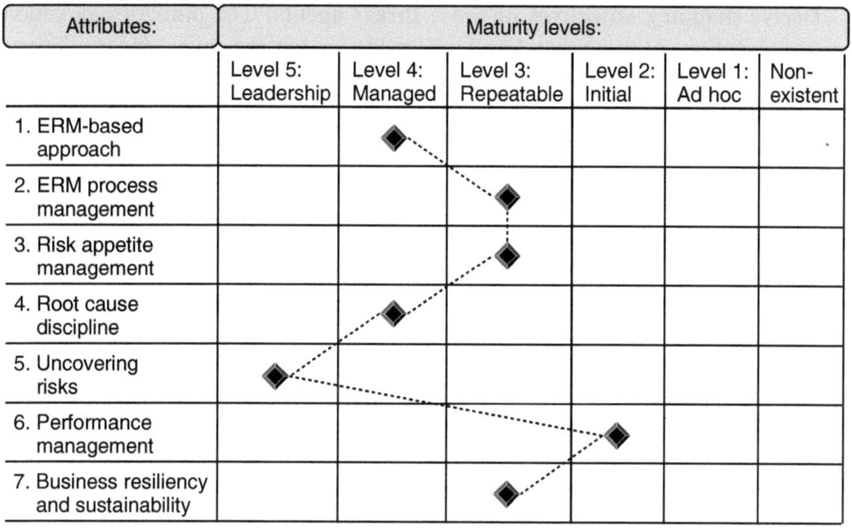

Fig. 4.8 Example maturity of an ERM

4.3.3.8 TARA

The Threat Agent Risk Assessment (TARA) is a risk-assessment framework that was developed by Intel (2009). It helps companies to manage risk by distilling the immense number of possible information security attacks into a digest of only those attacks that are most likely to occur. The basic idea is to **filter** the huge amount of possible risks into only the most important ones. Generally, the mitigation of all possible risks is not reasonable from the economic perspective. With the TARA, only the most critical attacks are targeted in order to apply the resources efficiently for maximum results in risk management. In contrast to traditional vulnerability assessments, TARA concentrates on threat agents and their motivation, methods, and objectives, and how they map to existing controls, not on the weak points themselves.

The TARA framework provides a process guidance with **six steps** for identifying the critical areas of exposure that are derived from likely attacks (Intel 2009, pp. 5 f.):

1. **Measure current threat agent risks to the company:** A panel of senior experts regularly reviews and ranks the current threat levels at the company. This leads to a general understanding of current risks and creates a baseline for further steps.
2. **Distinguish threat agents that exceed baseline acceptable risks:** If a new project is started or if the current baseline seems to be insufficient, new threats will have to be measured. Thereby, the threat agents that exceed the current or new baseline threat level for the areas being evaluated can be identified.

3. **Derive primary objectives of those threat agents:** The primary motivations and objectives of those threat agents identified in the previous steps are derived, for example, by using an existing library of threat agent methods and objectives. Examples for threat agent objectives are theft, exposure, data loss, sabotage, operations impact, and embarrassment.
4. **Identify methods likely to manifest:** In this step, the likely methods by which an attack might occur are identified. Again, an existing library of threat agent methods and objectives can be used.
5. **Determine the most important collective exposures:** At first, attack vectors caused by vulnerabilities without controls have to be found. For this purpose, an exposure library that enumerates known vulnerabilities and exposures, and maps them to existing controls can be used. The intersection of these attack-vectors and the methods determined in step 4 define likely exposures. These likely exposures are ranked according to their severity of consequence. In result, a list of the most important collective exposures can be created.
6. **Align strategy to target the most significant exposures:** In this final step, analysts and management shall use the results of the TARA analysis to concentrate their information security strategy on the most important areas of concern and allocate information security resources in the most effective manner.

The risk assessment data that the TARA can provide when assessing information security risks associated with a particular project can be **visualized** as shown in Fig. 4.9. The center represents low risk. The risk level increases towards the outer rim of the circle. The grey area represents default risks that existed before the project began. The black area shows the elevated risks associated with the project.

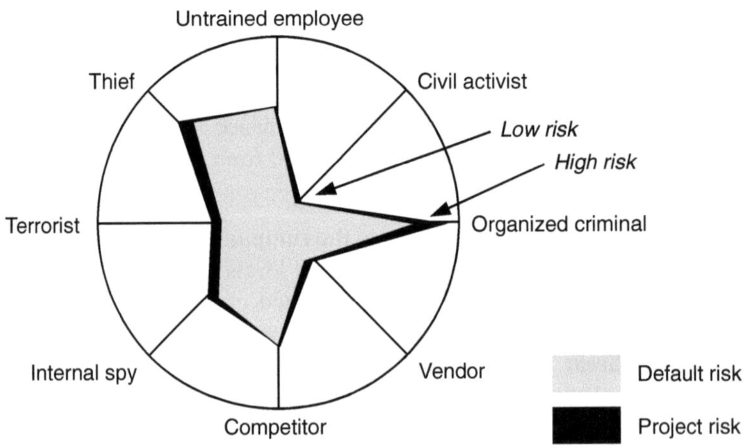

Fig. 4.9 Example of risk comparison for threat agent profiles

4.3.4 Risk Indicators

Similar to the asset value, which is also an important input to the risk analysis, the risk can be measured quantitatively and qualitatively. The key prerequisite for the measurement of risks is their **identification**. This can be systematically performed by moving along the chain of the terms asset, vulnerability, exploitation, threat, risk and safeguard, as shown in Fig. 4.10.

The **asset** should already be known. The question is if the asset has a **vulnerability** that can be **exploited** by an attacker or by environmental factors. If the answer is yes, there will be a **threat** for the asset. The threat gives an indication about the impact. Under consideration of the probability of occurrence, the impact forms the basis for a **risk**. **Safeguards** can be used to mitigate the negative aspects of a risk—the probability that an undesirable event occurs and the potential damage caused by this event shall be minimized.

Before appropriate safeguards can be selected from the economic perspective, the risk has to be evaluated and measured. Only if the potential damage succeeds the costs of the safeguard, the implementation of this safeguard will be financially reasonable. Therefore, a **risk measurement** serves as a decision support for decision makers that seek a reasonable approach to handle identified risks. The risk measurement can be performed in a quantitative or a qualitative way:

- The **quantitative** measurement includes the use of various metrics and cost functions to assess risks in monetary terms. Important inputs are the economic value and the potential loss related to asset objects.
- The **qualitative** measurement does not consider concrete value amounts, but rather uses scenarios to classify risks on a scale. Thereby, the impact of undesirable events can be measured from a qualitative point of view. Within this measurement, expert judgment, experience and intuition are considered.

In practice, the qualitative measurement is often **chosen** over quantitative ones. The reasons are that procedures for qualitative measurement are easy to design, implement and adjust. Nevertheless, these procedures have some disadvantages. In particular, they are based on expert opinions that are subjective and often biased.

After a procedure has been chosen and the risks have been measured, the risks should be **prioritized**. The highest risks should be marked with the highest priority so that the available resources can be concentrated on the biggest or most probable damages. If resources are too short to cover all reasonable risk mitigation opportunities, at least, the most important risks can be addressed.

Fig. 4.10 Chain of terms

4.3.4.1 Quantitative Indicators

The **risk** (*r*) is understood as the product of **impact** (*i*) and **probability** (*p*). It is often expressed as a monetary value:

$$r = i \times p$$
$$\text{where } r \in \mathbb{R}_+, i \in \mathbb{R}_+ \text{ and } p \in \mathbb{R}_+ \leq 1$$

The **impact** (*i*) can be calculated with knowledge about the **asset value** (*av*)—see Sect. 4.2 for details on measuring—and the **exposure factor** (*ef*). It is often expressed as a monetary value, too. The exposure factor indicates how high the financial loss can be upon the occurrence of a threat. It is expressed as a percentage of an asset value. Hereby, the situation is considered that an asset object can be just partially damaged. The impact shows in monetary terms how much loss or damage regarding an asset value will occur due to a threat.

$$i = av \times ef$$
$$\text{where } i \in \mathbb{R}_+, av \in \mathbb{R}_+ \text{ and } ef \in \mathbb{R}_+ \leq 1$$

The **probability** (*p*) can be calculated by determining the rate of occurrence of a threat for a specified period. For example, the period can be one year. Then, the **days** (*d*) are counted where a negative impact is expected to occur. In this case the formula is:

$$p = \frac{d}{365}$$
$$\text{where } p \in \mathbb{R}_+ \leq 1 \text{ and } d \in \mathbb{N}_0 \leq 365$$

The level of detail and the period can be adjusted arbitrarily. For example, instead of the days, the **minutes** (*m*) of occurrence can be counted. In addition, instead of a period of one year, a period of one day can be used. In this case the formula is:

$$p = \frac{m}{1440}$$
$$\text{where } p \in \mathbb{R}_+ \leq 1 \text{ and } m \in \mathbb{N}_0 \leq 1440$$

The probability of occurrence of a threat within a year can also be named **annualized rate of occurrence** (*aro*). This variable is no percentage, but a whole number. A zero represents that the threat never occurs. The maximum value of the *aro* is not limited upwards because, theoretically, the threat can even occur several times daily. The probable financial loss due to the occurrence of a threat is called **annualized loss expectancy** (*ale*).

$$ale = i \times aro$$
$$\text{where } ale \in \mathbb{R}_+, i \in \mathbb{R}_+ \text{ and } aro \in \mathbb{N}_0$$

If the *ale* is calculated before and after the implementation of an adequate safeguard, the benefit of this safeguard can be shown. The reduction of the *ale* can be compared to the **costs of the safeguard** in order to find out if the safeguard is reasonable from the monetary perspective. Because the benefits of a safeguard can be compared directly to its costs, a meaningful indication about its reasonableness can be made. In general, only if the costs of the safeguard are lower than the change in the *ale* that was caused by implementing the safeguard—the difference between ale_1 and ale_2, the safeguard will be worthwhile.

$$ale_1 - ale_2 = maximum\ safeguard\ costs$$
$$\text{where } ale_1, ale_2 \in \mathbb{R}_+$$

In order to make the costs of the safeguard comparable to the *ale*, they have to be related to a period of one year, too. The particular value is called **annual costs of the safeguard** (*acs*). When assessing the cost/benefit relation, it can be checked if the *acs* is lower than the change in the *ale*—the maximum safeguard costs. In other words, if the following formula has a positive outcome, the safeguard will be worthwhile:

$$ale_1 - ale_2 - acs > 0$$
$$\text{where } ale_1, ale_2, acs \in \mathbb{R}_+$$

Table 4.6 gives an overview about the variables and acronyms used for quantitative risk assessment.

4.3.4.2 Qualitative Indicators

With the qualitative risk analysis, impacts and probabilities can be allocated on a **scale**. Thereby, the risks are analyzed from a qualitative point of view. In contrast to the quantitative analysis, the potential damage cannot be directly derived from the lost profit. Besides, more qualitative impacts, like reputation, are playing an important role here. Generally, expert judgment, experience and intuition are considered to support the qualitative analysis and help to perform the allocation of impacts and probabilities.

The **techniques** that are often used in the qualitative risk analysis are, among other things, interviews, surveys, brainstorming and the Delphi technique:

- In **interviews**, experts are questioned directly face-to-face or via phone. The validity of the answers is usually very high because they reflect the genuine and unfiltered subjective perception of the experts.

- **Surveys** provide questions that shall be answered in writing. Advantages are that big groups or the entire company staff can be reached easily and the answering can be performed time-independent. The questions and answers should be designed in a way that supports the collection of valid data. An important prerequisite is that the questions are understood by the respondents. If scales are used, they should represent existing distributions. Respondents normally think that the specified scale is useful and reflects the actual distribution of the population. If a scale is, for example, extremely detailed in low value ranges, the respondents will believe that most people choose an answer in the low range and distort their response accordingly.
- **Brainstorming** is a technique for searching new ideas within a creativity-inspiring environment. Spontaneous inspirations of the participants are collected without criticism.
- The **Delphi technique** involves a repeated survey of experts. By distributing anonymous answers into the whole group of participants, the opinions of multiple experts shall be brought together.

The result of a qualitative risk assessment is normally demonstrated by a **risk matrix**. Within this risk matrix, the probability and impact of an undesirable event are assigned to specific categories, e.g. low, medium and high. The position of this event within the matrix represents the concluded evaluation of the belonging risk. The event can also be assigned to a specific risk class, which is derived from the risk matrix.

For **example**, the risk classes can be assigned as shown in Fig. 4.11: The risk class low can include risks with low probability and low impact, low probability and medium impact, or medium probability and low impact. The risk class medium can include risks with medium probability and medium impact, low probability and high impact, or high probability and low impact. The risk class high can include risks with high probability and medium impact, medium probability and high impact, or high probability and high impact.

From the risk class the acceptable **implementation time** can be derived. In general, the highest risks should be addressed fastest.

4.4 Cybersecurity Costs

Mostly, **costs** are money in a specific value that is needed to develop, implement or produce something. They are directly or indirectly necessary for the operational performance of a company. On the one hand, cybersecurity investments are strongly related to costs because they induce them and they provide a benefit that is often connected with the reduction of future costs. On the other hand, missing cybersecurity investments can lead to breaches and subsequent countermeasures that induce even higher costs. In one way or another, cybersecurity leads to costs that must be covered. Figure 4.12 gives an overview about the costs of safeguards,

Table 4.6 Acronyms and terms of quantitative risk indicators

Acronym	Term	Description	Calculation	Value-range
r	Risk	The calculated risk is based on the probability and impact	$r = i \times p$	$\mathbb{R}_+$
i	Impact	The impact shows in monetary terms how much loss or damage regarding an asset value will occur due to a threat	$i = av \times ef$	$\mathbb{R}_+$
p	Probability	The probability represents the rate of occurrence of a threat for a specified period, e.g. one year	$p = \frac{d}{365}$	$\mathbb{R}_+ \leq 1$
av	Asset value	The asset value is the known value of a particular company's asset	Estimation or measurement	$\mathbb{R}_+$
ef	Exposure factor	The exposure factor indicates how high the financial loss upon the occurrence of a threat can be. It is expressed as a percentage of an asset value	Estimation or measurement	$\mathbb{R}_+ \leq 1$
aro	Annualized rate of occurrence	The annualized rate of occurrence is the probability of occurrence of a threat within a year	Estimation or measurement	$\mathbb{N}_0$
ale	Annualized loss expectancy	The annualized loss expectancy is the probable financial loss due to the occurrence of a threat	$ale = i \times aro$	$\mathbb{R}_+$
acs	Annual cost of the safeguard	In order to make the costs of the safeguard comparable to the *ale*, they have to be related to a period of one year, too	Estimation or measurement	$\mathbb{R}_+$

Fig. 4.11 Risk matrix

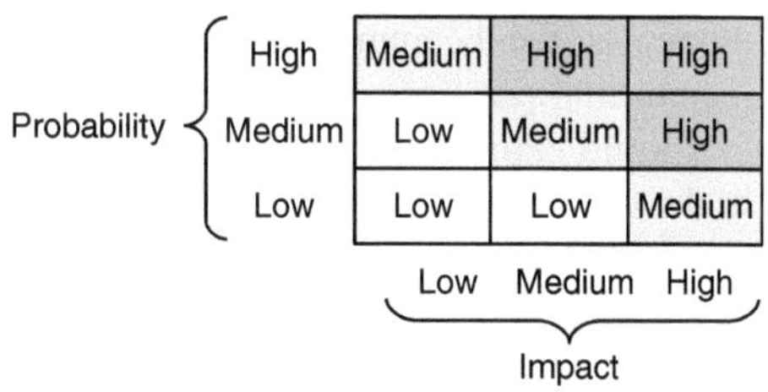

which are described in Sect. 4.4.1, and the costs of breaches, which are described in Sect. 4.4.2.

Generally, every company is interested in **preventing** breaches of any kind. However, as described in Sect. 2.3, a protection level of hundred percent is practically impossible. Normally, a company cannot fully exclude the possibility of a breach. Therefore, it should consider the consequences of a breach and necessary tasks after a breach occurred.

A company needs capital and liquidity to cover the incurred costs. The **own capital** of the company is the type of capital that is provided by the shareholders and can generally be used unrestricted by the company. Because own capital is a financial resource that can be used independently, cybersecurity investments that are funded with it can easily be performed. However, it could be difficult to defend the investment decision against the shareholders, who often focus on increasing their profits instead of minimizing the expected losses. **Borrowed capital** is the type of capital that is not provided by shareholders and not earned by the company. Instead, it is provided from other companies or people. It is timely restricted and causes interests. In order to pay back the borrowed capital, the company must earn it and related interests with their business transactions. In general, cybersecurity investments do not help to generate new profits. Instead, they are focused on securing the assets and processes of the company that are needed to generate profits. Therefore, cybersecurity investments have only an indirect benefit regarding profit generation. They reduce expected losses and, thereby, influence the profits of the company. However, this can be hard to explain to external capital providers.

The use of borrowed capital is **less favorable** than the use of own capital because borrowed capital incurs interests, which raise the overall investment costs. Besides, the company makes itself dependent on capital providers, which could try to influence company decisions. However, the company will have no choice than borrowing capital and paying interests if the own capital is not sufficient or not liquid.

Interests will occur if the time when cash is available does not match the time when cash is needed. If the cash is available before it is needed, interests will be paid by a bank or other debtors that will borrow the cash in the interim period. If the cash is available after it is needed, interests will have to be paid to a bank or other creditors that provide cash in the interim period. The time when cash is needed for a cybersecurity investment can be an important criterion in the selection, especially while choosing between similar alternatives. For example, to pay a big amount of money at the beginning is more unfavorable compared to a later payment or incremental payments.

Liquid capital has the form of cash and cash equivalents. This includes the cash at the company, the cash at a bank and credit balances with central banks minus current bank account liabilities. Liquid capital is available immediately. It will be very convenient if fast cybersecurity investments are made, for example, while dealing with new severe attacks. In this case, any day of waiting will increase the possibility of being affected by these attacks.

Besides, **opportunity costs** should be considered every time when spending capital. Opportunity costs are lost revenues that are caused because opportunities for using available resources cannot be used. The resources have already been bound. Within cybersecurity, the opportunity costs are important because the capital that is invested in cybersecurity cannot be used for new production processes that directly influence the profit generation. Especially if capital providers

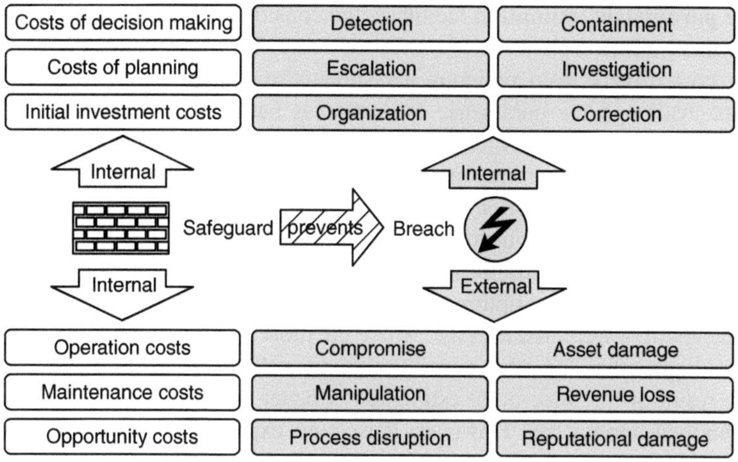

Fig. 4.12 Cybersecurity costs

must be persuaded, a concentration on the lost opportunities instead of the benefits from cybersecurity can be problematic.

However, the decision maker must not only know how the costs are defined and what components are included, but also he must acquire **reliable numbers** for the costs and benefits in focus. Common approaches to acquire the needed information are:

- The **expert judgement** is based on interviews and surveys with experts from the field. These experts use their own knowledge and experiences for providing a personal opinion to the decision maker. It is obvious that the resulting information is highly subjective. Often, the experts are biased and tend to over- or underestimate particular costs or benefits. The decision maker might get many disparate opinions. With a professional aggregation, he can create results that are more reliable. Nevertheless, the decision maker cannot eliminate the subjectivity. Therefore, a combination of expert judgements with other approaches is recommendable.
- The **analogous estimation** provides an objective estimation that reuses information about previous cybersecurity investments or other kind of investments in the company. The estimation can be improved if the decision maker adjusts it in order to consider known differences between the current and the previous investment. This type of estimation does not provide very precise numbers. Often, the investments are difficult to compare because of various known and unknown differences. If the decision maker can access comprehensive information about previous investments in the company, this estimation will be very quick and inexpensive. Because of the low reliability, it should only be used if the decision maker cannot get detailed information about the new investment.

- The **parametric estimation** facilitates the consideration of multiple parameters, e.g. time, affected clients, and protection level. These parameters are related to key cost drivers from previous investments, e.g. license costs and hardware costs. Although the parametric estimation is based on information about previous investments, too, it leads to numbers that are more reliable. The reason is that the parametric estimation enhances the estimation quality by using statistical data. This estimation is more complex and time-consuming than the analogous estimation, but it leads to much better results.
- The **three-point estimation** includes three variables to create reasonable numbers: most likely, optimistic, and pessimistic. The final estimation is calculated with a weighted average, where the most likely variable is weighted four times higher than the other ones: (optimistic + 4 × most likely + pessimistic)/6. The result of the three-point estimation is better than the results from the other mentioned approaches. However, it is more expensive to gather numbers for three reliable variables. For example, this approach can be combined with other approaches by using the estimations of other approaches as variables within the three-point estimation.

4.4.1 Safeguard Costs

Safeguard costs are caused during the whole lifecycle of a cybersecurity investment. These costs can be distinguished in costs of decision making, costs of planning, initial investment costs, operation costs, and maintenance costs. Besides, the opportunity costs should be considered.

- The **costs of decision making** must not be overlooked. From the problem identification until the alternative selection, the decision maker has to invest much time and effort in order to find a proper solution. Besides, experts that are integrated in the decision making process for providing expert knowledge and experiences also invest valuable working time. In particular, a proper asset appraisement, risk evaluation, and cost estimation can require much work, especially if the scope is very comprehensive.
- The **costs of planning** are induced by designing the solution, and finding a systematic approach for implementing it. Here, both functional and technical experts have to be involved. If the company cannot provide the required knowledge on its own, external consulting companies will be called in. The planning phase should be taken seriously because planning deficiencies that are realized later can lead to significant extra costs.
- The **initial investment costs** include expenses regarding hardware, software, infrastructure, organizational costs, and labor costs:

- **Hardware** is everything that is a physical part of an information system or belongs to it. An information system that performs security related tasks, and, therefore, has the role of a safeguard generally consists of a mainboard, a central processing unit (CPU), random access memory (RAM), a hard disk drive (HDD), a power supply unit (PSU), and a case. These parts can be purchased separately or within a complete system. The complete system can be purchased including an operating system and even including an application system. If the system is under exclusive maintenance by the vendor, it will be called appliance. The purchasing company sees an appliance as a black box because the employees use the provided application without knowing details about the underlying software or hardware. An appliance can be an additional security feature. It prevents manipulation from everybody except the vendor. Even the legitimate users are not able to change system parameters. Appliances can often be found in the cryptographic area, where substitution boxes (S-Boxes) are used to obscure the relationship between the encryption key and the cipher text. In addition to the system, the hardware segment also includes peripheral objects. They are everything used to create and deliver input data into the system, or display and transmit output data out of the system. Examples for input peripherals are mouse, keyboard, touchpad, microphone, video camera, scanner, and fingerprint sensor. Examples for output peripherals are monitor, beamer, printer and speakers. Also important for the data transmission into and out of the system are interfaces, which can be part of the mainboard or a separate expansion card. Examples are the universal serial bus (USB) and network ports. Interfaces are used to connect peripheral or to interconnect with other systems. While functioning as safeguards, systems can be required to meet special specifications. For example, a central monitoring system must be connected via error-free and fast data connections, e.g. provided by optical-fiber connections. Only by these specifications, monitoring systems can process security related tasks quickly and react within seconds.
- **Software** comprises programs and data that are necessary for operating an information system and providing the desired functionality. In a broader view, software also includes the documentation that is needed to use, adjust and maintain it. Software is distinguished in operating software and application software. Both have to be combined within an information system in order to enable or support a business process by the system. The operating system manages the hardware components of the system and allocates the resources, which are provided by the hardware components, to the application software, which runs on the system. On the one hand, the operating software has the function of an adapter between the various hardware components in the market and the application. Without this adapter, every application would have to be programmed so comprehensively that it could directly address all available hardware components. The operating system takes over this task by implementing drivers from vendors and providing a standardized interface for software developers. On the other hand, the

operating software manages the system resources in a way that allows multiple applications to run concurrently on the system. For example, CPU time, RAM areas and HDD space must be fairly divided and allocated to application software. Operating software is available as licensed software and open-source software. Licensed software is accompanied with license costs. Therefore, the initial costs are mostly higher. In contrast, licensed software might be supported and accepted better and, subsequently, might cause lower operation costs. While operating software is mostly bought as standard software "off the peg", application software is often developed individually for the company. Both standard software and individual software bring advantages and disadvantages. The decision primarily depends on the objectives and environmental situation of the company. For example, highly specialized software might be hard to find in the market, while software for standard business processes often leaves nothing to be desired. The most important advantages of standard software are the high availability, transparent costs, no development risks, high functionality, standardized trainings, and further development, test and support by the vendor. The most important advantages of individual software are the exact fulfillment of requirements, high customization, independence regarding further adjustments, potential advantages over competitors, and strategic benefits.

– **Infrastructure** covers everything that is needed to provide network connections to other systems and to ensure the necessary environmental resources and conditions. In a broader view, also hardware and software are part of the infrastructure. The network connections within companies are mostly wired with optical fiber cables or copper cables. Wired connections provide higher bandwidth and higher security. The access to network ports within offices is mostly secured physically, too. In contrast, wireless connections are more flexible to use. Devices that are connected via wireless technology are not bound to a specific location. While a wireless LAN requires the physical presence within company premises, other wireless communication, e.g. via Long Term Evolution (LTE), Universal Mobile Telecommunications System (UMTS) and Global System for Mobile Communications (GSM), will be usable worldwide if a cell tower is within reach. For the network within the company—the LAN, particular network devices are necessary, too. Switches and hubs are used to transfer data within a network or between network segments. Switches can transmit data more targeted because they already know the right route to the target systems. Hubs are only broadcasting the data within the network. Routers are used to transmit and filter data on the transition between the LAN and external networks, like the Internet. This transition between networks is also called the network perimeter. In addition, particular environmental resources must be provided. One of the most important ones is the power supply. With the help of redundant power supplies, uninterruptable power supplies (UPS) and generators, the continuous power supply can be ensured, even in case of disruptions of the external power supply. Furthermore, certain environmental

conditions must be ensured. Heating, ventilating, and air conditioning (HVAC) should be used to control temperature and humidity of sensitive information systems, like important servers. An adequate cooling is important because too high temperatures can affect the stability of systems and often lead to crashes. A high humidity must be prevented because it can cause corrosion. A low humidity can lead to discharge of static electricity. Sensors can be used to monitor the environment and to alert in case of deviations.
- **Organizational costs** include expenses that address necessary adjustments around the organizational structure within the company. Among other things, new teams or positions can be needed to develop, operate and maintain a safeguard. New processes or process changes can be implemented to build-in additional security features and controls. New procedures and guidelines complete changes because they make clear what is expected from the employees. Besides, training needs can lead to costly trainings that are provided externally, internally or via web interfaces.
- **Labor costs** are induced continuously within all activities. For example, the installation and testing of hardware, software and infrastructure often requires a high amount of working time. Trainings induce labor costs because they do not only bind the time of trainers, but also the time of all participants.

• The **operation costs** are caused by all actions that ensure the continuous operation of the safeguard in the long-term. Thereby, the protection level that was built with the safeguard initially can be hold up. Mostly, if no subsequent activities are performed after the initial implementation of the safeguard, its effectivity will steadily decrease. For example, antivirus software that is not monitored or supported, might not receive further signature updates after a failure. In consequence, it will not detect new viruses anymore. The operation costs include costs for licenses, administration and support:

- **Licenses** are necessary for the legitimate acquisition and use of application software and operating software from external vendors. They confirm the obtained right to use the software. License costs can become due at the initial investment or even once a year. In the last case, they cause repeated expenses. A non-payment of license costs does often not result in an immediate deactivation of the software, but a company that uses unlicensed software would be considered immoral and be liable to prosecution. If an illegal use of a software is detected within a license audit, the company will have to face legal consequences and, often, it has to pay penalties to the vendor. License costs can be avoided fully if the software has been developed individually so that it became property of the company during or after the development.
- **Administration** is important to configure and setup the safeguard. For example, new users might have to be created or deleted, e.g. within an access control system, or security parameters might have to be changed, e.g. filter

rules within a firewall. In addition, all manual tasks that are needed to operate the safeguard continuously have to be carried out, e.g. a tape swap for backup creation. Furthermore, necessary maintenance tasks have to be carried out. It is important to ensure a steady protection level and proper functionality of the safeguard. The safeguard will be analyzed periodically in order to check if it functions as required. For example, hardware components must be exchanged before they reach their expected end of lifetime. Often, the technical execution of maintenance tasks lies in the hand of the administrators, too.

  - **Support** has two perspectives: the user and the company. From the perspective of user support, the user must be supported if he has troubles in his work that are related to the safeguard. For example, the user cannot log on to an application due to problems within the authentication system. He might have forgotten a password or lost a physical access token. These are examples for scenarios when a user needs support that can mostly be provided by the first or second level support within the company. From the perspective of company support, the company must be supported in problems that cannot be solved internally by the company itself. These problems can be complex technical problems on particular systems that cannot be solved with internal resources and must be solved by the vendor. The subsequent support is called third level support. In addition, company-wide problems might occur, like incompatibilities to other applications after a new update. In this case, also the vendor has to become active and change the relevant source code.

- The **maintenance costs** are related to changes of the safeguard that are performed in order to eliminate actual or potential errors, achieve improvements and adapt to new environmental factors. Changes can be necessary if, among other things, business processes change. Then, the safeguards have to be made compatible to these changes. The amount of costs that are caused by changes depends on the complexity of the change and the property of the safeguard. More complex changes will require much more effort, e.g. if an access control system is changed from key usage to biometric authentication. In addition, changes have to be documented sufficiently. This includes not only a documentation about the new set-up, but also an update of user manuals, policies, procedures and guidelines. Because users are expected to cope with the changed safeguards, often, user trainings are needed, too. Furthermore, indirect costs will occur if users spend time for learning the use of changed safeguards or if they help their colleagues. If a safeguard is company property or open source, the company itself can perform the change of source code or internal parameters. If a safeguard is only licensed, the vendor must be requested to perform the change. This can lead to high costs and long waiting times.
- The **opportunity costs** are incurred whenever capital is invested. When capital is invested in a safeguard, it is bound to a specific purpose and cannot be used for other purposes. Therefore, profits that could be gained due to alternative

investments cannot be gained anymore. These lost profits are the opportunity costs. For example, a safeguard that is underperforming might incur high support costs. In this case, the high support costs that would not have been incurred by another safeguard and the interests that would have been earned by investing the money elsewhere are the opportunity costs. They should be evaluated regularly. New technologies and improved security products can lead to much more favorable safeguards. At least, if the opportunity costs of an old safeguard are higher than the migration costs to a new safeguard, the old one should be replaced.

4.4.2 Breach Costs

Any kind of incident that has a major negative impact on an important cybersecurity goal of a company is called a **cybersecurity breach**. Normally, it is connected to or preceded by an unauthorized access by a person or system with a malicious or fraudulent background.

The most important cybersecurity **goals** can be directly derived from the basic cybersecurity principles (see Sect. 2.2.1). Therefore, a breach is present when the confidentiality, integrity or availability of important data or systems have been impaired. In addition, a company can also consider other goals, e.g. goals derived from the extended cybersecurity principles (see Sect. 2.2.2), so that a related negative influence can be seen as a breach.

If a security breach occurs, the affected **company** can face tremendous costs. The company could be affected by significant financial and non-financial damages. Often, the negative consequences can only be eliminated after years. In the worst case, the company and its owners cannot compensate the subsequent losses and the company has to go out of business. However, not only the company and its property are at risk, but also **individuals** can be affected. A breach at a company can result in the compromise of personal data, which infringes personal privacy. It can also result in financial fraud, which threatens personal financial assets, and even in serious threats to health and life, especially if the company operates in the health sector. Although the following explanations are focused on company losses, a company that is directly or indirectly responsible for the personal integrity of individuals cannot only consider its own condition.

The impact for a company that is caused by a breach can be divided into internal and external costs. The **internal costs** are related to the tasks that are recommendable after a breach has occurred. These tasks require company resources. In particular, the detection, escalation, organization, containment, investigation and correction should be performed as soon as possible:

- The **detection** of the breach is necessary for triggering the subsequent tasks. All kind of detective safeguards, e.g. a log-monitoring tool, can help to detect a breach. Primarily, labor costs incur during the detection. Often, only indications and suspicions exists. By gathering more information and analyzing it thoroughly, security administrators can become relatively certain if a breach actually occurred.

- The **escalation** is an important first step in dealing with the breach. The employee that detected the breach reports it to his supervisor or the security officer. The escalation procedure continues until the senior management is informed. On the one hand, the escalation creates transparency about the current state of the company. The senior management needs transparency for building a good enterprise governance. On the other hand, the senior management can assign the necessary resources for dealing with the breach. Often, the required tasks are too time-consuming for performing them in parallel to the normal business operations. However, the senior management can assign employees completely to the tasks that need to be performed after a breach.
- The **organization** should only be performed after the senior management supports the containment, investigation and correction of the breach. With this support, the organization of the subsequent tasks can be planned. The persons that will perform these tasks should be experts with adequate skills. Therefore, identifying and selecting internal or external staff can be challenging and should not be underestimated. Besides, time is a crucial factor in dealing with the breach. The availability of the experts must be considered while organizing the tasks as fast as possible. Often, an emergency response team has already been organized before so that no extra time is needed for putting together a new team after the breach.
- The **containment** is one of the most important tasks while dealing with a breach. It is needed to get back the control over the attacked assets and to limit the negative consequences of a breach, in particular any damages. After a breach occurred, the damages can increase steadily. For example, an attacker that found an unprotected network service could exploit it repeatedly and tap or manipulate more and more data. By blocking the attacker quickly, the company can limit the damages. Which countermeasures are reasonable, depends on the specific attack and vulnerability. Vulnerable network services should be blocked at the perimeter firewall. Vulnerable software should not be used until a patch or workaround has been deployed. Hacked systems should be taken offline and restored to an intact condition.
- The **investigation** is needed to find knowledge that helps to prevent similar breaches in the future, e.g. about attack patterns that can be integrated into monitoring-tools. Besides, the investigators can search insightful information that can be used to understand and reconstruct the attack that led to the breach. Thereby, evidences are preserved in order to hold someone accountable. Subsequent lawsuits strongly depend on reliable evidences that have been preserved properly.
- The **correction** aims at resolving the negative state by recovering important systems and business processes, and by eliminating the vulnerability. Thereby, further attacks that are similar to the attack that led to the breach will be blocked. The recovery is supported by corrective safeguards, e.g. backups. It includes

tasks from the business view, e.g. moving to another location, and from the technical view, e.g. installing new servers.

The **external costs** are caused by external factors that are part of the breach or direct consequences. These factors are primarily compromise, manipulation, process disruption, asset damage, revenue loss, and reputational damage:

- The **compromise** of data leads to the case that an attacker gets knowledge of sensitive information. This can have a strategic and individual impact:
  - The **strategical impact** should be expected if the compromise affects the competitiveness of the company or if planned strategies are impaired. The competitiveness can be lost if particularly these assets are damaged that have caused or will cause a competitive advantage, like information systems for the company's core processes. By replacing these assets, the competitiveness can be lost temporarily or even permanently. For example, a profitable individual online shop could be hacked and subsequently replaced by a standardized online shop until the vulnerabilities have been closed. Besides, if strategically important information, like research results and sales plans, has been compromised and got into the knowledge of competitors, this information cannot be used as a competitive advantage anymore. This both affects the competiveness and impairs possible planned strategies. Planned strategies can also be impaired if new ventures have to be held up in consequence to a security breach. In particular, the breach can make required resources unavailable or frighten important business partners or capital providers.
  - The **individual impact** can lead to damages regarding the health and life, finances and personal privacy of individual persons:
  - The **health and life** of individuals can be damaged e.g. if security breaches lead to malfunctions of machines or to dangerous conditions. For example, a fire extinguishing system in a data center might release harmful carbon dioxide. Individuals can also be affected by breaches if critical infrastructure is attacked. A breach at any system that is used to support essential parts of our society or economy can result in hazards to life and health. This includes, among others things, systems used in public health, e.g. within hospitals and ambulances, systems providing essential supplies, e.g. drinking water and food, and systems that support other crucial systems, e.g. by providing electricity.
  - The **finances** of individuals can be damaged e.g. if financial data from employees have been compromised or manipulated after a breach. Mostly, companies store and process financial data from employees for payroll accounting.
  - The **personal privacy** of individuals can be damaged if personal data about individuals have been compromised. Normally, companies store not only addresses of employees, but also further information, e.g. performance

evaluations. A compromise can result in the misuse of this information by dubious organizations.

- The **manipulation** of data or systems can be part of an attack where the attacker tries to make fraud by altering data or to harm the company by making the data unusable. If the goal of the attacker is fraud, he will alter specific data and cover up his tracks with the hope that the fraud will stay undetected. For example, an attacker that aims at payment fraud can try to manipulate single transactions secretly in order to make money. In contrast, the actions of an attacker that performs a manipulation that is harmful to the company will be discovered in most cases. Even if they were not, the company would notice a comprehensive manipulation quickly. One way or another, a successful manipulation is very serious for the affected company. The company cannot trust the data on manipulated systems anymore. This leads to a time-consuming recovery to a trustful system state. The company can also face data loss if the backups are faulty or new data has been stored after the last backup. The data can have a high value to the company, especially data that is related to customers. The new acquisition of the data might be the only reliable way. However, it might negatively affect the company's reputation.
- Mostly, the **process disruption** is also a result of a breach. The processes that are important for the business operation of the company can be disrupted shortly or permanently. For example, malware can infect the payment processing system so that customer payments can only be accepted in cash. A security breach can also result in the loss of management control and subsequent infringements of operational standards and procedures. The employees can create workarounds, which enable to continue the operations independently from affected systems. The problem is that important security safeguards or legal frameworks can be bypassed knowingly or unknowingly. For example, if the electronic payments are normally the only acceptable payment option at a company, this company will probably be not prepared for handling cash at checkouts. If the employees decide on their own to accept cash, this workaround will lead to new vulnerabilities to theft and fraud. In addition, unpredictable expenses can be necessary to recover normal operations quickly. For example, additional anti-virus software has to be purchased to handle a new virus. All efforts that are made to continue operations despite of the security breach or to recover normal operations bind employees and resources. In result, providing services and delivering goods to customers can be delayed. These delays can infringe existing contracts so that contractually agreed penalties must be paid and, possibly, legal liabilities must be paid. Especially business customers that are part of a large supply chain can be affected by high losses due to production downtime and empty storages. The company that is directly or indirectly responsible for these losses can be legally required to compensate the resulting financial damages. Besides, the consequences of a breach can influence the work of employees that is important to perform business processes. On the one hand, employees can be bound to recovering tasks, troubleshooting and security

improvements that are necessary after the breach. In result, the employees are not available to be highly productive regarding the revenue or profits of the company. For example, the IT department is not available to improve business processes, like optimizing the information management along the supply chain. On the other hand, employees might be not willing to work productively anymore and, instead, work to the rule. This can be caused by losses of confidence in the company. It might be not seen as a reliable and future-proof anymore. In addition, bad press can influence the morale of the employees. In particular, the identification of the employees with the company can decrease severely.

- The **asset damage** will occur if a tangible or intangible asset is damaged partially or completely. The extent, to which an asset is damaged, is also considered in the calculation of quantitative risk indicators (see Sect. 4.3.4.1). In this perspective, the reduction in the value of an asset equals the impact of the breach. Therefore, the asset value must be measured before and after the breach. The value before the breach can be measured by considering the initial costs and the value changes over time. In the case of information, direct or indirect indicators can be considered (see Sect. 4.2).
- The **revenue loss** is a result of all consequences that are related to the interruption of business processes and fraudulent behaviors of attackers. Lost revenues are connected to the disability of a company to perform regular business operations, e.g. selling goods or providing services to customers. Besides, conditions can occur that complicate business operations, e.g. inefficient workflows due to failed systems or corrupt data. Lost revenues are mostly accompanied by lost profits. In order to recover and repair failed systems, costly resources and much effort can be necessary. In some scenarios, the company might have to face high penalties resulting from a cybersecurity breach, e.g. as defined in contractual agreements with business partners. In addition, the company can be held liable for losses or damages at other parties that occurred subsequently to the cybersecurity breach. To cover the incurred costs of a breach, the company can be forced to change its invested capital into liquid financial resources. Subsequently, planned investments can be delayed and business goals might be missed. In the worst case, the company will not be able to raise sufficient financial resources. This can result in the bankruptcy of the company.
- The **reputational damage** occurs when the image of the company to external parties is negatively impacted. A security breach can dramatically change the public opinion about the company. Especially if customers have been affected by the security breach, the company can be seen as dubious, careless or irresponsible. A bad reputation does not directly harm the company, but it leads to many undesirable consequences, which might only be stopped after a long-term interaction with the public. Customers can move to competitors so that the amount of customers can steadily decrease. In detail, the number of sales and orders can decline. Business partners can cancel their contracts with the company or allow their contracts to expire. Key institutions can lose the confidence in the company so that important support or cooperation can be difficult to get,

e.g. raising a credit. In addition, if the company is a stock company, the share price can dramatically decrease. The specific amount of damage depends on the business relationships of the company. The reputation will be of crucial importance if the company is in business with many customers that are normally performing short-term transactions. In contrast, if the company is only connected with few parties and normally provides long-term contracts, e.g. for many years, the reputation will rather be of low importance. In any cases where the customers' opinions strongly influences the revenue and subsequently the profits of a company, reputational damage can be severe. Cybersecurity breaches that are going public are generally very influential to the customers. Therefore, a company should not only be concerned in preventing breaches but also in controlling the public opinion because even the suspicion or rumor about a breach can strongly influence customers.

4.5 Cybersecurity Benefits

Benefits must not be confused with profits. **Profits** are financial advantages gained by using capital or assets within productive processes. Therefore, profits can be seen as a specific type of benefits that are financial and quantifiable, and that lead to an increase of important performance indicators.

Benefits have a more general meaning than profits. Benefits are improvements that are seen positive or worthwhile by a stakeholder. Normally, they are delivered by an asset or investment, e.g. a cybersecurity investment. The benefits of cybersecurity investments, which include reasonable safeguards, are the result of a risk mitigation or elimination. Breaches are prevented and, thereby, the subsequent breach costs are reduced. By considering the probability of the occurrence of a breach, the expected losses can be calculated. Related to one year, the expected losses can be shown by the annualized loss expectancy (see Sect. 4.3.4.1). In this case, the benefits are the difference between the initially expected losses (before the implementation of a safeguard) and the residual expected losses (after the implementation of a safeguard):

$$benefits = initially\,expected\,losses - residual\,expected\,losses$$

As shown in Fig. 4.13, the initially expected losses depend on the initial risk and its evaluation. The safeguard leads to a mitigation of this risk. In an extreme case, the safeguard can even eliminate the risk fully. The residual risk represents the risk that exists after the safeguard has been transited into an operational state. The benefits from the investment in the safeguard are expressed with the difference between the expected losses related to the initial risk and the expected losses related to the residual risk. These benefits should be compared to the safeguard costs in order to achieve a reasonable decision.

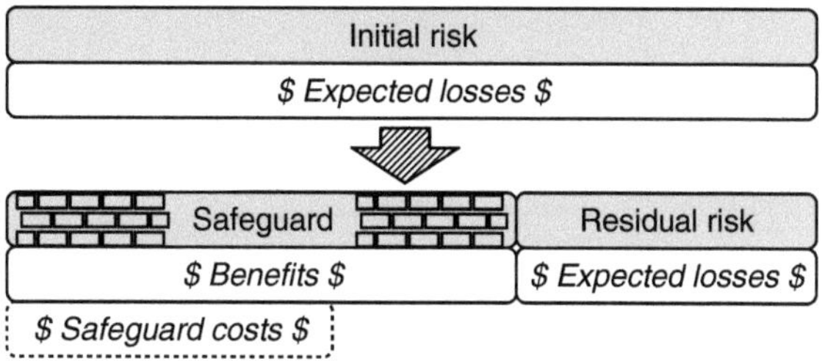

Fig. 4.13 Trade-off between benefits and costs

Like other benefits, the benefits from cybersecurity investments can be **financial**, e.g. in the form of prevented losses, or **non-financial**, e.g. in the form of protection of the company's reputation. While some benefits are quantifiable easily, e.g. the number of prevented attacks, others can be described only qualitatively, e.g. the image of a secure company.

Generally, **cybersecurity investments** cannot be used to generate profits. They only help to secure assets used within the production processes. They help to prevent interruptions and financial losses caused by problems within these processes. Often, they are not necessary for starting business operations, but rather they are necessary to keep them running without compromise, manipulation and interruption. Preventing negative effects can have a significant influence on the value generation of the company. Therefore, cybersecurity investments generate benefits, which can be very favorable for the company. However, the benefits must be compared to the incurred safeguard costs. A trade-off between benefits and costs should be performed before making an investment decision. If the costs are greater than the benefits, it will not be reasonable to make the investment in a safeguard. Instead, it will be more reasonable to accept the expected losses. Even if these losses actually occur, the company will have to face fewer costs than it would have spent for the safeguard.

Chapter 5
Foundations of Decision Making

5.1 Motives

In the daily business of small, medium or big companies, cybersecurity investment decisions are sometimes based on inopportune justifications. Their cause is mostly originated in **fear, uncertainty and doubt**—also known as FUD. Some unethical sellers even enhance these conditions to increase their sales. They use comprehensive and often subtle and subliminal disinformation. Among other things, neutral sources are referred, but the significance for the enterprise is greatly exaggerated or is presented in a wrong context. The result can be an expensive and inadequate investment in a suboptimal safeguard.

On the other hand, **hastiness and poor preparation** can lead to an inopportune justification, too. If managers must quickly react because of severe threats, there will be a danger that experts are not consulted prior to the investment decision. In this case, poor decisions are very common. Subsequently, the expenses are high without generating the expected security enhancement.

The best way to avoid an inopportune decision justification is a well thought decision procedure including recognized **techniques** from the areas of decision theory and investment management as well as the involvement of experts. In order to find the most appropriate investment, the decision maker must be able to evaluate several alternatives and to identify and select the best one. The selection of an alternative is based on the evaluation of multiple qualitative or quantitative attributes. Therefore, a technique is handy that provides a structure for handling these attributes and evaluating the existing alternatives accordingly. The attributes are weighted so that the evaluation of the alternatives can be performed under consideration of the individual preferences of the decision maker. The **advantages** of using a technique over a non-systematic procedure are:

- The decision problem must be defined before actually starting the evaluation.
- The identification and use of attributes facilitate the consideration of different perspectives within the evaluation.

S. Beissel, *Cybersecurity Investments*, Progress in IS,
DOI 10.1007/978-3-319-30460-1_5

- The decision making process is organized with transparent steps that can be understood by third persons.
- The decision making process is divided into subparts that require the decision maker to develop intermediate results that are aggregated in an understandable way to an overall result.

The most common **decision making techniques** for selecting an alternative with multiple attributes are the simple additive weighting and the analytic hierarchy process. Both techniques are based on the same general sequence: the decision problem identification, attribute identification and evaluation, alternative identification and evaluation, and selection of the best alternative. The difference lays in the calculations of the evaluations. The simple additive weighting uses calculations that are based on independent evaluations of separate attributes and alternatives, while the analytic hierarchy process uses pairwise comparisons of two attributes or alternatives at a time. Since these different techniques include different calculation methods, the same alternatives can lead to dissimilar results, e.g. the same alternative could be the most appropriate according to simple additive weighting, while it is only the second choice according to the analytic hierarchy process. Especially, evaluation results with alternative scores that are close to each other can lead to this situation.

There are also other decision techniques in the scientific field, e.g. the ANP (Analytic Network Process) by Saaty (1996), TOPSIS (Technique for Order Preference by Similarity to Ideal Solution) by Hwang and Yoon (1981), and DEA (Data Envelopment Analysis) by Charnes et al. (1978). However, the simple additive weighting and the analytic hierarchy process provide the best balance between an ease of understanding and thoughtful application for the **practical use** in the enterprise sector.

5.2 Simple Additive Weighting

The simple additive weighting (SAW) is also known as the weighted sum method (Fishburn 1967). In this technique, a mathematical function is used to model the preferences of the decision maker and evaluate the considered alternatives regarding multiple attributes. It is a very common and straightforward procedure for an attribute-based decision making that aims at the selection of an alternative.

For each alternative, an overall **score** is calculated by summing the weighted sub scores that are related to the specific characteristics of the alternative. The alternative with the highest overall score is finally selected. Due to the restriction on basic arithmetic operations, the SAW can be used without a special software tool.

At first, the relevant **attributes** must be identified and evaluated. The evaluation leads to attribute weights, which are defined to represent the importance of each attribute from the perspective of the decision maker. Normally, but not necessarily, the weights are positioned on a scale from 0 to 1. Then, the relevant alternatives must be identified. Afterwards, all attribute values of each alternative must be evaluated with a sub score. Again, a scale is used, e.g. from 0 to 4. In order to calculate an overall score, the sub scores regarding the single attributes must be aggregated with a utility function. Often, a straight linear aggregation is preferred over a nonlinearly one. The linear **aggregation** can be executed with the following formula:

$$O_y = \sum_{z=1}^{n} W_z S_{yz}$$

$O_y \in \mathbb{R}_+$ is the overall score of the alternative y. $W_z \in \mathbb{R}_+ \leq 1$ is the weight of the attribute z and, for example, $S_{yz} \in \mathbb{N}_0 \leq 4$ is the sub score of the alternative y regarding the attribute z.

By ordering to the overall scores of all alternatives, a **ranking** can be made, which shows the alternative with the highest overall score on the top. This is the best and, therefore, the most adequate alternative.

The straightforward SAW can be processed by just using basic mathematical operations. A special software tool is not necessary. However, the SAW also comes with some **disadvantages**:

- The addition of the sub scores implies the independence of the attributes. However, **dependencies** between attributes, such as competitive or complementary relationships, often cannot be completely avoided. For example, the resilience of a system is not only determined by fail-safe or redundant hardware, but also by error-free software. In addition, the general dependency of economic parameters can be influential. For example, if a costly safeguard system is hacked, the financial loss will be additionally raised because of the protection loss of sensitive assets. Consequently, there is a risk that strongly dependent attributes lead to an unintentional over- or undervaluation of alternatives in the evaluation.
- The SAW is also characterized by many possible ways of **manipulation**. Because precise figures and calculation methods are used, objectivity can be faked. Due to the general subjectivity in the weighting and evaluation of attributes, the result can be significantly affected by undetected manipulation. Although the subjectivity can be reduced by including experts, it cannot be eliminated. In addition, the decision maker has the freedom of choice regarding the attribute selection.
- The accumulation of the sub scores and the linear evaluation lead to a possible **substitutability** of the sub scores. In particular, sub scores that are derived from very bad characteristics of an alternative can be substituted with sub scores from very good characteristics. Therefore, single attributes might be neglected. If the attributes are divided into exclusion and comparison attributes, this problem can be eliminated only partially. The comparison attributes are still affected by a possible substitutability.

- The overall result of the SAW is subject to **leveling**. It is likely that the weaknesses or strengths of the best alternative are no longer recognizable in the result. The more attributes are considered, the more likely the results are positioned in the middle region of the range of the possible overall scores.
- Due to the assessment of alternatives with individual attributes, the overall problem will be broken down into many single problems. This **decomposition** is questionable because, firstly, the overall problem is no longer clear and, secondly, there is a risk that the assessments of many single problems lead to an undesirable overall assessment. If the attributes are in a competitive relationship to each other, the improvement of a sub score regarding a single attribute can lead to the situation that the evaluation of a competing attribute will result in a lower sub score. Exemplarily, the reduction of false positive events in biometric access control systems mostly leads to an increase of false negative events.

Because of these disadvantages, the SAW should be seen **skeptical**, especially in case of crucial decisions, e.g. during the evaluation of safeguards that are needed to mitigate severe risks for the whole company.

5.3 Analytic Hierarchy Process

The analytic hierarchy process (AHP) (Saaty 1994, 2000) is a technique for a complex decision making wherein **pairwise comparisons** are used for thoughtful and consistent evaluations of attributes and alternatives. Similar to the SAW, the AHP facilitates the evaluation of alternatives with respect to clearly defined attributes while the level of importance for each attribute is taken into account. It helps to aggregate sub scores regarding single attributes into an overall score for each alternative.

The biggest difference between the SAW and the AHP lies in the **evaluation technique**. The SAW uses single and, mostly, isolated decisions regarding each attribute and each alternative. In contrast to this, the AHP always uses pairwise comparisons, which lead to evaluations that are more thoughtful.

In AHP, the **evaluation result** of each pairwise comparison is represented with a value from Table 5.1. The values from this table will be used to express if an

Table 5.1 Evaluation results

Values	Description
1	Equally important
3	Moderately more important
5	Strongly more important
7	Very strongly more important
9	Extremely more important
2, 4, 6, 8	Intermediate values
$\frac{1}{2}, \frac{1}{3}, \frac{1}{4}, \frac{1}{5}, \frac{1}{6}, \frac{1}{7}, \frac{1}{8}, \frac{1}{9}$	Reciprocal values

attribute or alternative is more or less important than another attribute or alternative. Regarding alternatives, being more important is also understood as being better.

The value from each pairwise comparison of n comparison objects has to be inserted into the **evaluation matrix**, which has the following structure:

$$A = \begin{pmatrix} a_{11} & \ldots & a_{1j} & \ldots & a_{1n} \\ \ldots & \ldots & \ldots & \ldots & \ldots \\ a_{i1} & \ldots & a_{ij} & \ldots & a_{in} \\ \ldots & \ldots & \ldots & \ldots & \ldots \\ a_{n1} & \ldots & a_{nj} & \ldots & a_{nn} \end{pmatrix}$$

$$\begin{aligned} \text{where} \quad & \forall i = 1, \ldots, n \quad \forall j = 1, \ldots, n: \quad a_{ij} > 0 \\ & \forall i = j: \quad a_{ij} = 1 \\ & \forall i = 1, \ldots, n \quad \forall j = 1, \ldots, n: \quad a_{ij} = a_{ji}^{-1} \end{aligned}$$

In order to complete the evaluation matrix, $\frac{n \cdot (n-1)}{2}$ pairwise comparisons have to be performed. Along the main diagonal, all values are set to one because, normally, the comparisons are reflexive. Below the main diagonal, the values are set to the reciprocal values of the values that are above the main diagonal because, normally, the comparisons are symmetrical. The matching between the above and below values can be done by using the main diagonal as a center for mirroring.

Afterwards, the values from the evaluation matrix have to be aggregated. For this purpose, the sum of every column j has to be calculated with the following formula:

$$\sum_{i=1}^{n} a_{ij}$$

The **normalization** of the matrix has to be done by dividing every value by its column sum:

$$N = \begin{pmatrix} \frac{a_{11}}{\sum_{i=1}^{n} a_{i1}} & \ldots & \frac{a_{1j}}{\sum_{i=1}^{n} a_{ij}} & \ldots & \frac{a_{1n}}{\sum_{i=1}^{n} a_{in}} \\ \ldots & \ldots & \ldots & \ldots & \ldots \\ \frac{a_{i1}}{\sum_{i=1}^{n} a_{i1}} & \ldots & \frac{a_{ij}}{\sum_{i=1}^{n} a_{ij}} & \ldots & \frac{a_{in}}{\sum_{i=1}^{n} a_{in}} \\ \ldots & \ldots & \ldots & \ldots & \ldots \\ \frac{a_{n1}}{\sum_{i=1}^{n} a_{i1}} & \ldots & \frac{a_{nj}}{\sum_{i=1}^{n} a_{ij}} & \ldots & \frac{a_{nn}}{\sum_{i=1}^{n} a_{in}} \end{pmatrix}$$

For every attribute or alternative, the impact v_i has to be calculated. For attributes, this impact will be used as a weight when the overall score of an alternative will be calculated. For alternatives, this impact represents an unweighted sub score that will be weighted and aggregated subsequently. For calculating the impact, the line sums of the normalized evaluation matrix N are calculated and divided by the number of attributes or alternatives (n):

$$v_i = \frac{\sum_{j=1}^{n} a_{ij}^{norm}}{n} \quad \text{where} \quad a_{ij}^{norm} = \frac{a_{ij}}{\sum_{i=1}^{n} a_{ij}}$$

The calculation results are **approximations**. Results that are more precise can be obtained by using an iterative approach, as integrated in dedicated AHP software, e.g. Expert Choice. The deviations between the approximation results and the precise results can mostly be found in the second or third decimal.

While the SAW can be handled just by processing basic mathematical operations, the AHP requires **advanced computations**. Therefore, a computer-based implementation of the AHP is strongly recommended.

Although the AHP leads to more thoughtful and consistent evaluations, it cannot eliminate the **disadvantages** of the SAW fully. Therefore, the following possible disadvantages should be taken into account while processing the AHP evaluation results:

- The AHP also suffers from the problem that strongly **dependent** attributes can lead to alternatives that are unintentionally overvalued in a positive or negative way.
- The AHP is characterized by **manipulation** opportunities, too. The evaluations, the structuring of the decision, the definition of attributes and the identification of decision alternatives are characterized by the freedom of choice of the decision maker. However, this is not a special weakness of the AHP technique because there is no technique that can independently make these essential decisions on behalf of the decision maker.
- The problem of the possible **substitutability** of attributes with each other is similar to the one within the SAW.
- In addition, **leveling** is also a potential problem. Like in the SAW, a high amount of attributes probably leads to evaluation results that are positioned in the middle region of the range of the possible overall scores.
- Like in the SAW, using individual attributes causes a breakdown of the overall problem into many single problems. Therefore, this **decomposition** can be questionable in the AHP, too.

However, the AHP has the following **advantages** that can increase the decision quality noticeably:

- Inconsistencies and contradictions within the decision making can be recognized. For this purpose, a **consistency check** of the evaluation scores is offered by the AHP.
- The AHP offers a **bigger range** of possible evaluations than the SAW. However, the AHP does not dramatically increase the complexity. This leads to a more sophisticated evaluation without losing the user acceptance.
- The pairwise comparisons require the decision maker to think thoroughly before the single evaluations will be made. The necessity to deal with every part of the decision problem more closely leads to **high quality** decisions.

5.4 Decision Difficulties

Independently from the disadvantages of the particular decision making technique, general **difficulties** can occur during the selection of a cybersecurity investment. As so often, the company is influenced by cost, time and quality aspects while performing the decision making. Besides, substantial interdependencies to other parties should be considered. Although the difficulties cannot always be eliminated, it is crucial that they are understood and handled appropriately. From the aspects of cost, time, quality and interdependencies, particularly the following issues should be considered before and during the decision making.

5.4.1 Cost Aspects

The decision making **costs** must not be neglected. During the decision making, company resources, e.g. skilled professionals and software tools, are needed. There is a risk that the company only focuses on the costs that will be incurred by the cybersecurity investment itself. In this case, the costs that are needed to select the best investment are often neglected. Especially if complex decisions are made, e.g. under consideration of a large amount of abstruse attributes, the company will have to face high costs. Finding a good decision has a certain value to the company. For example, another alternative can be selected that provides the same functionality as the previous one, but is less expensive. Then, the decision value equals the saved costs. If the costs of the decision making exceeds the decision value, the decision making will not be worthwhile. In general, the company should always ensure that the decision making costs do not exceed the decision value. However, the precise decision value is often hard to determine before the decision had been completed. For example, it can be unclear how much cheaper another appropriate alternative will be. Therefore, the decision value should be estimated so that a limit for the decision making costs can be established. While controlling these costs, particularly these factors should be considered:

- The engaged **human resources** can be a high cost factor. One or more decision makers have to concentrate on the decision making process. Besides, interviewees and testers might be needed at least partially. In some cases, external consultants might also be called in for performing sophisticated analyses. Besides, trainings in decision making can be useful in order to ensure a proper and accurate process.
- The **work equipment** consists of everything that the persons involved in decision making need for their work. They have to be equipped with desktop or mobile computers if not already done. In addition, certain evaluations require the use of test systems. In this case, test systems have to be provided at least temporarily. The computers also have to be deployed with adequate software. Besides the operating system, cross-functional and dedicated software can be

necessary. Cross-functional software includes software that generally supports professional work, e.g. software for office communication, collaboration, project management, and portal sites. Dedicated software addresses only the decision making process in a narrower sense, e.g. AHP tools.

- The integration of a high **diversity** into the decision making can be a good idea from the quality view, but it can strongly increase the costs. More diversity can be achieved with more resources or more considerations of technical aspects.
  - More **resources** can mean that more experts from various departments or companies are involved. This leads to better results because the subjectivity is reduced and more opinions can be considered. More resources can also mean that more equipment is used, e.g. various test systems.
  - More considerations of **technical aspects** can be applied to different subtasks of the decision making. For example, expert opinions can be collected in different ways, e.g. with interviews and surveys. The evaluation of attributes and alternatives can be performed with various decision making techniques, e.g. with the SAW and AHP. Due to the increased effort that is accompanied by more considerations of technical aspects, more resources are needed here, too.

Because integrating diversity directly or indirectly requires more resources, it is generally accompanied by higher costs. Besides, diversity can also be advantageous in the selection of the cybersecurity investment. If various safeguards are combined, the possible damages of exploited vulnerabilities will be limited because the safeguards will not share the same vulnerabilities. Of course, this also increases costs. Operation and maintenance costs will increase and the purchasing costs can hardly be decreased with volume discounts. However, suitable alternatives for a combination might not be available if the market is not very competitive and one vendor dominates it.

5.4.2 *Time Aspects*

The **time** required for decision making can also be affected by difficulties. Primarily, all activities that slow down the decision making for unforeseen reasons are disadvantageous from the time perspective. The main reasons for time issues are changes, process deficiencies and resources:

- **Changes** can be caused by internal factors from inside the company or external factors from the environment. In result, additional time has to be spent in order to analyze these changes and evaluate the effect on the current decision making. In the worst case, requirements change dramatically so that the complete decision making process will have to be revised. A crucial problem that is often connected with changed requirements is the scope creep. Here, the requirements are changed repeatedly so that the process also has to be revised repeatedly.

In consequence, there is a risk that the process is delayed extremely or cannot even be finalized in the long-term.

- **Internal factors** are mostly related to changes in the organization, objectives or opinions of the company or important stakeholders. For example, the sponsor can be replaced and, at the same time, fundamental aspects of the decision problem can be changed. Possibly, users of a new solution can identify additional requirements during the testing or first use, e.g. time restrictions for the response times of a system.
- **External factors** can be related to, among other things, new behaviors, technical trends, or regulations. For example, cloud computing became very popular because many companies were able to save high costs that were accompanied by systems on premises. In result, many safeguards could only be implemented by the cloud service provider, who took over the hosting and, on request, even the administration of the systems. DevOps, mobile devices, social media, and the Internet of things are more trends that influenced cybersecurity investment decisions. Besides, because of new or updated regulations, the company can be suddenly bound to new requirements, e.g. certain protocols can be prohibited.

• **Process deficiencies** during the decision making can cause, among other things, unnecessary waiting times and unforeseen delays. By checking the applicability of general approaches for reducing processing times (Bleicher 1991, p. 196), potential deficiencies in the decision making process can be identified and eliminated:

- The approach of **removing** activities will be suitable if unnecessary or redundant activities are performed in the process. Every activity that does not lead to a benefit in the decision making outcome should be removed. For example, a sensitivity analysis right after the attribute evaluation will be unnecessary if another sensitivity analysis for all evaluations is done at the end of the process.
- The **outsourcing** of activities can be advantageous because the process can be accelerated if particular activities are performed by a third party. For example, the creation and analysis of comprehensive surveys during the alternative or attribute identification can be performed faster if a specialized service provider performs the related activities.
- By **combining** activities, the setting-up times can be reduced. For example, if the same persons handle the identification and evaluation of alternatives, they will only have to become acquainted with the needed background information about the alternatives once. If different persons or systems are involved for different tasks, the input and output data of the activities must be transmitted over interfaces. This will also cause additional time.
- Activities should be **parallelized** if they are sequential but independent from each other. If sufficient resources are available for parallel processing, the overall processing time can be reduced. For example, the alternative and

attribute identification can be parallelized. However, during parallel processing, different activities are performed by different persons. Therefore, there can be conflicts with the approach of combining activities.
   - Because the sequence of activities might not be optimal, **shifting** them to another position in the process can be advantageous. Especially if waiting times are filled up with other activities, the overall processing time will be reduced. For example, the decision maker might have to wait until all relevant stakeholders are available before starting the attribute identification and evaluation. If the alternative identification is shifted before the attribute identification, he can reduce the waiting time. However, possible dependencies can forbid the shifting of certain activities.
   - Often, various possibilities can be used that help to **accelerate** single activities. Some activities can be accelerated with automation, while others will use less time if more or better resources are provided. In the decision making, skilled professionals can often complete activities faster than untrained workers can do. Providing dedicated decision making tools can also accelerate activities. In particular, the evaluation activities in the AHP can be accelerated with these tools.

- **Resources** can be fully utilized or unavailable so that undesired waiting times arise. It should be considered as soon as possible which resources would be needed with which utilization for particular activities in the decision making process. Otherwise, insufficient availability or capacity can lead to delays or even the cancelation of the process.

   - If resources are fully **utilized**, bottlenecks and queues with waiting times will arise. Generally, this can be inconvenient but not dramatic. Only if the bottlenecks are overlooked and important deadlines cannot be met, serious impacts can be caused. For example, if the decision maker wants to complete the attribute identification but does not get answers from busy stakeholders, he will have to wait. However, if the sponsor requires a timely completion of the process or if deadlines arise from external factors, e.g. new regulations, the additional waiting time can become a severe issue.
   - Resources can also be temporarily or permanently **unavailable**. The reasons for the unavailability can be manifold. For example, resources can be defective, not accessible, under maintenance, reserved for other projects, sold, lost or damaged. In case of unexpected issues with the resource availability, the decision maker has to cope with delays. In the worst case, the needed resource is permanently unavailable and cannot be replaced. Then, the decision making process might have to be canceled. For example, if specific systems shall be protected with a new safeguard, e.g. hardware encryption, these systems must be available in order to analyze technical compatibilities and derive information for a test setup. If these systems are not available because their hosting and operation have been outsourced, the collectable information for the decision making will not be sufficient and the decision making process will have to be canceled.

5.4.3 Quality Aspects

The **quality** aspects of a decision strongly influence its value. Only thoughtful decisions are truly beneficial for the company. If the decision making is characterized by errors, the decision will often not lead to a good choice. Besides, overlooked information can cause a completely different ranking of alternatives. The quality also depends on aspects that are related to cost and time. For example, untrained employees are less expensive and quickly available, but the quality of the decision will be probably affected by errors or missing information. Regarding the quality aspects of decision making in the narrower sense, the following factors should be considered:

- The **qualification** of the involved professionals is important. On the one hand, they should be adequately trained. If the professionals do not have knowledge about decision making techniques or common problems and solutions from the industry sector, they will probably not succeed in performing the decision making process systematically and faultlessly. Besides, soft skills are important when they collect information in interviews, meetings or workshops.
- The **motivation** of the professionals can also influence the decision quality. If the motivation is high, the professionals will be encouraged to deliver good outcomes. If it is low, they will not care much about the outcome. For example, the motivation can influence the professionals' willingness to perform additional overwork in order to check the critical parts of the decision. Among other things, missing information, hastiness, and clerical errors can be caused by low motivation. In order to understand and improve the motivation, intrinsic and extrinsic motivation should be distinguished:
  - If a professional is motivated **intrinsically**, he will have an interest in the performance on his own. From work, he receives a self-fulfillment because, in his own understanding, he likes the work or he believes that it is natural.
  - The **extrinsic** motivation is driven by external factors. They include, among other things, financial compensations, external expectations and an interest in the company success.
- Insufficient **clarity** in the objectives that are related to the decision making is also problematic. Even highly motivated professionals can fail to meet the objectives if they are not expressed in an understandable way. According to Doran (1981), well-expressed objectives should meet the **SMART** criteria, which start with a letter from the acronym (see below). In decision making, they can have e.g. the following meaning:
  - A **specific (S)** objective leads to a consistent understanding among all involved stakeholders. For example, the objective "identify attributes" is not very specific, while "identify at least 10 attributes that represent the user requirements on a new access management system" is more specific.

- If an objective has actually been met, can only be seen if it is **measurable (M)**. Some objectives can be measured directly, e.g. the number of considered alternatives. Others can only be measured indirectly, e.g. the satisfaction of the sponsor with the decision. Here, substitute metrics must be used, e.g. the number of denials or time until approval.
- An objective will be **achievable (A)** if the needed resources are available in the right capacity and on time. Besides, the cooperation from relevant stakeholders must be given. For example, a decision maker cannot meet the objective of collecting user opinions if the users do not cooperate.
- An objective will be **relevant (R)** if it matches to the overall business goals or specific personal goals of the person who has to meet the objective. An irrelevant objective in decision making would be to provide user support for application software that is not related to the decision.
- A **time-bound (T)** objective is dated so that everybody who is involved knows when the objective is expected to be complete and when it can be measured. When an objective is dated, relevant internal factors, e.g. the availability of resources, and external factors, e.g. the binding date for complying with new laws, should be considered.

- Another factor is the conscious or subconscious **manipulation** of the decision making by single stakeholders. In result, the decision might not only represent facts but also falsified information that lead to the selection of a suboptimal alternative.

  - The **conscious** manipulation is related to certain interests that are pursued by a stakeholder, e.g. a vendor that manipulates product information. The particular reasons that lead to an actual manipulation attempt can be derived from the fraud triangle, which is described in Sect. 6.6. If a stakeholder has interests in a proper decision making and, at the same time, interests that lead to a manipulation, a conflict-of-interest will occur, as described in Sect. 6.8.
  - The **unconscious** manipulation is caused by a possible response bias, which leads to deviations in the evaluation results of the involved stakeholders. As described in Sect. 6.8, the reaction of evaluators can be characterized by tendencies, which can reduce the information value of the results.

- In addition, the influence of the **communication** between stakeholders on the decision quality should not be underestimated. Multiple issues that are related to communication can cause difficulties in the decision making:

  - The **data collection** can be hampered if the needed data is not available or not approved for disclosure. In cybersecurity, statistics about attacks can be hard to get. Companies that have been attacked often do not publish related information. Besides, reliable data about the newest cyber threats mostly do not exist. Therefore, there is a risk that the selection of a cybersecurity investment is based on incomplete or obsolete data. It should also be considered that data from multiple sources could be hard to compare if they have different bases. For example, an antivirus software that has a detection rate of

  95 % cannot be compared to one with a rate of 98 % if the rates are based on different sets of malware, e.g. viruses, worms, Trojan horses and rootkits.
  - In contrast, the **amount** of the relevant information for the decision can be too big. The decision maker can be overstrained with structuring and analyzing the data. Distinguishing useful from useless data and aggregating large amounts of data can be very challenging. Often, sophisticated pattern-based analyses are necessary to gather useful information from these data.
  - If too less communication is performed with important stakeholders, e.g. the sponsor, the **transparency** towards the decision maker can be significantly impaired. For example, important requirements or expectations that are not communicated at the beginning of the lifecycle can lead to a denial of the decision paper eventually.

- The **outsourcing** of the decision making process or separate subtasks of this process mostly influences the decision quality, too. On the one hand, a service provider who is focused on decision making normally provides experts from the field. In contrast to generalists, these experts are able to achieve a higher decision quality. On the other hand, interfaces between the outsourcing company and the service provider must be created. Because of that, understanding and interpreting the transmitted data can be impaired. Besides, if significant tasks are performed externally, the outsourcing company cannot benefit from lessons learned. Therefore, less knowledge can be built by internal professionals so that the company can hardly improve its own decision quality and decision making process in the future.
- Another factor is the unforeseen **future** of cybersecurity trends. Good solutions can become obsolete quickly for various reasons. For example, vendors can go out of business and stop supporting their product, new approaches from attackers can change the protection requirements, or shifts in business strategies can lead to changed company risk profiles. In case of major changes in the future, it often will not matter how good the decision has been before. Moreover, the decision will have to be reevaluated under consideration of the new conditions.
- Cybersecurity investments, especially those that are purchased from a vendor, are normally accompanied by various **terms** of licenses, agreements or contracts. Inopportune terms can lead to very unfavorable consequences for the company. Therefore, neglecting or overlooking terms completely or partially can impair the decision quality. For example, terms that address the liability in case of failures can have a high importance. A company that was severely damaged by a successful cyber-attack because of a faulty security product might not be able to claim damages if it agreed to inopportune terms previously. Besides, the place of jurisdiction, which depends on the place of business of the contractual partners, can affect the legal enforceability of licenses, agreements and contracts.

- Naturally, **quality controls** within the decision making process strongly influence the decision quality. If quality controls are integrated, errors can be made visible before finalizing the decision. In general, the sensitivity analysis should always be applied in order to identify and check critical data. Besides, some decision making techniques offer additional checks, e.g. the consistency check in AHP.

5.4.4 Interdependencies

Often, the company that performs the decision making is **interdependent** to other parties in the industry. Subsequent to these interdependencies, effects related to cybersecurity investments can occur. From the perspective of time, effects can lead, accompany or follow cybersecurity investments.

- Effects that can **lead** the cybersecurity investment are based on a previous relationship between parties or previous actions of relevant parties. Before an appropriate cybersecurity investment will be selected, these effects should be understood. Sometimes, evading these effects can be a reasonable solution for the company, e.g. by renegotiating cybersecurity terms in contracts. Some examples that illustrate leading effects are:
  - The company provides services to powerful customers who transfer their **risks** in an excessive way towards the service provider. Due to contractual agreements, possible damages from security breaches have to be covered by the service provider. This fundamentally affects the risk situation, which in turn affects the decision attribute identification and evaluation.
  - Hackers who create new **attacks** can strongly influence the evaluation of cybersecurity investments. Safeguards that cannot protect the company against these new attacks can suddenly become unsuited. Therefore, the requirements for an appropriate cybersecurity investment depend on, among other things, the advances in the hacker community.
  - **Regulations** that are binding for the industry or specific sectors also have effects on the selection of the cybersecurity investment. On the one hand, various requirements have to be covered by suitable safeguards, e.g. the protection of sensitive data. On the other hand, public regulations might also influence the decision making process itself. For example, § 202c of the German criminal code forbids, among other things, producing, acquiring, selling and software for data espionage. This also influences research by cybersecurity consultants so that finding an appropriate safeguard becomes more difficult.
- Effects can **accompany** the cybersecurity investment so that a company influences the situation at or relationship to third parties at the same time as the investment is performed. These situations should not be overlooked. Moreover,

it should be explicitly considered during the decision making. Examples for concurrent effects are:

- The feasible **protection level** of the company depends on the protection level of other parties. For example, the company cannot decide on its own that transmitted data shall be encrypted. The receiver and sender must both implement encryption solutions that can cope with the same algorithms in order to exchange encrypted files.
- A cybersecurity investment can be **beneficial** for other parties, too. For example, new guidelines from the payment card organizations are often published in the whole industry so that others can benefit from free additional guidance. Besides, not only new customers but also regular customers can benefit from publicly available security enhancements of software products, e.g. in the form of security patches.
- Due to cybersecurity investments, the company can become more **competitive** in the market. For example, if certain well-recognized standards, e.g. ISO 27001, are met, customers will probably be more interested in the provided services.

• Besides, various effects can **follow** cybersecurity investments. The behavior of other parties can change because of a company's decision regarding cybersecurity. Examples for effects that occur after cybersecurity investments are:

  - If the company's safeguards cannot sufficiently prevent breaches, not only the company itself can be **damaged** but also the business partners or customers. For example, if customer databases are compromised, the customers can be affected by social engineering from attackers who will exploit contact information.
  - By selecting a good cybersecurity investment, the company can hold an **exemplary** role in the industry. Other peers in the market might copy the company's strategy related to cybersecurity. This would improve the overall protection level in the market. For example, providing secure web site connections became a de facto standard for online shopping.
  - Hackers who become aware of recently implemented safeguards often adapt their **attack strategy**. They try to circumvent the company's protection and search new vectors for their attacks. For example, after a company invested in its network perimeter and endpoint security, hackers might focus on social engineering attacks.

Chapter 6
Lifecycle of Cybersecurity Investments

6.1 Overview of Lifecycle Steps

The **lifecycle** covers every step from the initiation until the termination of a cybersecurity investment. The steps 3–8 represent the core steps of decision making (see grey boxes in Fig. 6.1).

The steps of the **lifecycle** of cybersecurity investments address the following subjects:

1. **Initiation** (Sect. 6.2): At first, a cybersecurity investment is recognized as desirable. This can be caused by an internal or external event as well as a self-assessment or just by the idea of a responsible member of the company in focus.
2. **Sponsoring** (Sect. 6.3): Generally, the procedure for performing the following lifecycle steps needs funding. Often, multiple experts have to be involved at different levels, from consulting to decision making. This can cause noticeable costs for the company, which can be seen as misspent if not approved in advance. In order to avoid complications, the procedure must be sponsored and the approval must be granted by senior management.
3. **Decision Problem Identification** (Sect. 6.4): Although the decision problem might be clear in the mind of the initiator, it might be very vague in the mind of other important contributors. An accurate identification of the decision problem helps to create a common and clear understanding by every involved contributor and, at the same time, prevents the undesirable situation that crucial aspects of the decision problem like scope and required protection level have not been entirely recognized. The decision making technique that shall be used—often the SAW or the AHP—is also selected in this step because further steps can differentiate in accordance to the selected decision making technique.
4. **Attribute Identification** (Sect. 6.5): The identification of adequate attributes is a very important and influential part of the overall decision. In this step, all

S. Beissel, *Cybersecurity Investments*, Progress in IS,
DOI 10.1007/978-3-319-30460-1_6

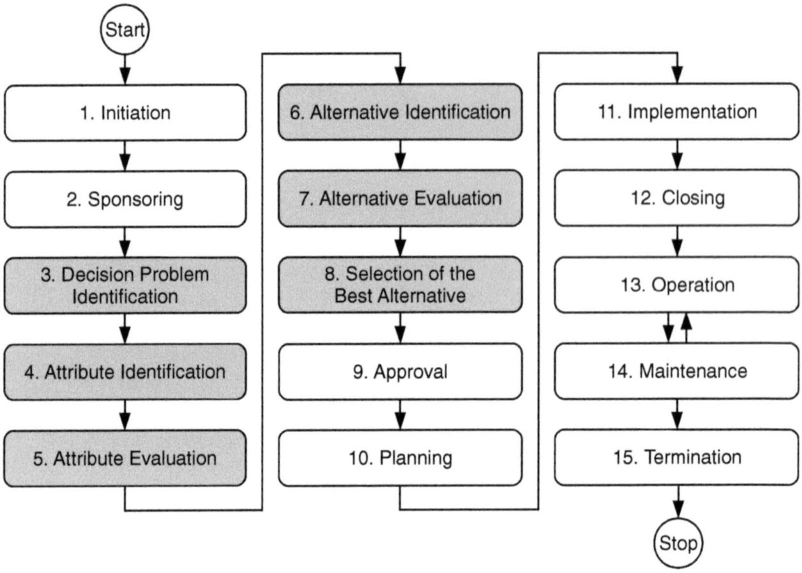

Fig. 6.1 Cybersecurity investment lifecycle

attributes that shall be considered during the decision making process must be identified. Overlooking relevant attributes can affect the quality of the decision and the appropriateness of the selected alternative severely. The identified attributes should address the functional, technical and economical perspective. For example, the selection of a client-based software that is incompatible to the deployed operating system or a server hardware that has a short mean time before failure can be falsely seen as appropriate if relevant attributes are missing. Under economic aspects, financial indicators should be included as attributes in order to consider the costs and benefits sufficiently. The attribute identification is very subjective. Therefore, the decision maker should involve experts or consider relevant standards or best practices for reducing the subjectivity and improving the identification.

5. **Attribute Evaluation** (Sect. 6.6): The evaluation of the identified attributes is needed to assign a weight to each attribute. The weight reflects the relative importance of an attribute in comparison to other attributes. Thereby, the preferences of the decision maker, who considers the previously identified problem, can be taken into account. In this step, involving experts from different departments can improve the results by decreasing the subjectivity, too. A weight that is too low or too high can lead to the selection of an unfavorable alternative. The distinction between exclusion and comparison attributes allows the decision maker to ensure that alternatives meet particularly important attributes before the alternatives are actually considered within the comparison procedure.

6. **Alternative Identification** (Sect. 6.7): In this step, a proper market analysis is essential. The decision maker should gather and analysis as much relevant information as possible. The sources for relevant information are very comprehensive, e.g. internet research, vendor presentations, product brochures and customer experiences. Only alternatives that are identified in this step are further evaluated. The set of identified alternatives should be as adequate as possible. Only if appropriate alternatives are considered in this step, the selected alternative can be appropriate, too. Import preliminary information for identifying alternatives has already been found in the decision problem identification. This information should be used for improving the outcome of this step. Among other things, the strategy, including the protection goal, protection level, safeguard type etc., and the protection requirements are strong drivers for the alternative identification.
7. **Alternative Evaluation** (Sect. 6.8): This step is the fundament for a sound decision. The identified alternatives from the previous step are evaluated with the identified attributes. Thus, each alternative gets a sub score regarding every attribute. When all sub scores of an alternative are weighted and summed, the alternative gets an overall score. The higher this overall score is, the more favorable the alternative is for the company. The overall scores from the evaluation are an essential perquisite for the selection. They allow a ranking of the alternatives regarding their favorability.
8. **Selection of the Best Alternative** (Sect. 6.9): The inputs from the previous steps are the set of alternatives with according overall scores from the evaluation. Based on these, the final selection of the best and, thereby, most favorable alternative can be made. If more than one alternative share the best overall score, the decision maker will have to find further attributes for choosing one alternative that stands out from multiple best alternatives.
9. **Approval** (Sect. 6.10): Now, the most favorable alternative has been selected. The previous steps, including the decision making in the narrower sense, should have been performed and completed in an understandable and transparent way. The final decision still has to be made by the senior management of the company. The previous steps have rather been used to make a decision template that now has to be finally approved. The more transparent and understandable the previous steps have been performed, the fewer aspects of the results will be questioned or doubted.
10. **Planning** (Sect. 6.11): The planning step is needed to determine every detail that is needed to implement and operate the safeguard, which will be the output from the cybersecurity investment. Hereby, the technical and business view should be covered. The technical view includes the installation and configuration options. For example, it has to be determined which services have to be deactivated, which standard passwords have to be changed, and which users have to be created. The business view includes the alignment of the new safeguard to the existing business processes. The business must not be disturbed by the new safeguard. In particular, the performance within the value

generating processes should not be affected negatively. An important aspect in the planning process is the consideration of user trainings that shall impart knowledge regarding new security tools and procedures.

11. **Implementation** (Sect. 6.12): The implementation must not be seen as trivial. Only by deploying a new safeguard gradually, the implementation risk can be minimized. A rollout that affects all workstations at the same time can severely interrupt business processes. Incompatibilities or errors that have not been considered before the rollout can lead to outtakes and, thereby, to lost revenues. Therefore, the rollout should be performed systematically. At first, only a small group of workstation or users should be addressed by the new safeguard. After a few days of thorough monitoring, the rollout can be continued with the next group, which is possibly even bigger. Again, a few days should be used for monitoring. Depending on the overall company structure, more or less groups can be defined. They should be addressed gradually until the rollout has been completed.
12. **Closing** (Sect. 6.13): The closing step is used to complete the implementation of the safeguard formally. The previous steps are often handled as a project because they are temporary and unique with a defined scope and restricted resources. In this case, this step is also a project closing. Important tasks in this step are the review, the final approval of the sponsor and the completion of the documentation.
13. **Operation** (Sect. 6.14): When moving to this step, the temporary work that was related to the project is completed and the routine operation begins. This includes monitoring the performance of the safeguard, dealing with incidents and problems, and securing the reliable operation. Mostly, minimizing disruptions of the business operations and ensuring a steady operation have the highest priorities here. Besides, a responsible management of possible changes is essential in order to decrease potential negative effects from changes and securing relevant assets while and after implementing a change.
14. **Maintenance** (Sect. 6.15): After the previous steps, the cybersecurity investment has been performed and a safeguard has been transformed into an operational state. However, the lifecycle is still not completed. In recurring maintenance steps, the safeguard must be checked and maintained in regular intervals. If needed, repair work must be performed or replacement parts must be obtained. This step is very important to ensure a high level of continuous protection. After maintenance, the safeguard gets back into an operational state.
15. **Termination** (Sect. 6.16): Eventually, the safeguard will be terminated. Many reasons can cause its termination, e.g. a bankruptcy of the company or a technologic innovation that provides a more efficient way of safeguarding an asset. A proper termination ensures that the safeguard in focus is removed completely without leaving crucial functional or security problems. If the safeguard is left in place unused, it should still be managed. Therefore, unnecessary administration effort would occur. In contrast, unmanaged safeguards can lead to new potential attack vectors.

Generally, these steps are performed in a sequence. However, the contents of particular steps can require a **return** to previous steps. Especially the following returns can be necessary sometimes:

- A return from **approval** (step 9) to **decision problem identification** (step 3) will be required if the sponsor does not approve the decision result and the derived safeguard selection. A sponsor that denies the selected solution mostly has specific reasons for this. In this case, it is unfortunate that these reasons have not been considered before. In consequence, a return to the step of decision problem identification would be recommendable. Now, the sponsor should express the unconsidered requirements or problem characteristics. Thereby, the decision making process can be repeated with a sufficient consideration of the sponsor's needs.
- A return from **implementation** (step 11) to **planning** (step 10) will make sense if significant problems occur during the implementation step. For example, the calculated duration of client installations might have been wrong so that the implementation cannot be performed on schedule. In some situations, e.g. high incompatibilities between the selected safeguard and the company infrastructure, it can even be necessary to return to the previous decision making steps. For example, a return to the attribute identification (step 4) can be used to add the attribute "Compatibility with Windows 8".
- A return from **maintenance** (step 14) to **operation** (step 13) is a regular action that has to be performed every time after maintenance work took place. After completing a maintenance task, the safeguard has to be set back into an operating state. Sometimes, the maintenance can be performed in parallel to the operation so that the operation is not interrupted. For example, a redundant array of independent disks (RAID) prevents outtakes when a disk fails and, thereby, it allows the swapping of particular disks for maintenance without affecting the operation.

The following subchapters start with numbered **key questions** that give an impression about the main issue that should be answered in each particular phase of the cybersecurity investment lifecycle. All key questions can also be found in Sect. 7.3, which includes a checklist that can easily be used in practice. The division of the key questions in accordance to the lifecycle steps allows an individual consideration of relevant issues. For example, a concentration on the core steps of decision making in the narrower sense can be facilitated.

Case Study

In the following subchapters, a case study expands the explanations of the lifecycle steps. The case study information is printed in italics. The example company in the case study is a fictitious payment service provider (PSP), who is specialized on offering services to merchants for processing card payments. Merchants that want to accept credit and debit cards can use the services of the PSP for providing a payment interface to customers in online shops, and physical stores. The PSP also offers the clearing and settlement of payment transactions. The evaluated safeguard alternatives are also fictional and named after the names of Greek letters.

6.2 Initiation

1.1 The reason to initiate the cybersecurity investment has been found.

Various events inside and outside of the company can affect the stakeholders' perception of cybersecurity. Often, stakeholders find a solid **reason** for a specific cybersecurity investment. As shown in Fig. 6.2, the most reasons for this investment are a breach, risk response, customer expectation, contract, competitive advantage, law or standard, and a new technology.

- Often, a **breach** has a major negative impact to the cybersecurity of a company. Important cybersecurity goals, like confidentiality, integrity and availability, might not be achieved if the company is affected by a breach. Among other things, unauthorized access by a person or a system can lead to negative consequences. Not only a breach in the company but also breaches at other companies in the market can be a good reason to invest in cybersecurity. If another company that performs its operational tasks similarly or makes business in the same industry is affected by a breach, it can be possible that the company in focus will also be affected by the same attacks and vulnerabilities that have been detected at other companies. With a cybersecurity investment that addresses primarily the risks that can lead to breaches, the company can strongly reduce the occurrence of breaches and the subsequent consequences that have to be expected.
- A **risk response** is normally a subsequent step after the identification and assessment of risks that can affect a company. Among other sources, COBIT can be used to organize the risk management. A cybersecurity investment helps to mitigate or eliminate risks. This is mostly the most secure and most favorable way to manage risks. Under consideration of the individual risk appetite of the company, risks also can be transferred, accepted or rejected. If the company has

Fig. 6.2 Initiation reasons

a high risk-appetite, risks will be mostly accepted so that an investment in cybersecurity safeguards will often be unnecessary.

- The way the company meets a **customer expectation** can have a strong effect on the revenues of the company. Especially if the expectation is shared by many customers and if the expectation is reasonable, the company should consider meeting it. Otherwise, the costumers might move to competitors. In cybersecurity, customer expectations mostly address the responsible handling of sensitive customer data. On the one hand, a cybersecurity investment can be used as an advertising measure to show the company's sense of responsibility. On the other hand, an investment in appropriate safeguards can lead to a high protection level that prevents breaches. If customer data have been compromised with a breach, the reputation of the company can be damaged. As a result, customers can avoid business transactions with the company.
- A **contract** with business partners, like vendors, service providers, and customers, does not only cover business agreements about services and deliveries but also the protection of the company. Often, breaches do not only affect the reputation of an insufficient protected company but also the reputation of its partners or subsidiaries. Therefore, contracts are commonly extended with requirements regarding the protection level. These requirements can be specific, e.g. a particular safeguard, or more general, e.g. the requirement to provide sufficient protection. One way or another, reasonable cybersecurity investments are necessary to meet most contracts.
- A company can achieve a **competitive advantage** with cybersecurity investments. The advantage is not caused just by investing in cybersecurity and operating any safeguards. This can be seen as a matter of cause today. Moreover, the selection of the most appropriate safeguard can make a noticeable difference against competitors. Better safeguards reduce the implementation and operating costs. These safeguards can be managed more easily and are more reliable. The saved capital can be invested in the core competencies of the company. For example, the research and development department of a company can benefit from additional investments. In result, the company can create new products, which can raise the revenue and improve the market position of the company.
- A **law or standard** can include requirements regarding cybersecurity that must be met in order to avoid negative consequences, e.g. fines from the authorities. While laws, e.g. HIPAA (Health Insurance Portability and Accountability Act), are binding, a company can choose freely if it wants to comply with standards. The compliance with standards can help to reach a high protection level. It can also be used as a competitive factor, e.g. by holding a certificate that can be presented to the customers. ISO 27001 is an example for a worldwide known standard in information security that is actually well respected by many customers. Besides, many industry-specific standards exist. They can de facto be seen as binding because companies that do not comply with them have to face high disadvantages in the market. Business partners can be more restrictive or expensive and customers can be very skeptical and hold back the purchasing of

the company's products. An example for an industry-specific standard is the PCI DSS. Companies that store, transmit or process payment card data have to comply with PCI DSS. Otherwise, they can hardly negotiate favorable conditions with merchants and payment card organizations.

- A **new technology** in the cybersecurity field can allow the use of safeguards that are more efficient. By investing in new safeguards and replacing the old ones, the company can reduce costs in the long term. Besides, the protection level can be improved. For example, the replacement of physical keys by smart cards had reduced the administration costs in many companies because the cards are programmable and can be adjusted more easily. The protection level can be raised because the cards can be locked directly without the need to retrieve the smart card physically. Hackers can also benefit from a new technology. They can use it to develop new attacks or to automate existing attacks. For example, tools that facilitate the development of exploits enabled many amateur hackers to use exploits in attacks. If hackers benefit from a new technology, the company will have to consider new cybersecurity investments. Regarding the increase of exploits, companies had to improve patch management so that the vulnerabilities that could be exploited were eliminated as fast as possible.

Case Study

The PSP secured the ***payment card data*** *that was at rest, in use or in motion in order to prevent fraud and to comply with the PCI DSS. Payment fraud that can be the result of a security breach had to be prevented because it would have led to financial and reputational damages at the PSP. If the PSP had not complied with the PCI DSS, the credit card organizations would have raised the interchange fees of payment transactions. Besides, the PSP would have had problems to compete against competitors in the market.*

The PSP conducted a self-assessment for identifying and evaluating existing risks in the company. The PSP encapsulated the payment card data within an encrypted database, which was operated in a separate network segment. Outside of the database, tokens were used to identify payment data. Although all payment data was supposed to be secured, the internal risk auditors identified unencrypted payment data. The accounting department stored ***unencrypted payment card data*** *regularly while processing chargebacks, retrieval requests and fraud-related requests. During this processing, the cardholder, merchant, PSP, issuing bank, payment card organizations and law enforcement agencies can be involved (see* Fig. 6.3*).*

- ***Chargebacks*** *can be requested by customers at the issuing bank that issued the payment cards to the customers. If they have a proper reason for questioning the rightfulness of a certain payment transaction, they will get a refund. Proper reasons are billing errors, claims and defenses. After a customer requested a chargeback, the issuing bank grants a provisional credit to the customer and contacts the PSP. The PSP requests information about the payment from the*

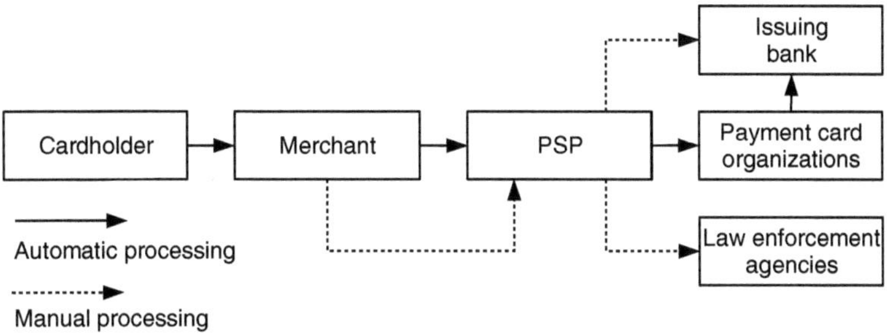

Fig. 6.3 Payment data flow

merchant. After receiving this information, the PSP analysis it and presents it to the issuing bank. The information also contains sensitive payment card data. The issuing bank makes the final decision by concluding whether the chargeback is valid or has to be rejected. According to this decision, either the provisional refund becomes final or it will be withdrawn.

- ***Retrieval requests** can be separate request, preliminary steps of chargebacks or part of chargebacks. Customers that need more information about a specific payment create retrieval requests at their issuing bank. The bank forwards the request to the PSP, which contacts the merchant for requesting additional information. As with chargeback processing, the PSP analysis the received information from the merchant and presents it to the issuing bank, which hands it over to the customer. If the retrieval request is not already part of a chargeback process, the customer can now decide if he wants to request a chargeback so that the according process will be started afterwards.*
- ***Fraud-related requests** are similar to retrieval requests. The process steps at the PSP are the same. The difference is that fraud-related requests are triggered by a law enforcement agency, while retrieval requests are triggered by the customer. Accordingly, the results will be handed over to the party who triggered the request. The reason for fraud-related requests can be a suspicion of illegal activities, e.g. misuse of payment cards or identity theft. Fraud-related requests can even be created after a payment has already been refunded due to a chargeback request.*

*The **documentation** that was often stored by the PSP for processing or verifying chargebacks, retrieval requests and fraud-related requests included:*

- *payment account number*
- *authorization code*
- *expiration date of the payment card*
- *name of the cardholder*
- *transaction date*
- *transaction time*
- *merchant name and location*

- *description of the purchase*
- *transaction amount*
- *shipping information*

*Here, much **sensitive data** were included, which had probably been misused if it would have been accessible by unauthorized persons. Especially the payment account number had to be protected. This was also stated by the PCI DSS. At the PSP, the transmission of the data was protected by using encryption. However, the data were stored **unencrypted** on the local hard drive of accounting staff members. Unencrypted payment data that were stored on hard drives led to a high security risk because workstations and notebooks could easily be stolen or lost. In consequence, the payment data would have been accessible by unauthorized persons. Besides, the storage of unencrypted payment data did not comply with the PCI DSS. In requirement 3.4, the standard stated explicitly that payment account numbers must be rendered unreadable anywhere they are stored (PCI SSC 2015, p. 40). As an alternative to strong encryption, the company was also allowed to use hashing, truncation, index tokens or pads.*

*The internal auditors **initiated** the cybersecurity investment lifecycle by reporting a risk for the finance and reputation of the company, and by showing a compliance issue regarding the PCI DSS.*

6.3 Sponsoring

2.1 The sponsor for the cybersecurity investment has been confirmed.

In the sponsoring phase, the initiator needs to get **acceptance and support** from the executive management in the company. Based on a clear identification and definition of the investment project, he should be able to demonstrate roughly how the investment will be in the interest of the company. Besides, a provisional cost estimation can be advantageous.

2.2 The sponsor has been found suitable for the sponsorship.

The **sponsor** has an important role that can strongly influence the success of an investment project. In order to support the project efficiently, the sponsor must be at an executive level and be able to fund the project. In particular, he must be able to approve and support the allocation of the required resources. Besides, he must be capable and willing to fulfill the common **key responsibilities** of a project sponsor:

- He must be aware of the company's overall **strategy** so that he can link the new investment to this strategy. He must be able to assess the appropriateness and to identify potential benefits of the investment regarding the company's strategy.

- He must have the authorization to allocate company **resources** to the project. Without the availability of sufficient resources, the project goals would not be achievable.
- He must **communicate** with the executive management and other stakeholders. Especially, he must explain project benefits and get commitments regarding the support of the project.
- He must provide **continuous** support over the whole lifecycle of the investment. His participation is most important during the early phases. The critical evaluation of the investment idea and the subsequent stakeholder communication are crucial success factors of the project. However, the sponsorship should not be restricted to these phases. Without continuous support, later problems can cause the project to fail. For example, all company resources might be allocated to another project that is sponsored by another executive manager. The sponsor has the responsibility to look after the investment project over its whole lifecycle.
- He must **monitor** the project critically. In case of any problems, he must intervene. Problems can be caused by external and internal factors. External factors include, among other things, changes in laws, standards and the public opinion. Internal factors include, among other things, delays in resource allocation and motivational issues.

The sponsor does not only support the investment project actively; he is also the **owner** of the project. However, the uncritical continuous support might not always be adequate. For example, if problems are caused by serious project flaws, the sponsor can decide that the project has to be canceled. Besides, the sponsor is obligated to consider the generated benefits from the sponsored project to the overall company. If the project shows itself as useless or even harmful to the company, the sponsor will have to cancel the project and stop his support.

Sometimes the sponsor might fail to fulfill his responsibilities. The most common reasons for an **insufficient sponsorship** are:

- The sponsor must have the **power** to allocate company resources and to make company-wide decisions. If the sponsor does not hold an influential position in the company, the sponsorship will not be effective. Mostly, a sponsor from the executive management is recommendable. However, if the investment is not very costly, other managers can also be a suitable sponsor, e.g. a department head.
- The sponsor neglects his responsibilities because he is already loaded by the responsibilities accompanied by his **primary role**. For example, he can be tightened by executive management tasks. In conclusion, he does not have free personal resources for a sufficient sponsorship.
- The sponsor is not devoting enough **time** for the sponsorship. He is in the wrong opinion that little time and effort are needed to sponsor an investment project. In consequence, he can evaluate the appropriateness of the investment incorrectly and not see serious problems within the project execution.
- The sponsor gets **involved** too deeply in the investment project. He assesses the details but loses the view of the overall strategy and the stakeholder support. He

does not understand that the detailed project management is in the responsibility of the project manager.

- The sponsor is **overextended** by the tasks of assessing the investment from the strategic view. He does not have enough knowledge about the company and the investment itself to make a good decision. He might also lack the knowledge and skills to monitor the project continuously.
- The communication and possibly the persuasion of stakeholders from executive management, other hierarchy levels and external organizations are important tasks of the sponsor. These tasks will probably not be performed sufficiently if the sponsor lacks **communication** skills. If crucial project information is communicated incompletely or in the wrong way, the motivation and support of crucial stakeholders can be affected. This can even cause the project to fail.

Case Study

The report from the internal risk assessment of the PSP was transferred straightly to the ***Chief Information Officer*** *(CIO) of the company. The CIO identified the need for a cybersecurity investment. He collected further information from the internal auditors and requested a recommendation that was supposed to focus on fixing the security issue. Based on this information, the CIO took over the sponsorship for the investment project.*

The CIO of the PSP was ***well suited*** *to take over the sponsorship. He was the most senior executive manager at the company that was responsible for information technology (see* Fig. 6.4*). He was able to make executive decisions regarding the*

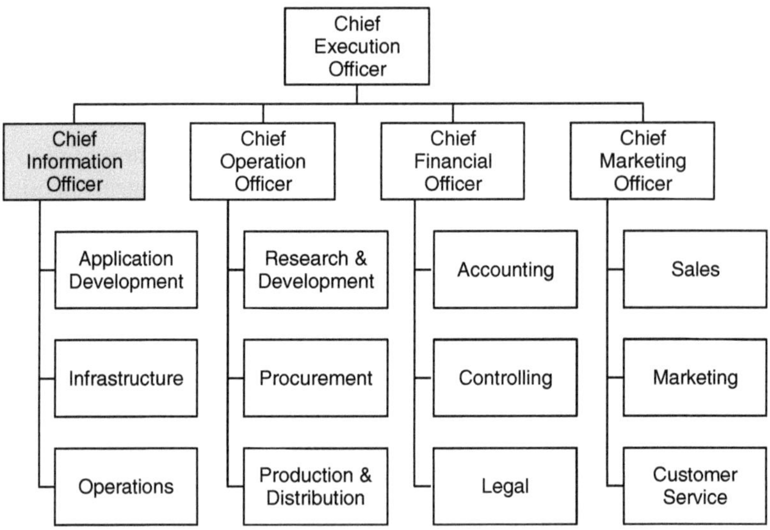

Fig. 6.4 Organizational chart

operation and development of information systems. His role included the analysis and re-engineering of processes supported or enabled by IT. The processing of chargebacks and fraud-related requests was a process supported by IT. The identification and development of new solutions that improved the company's performance or security were also part of the CIO's responsibilities. The cyber-security investment that needed sponsorship was aimed at the improvement of the company's security.

The CIO was able to fulfill the sponsorship ***responsibilities*** *sufficiently. He regularly communicated with other execution managers, i.e. the Chief Execution Officer, Chief Operation Officer and Chief Financial Officer. He was able to link the investment to the company's overall strategy. He had the authorization to allocate resources and he regularly monitored the performance of the IT department, which was supposed to be strongly involved in the new solution. Because of the demands against the CIO to create and uphold a cost-effective information infrastructure, he had a high interest in critically evaluating and monitoring the investment project.*

Alternatively, a ***manager*** *at a lower hierarchy level could have taken over the sponsorship, e.g. the Head of Operations. The concrete influence and power of the relevant manager in the company had to be considered. For example, it had to be clear that the manager was able to allocate sufficient resources for the investment and that he had enough power to defend the investment against criticism from the senior management.*

6.4 Decision Problem Identification

The **decision problem** contains multiple sub-problems that are built on one another. The attribute identification is needed to find appropriate criteria that can be used to compare alternatives. After the identification, these attributes have to be evaluated in order to consider different levels of importance. Next, some alternatives must be found that seem to be appropriate in general. These alternatives can be evaluated by using the knowledge about attributes. However, these fundamental steps of decision making cannot be performed without sufficient preliminary information. Which attributes are appropriate and how important they are, can only be answered if sufficient information about the decision problem has been gathered before. Besides, the selection of alternatives to be evaluated can be very complicated if no systematic procedure is performed. For example, finding an appropriate firewall system should be started by analyzing the products from well-recognized security companies. The preliminary information about which security companies are in the market and which of them are trustworthy or recognized can be very important.

In conclusion, gathering **preliminary information** before performing the traditional decision making steps should be considered as a separate step in the decision making process. The primary goal of this preceding step is the identification of the problem that shall be solved by the alternative to be selected. At first, the strategy and the scope of this problem must be determined. Afterwards, the values of the assets within this scope and their protection requirements must be measured. The risk analysis gives a clear answer to the question, which damages should be expected without any cybersecurity investment. Based on the discovered conditions, the most adequate decision technique can be chosen. Besides, the involvement of stakeholders should be considered because it can be a crucial success factor for the investment project.

The preliminary information that shall be gathered in this step will have a major **influence** on the subsequent steps of the decision making process. In particular, the attribute identification, attribute evaluation and alternative identification will strongly depend on this information.

- The **attribute identification** is focused on finding all attributes that are needed to cover every important aspect sufficiently in order to select the best alternative. For example, if the strategy is finding a suite of security software, the attributes will often be more comprehensive than if the strategy is finding a very specialized security software. Similarly, the more comprehensive the scope is, the more attributes have to be considered.
- The **attribute evaluation**, which prioritizes the identified attributes according to their importance, also depends on preliminary information. For example, if the protection requirements are focused on protecting the confidentiality of information, the attributes that address the availability and integrity of information will be seen as minor important. The decision technique that has been found adequate influences the method to perform the evaluation. While the SAW technique requires the determination of independent scores, the AHP technique is based on pairwise comparisons of attributes.
- The **alternative identification** would be very difficult without preliminary information. In the market, very many different safeguard solutions are available. Without any parameters that can be used to restrict this huge amount of possible solutions, the decision making process would be much too comprehensive because too many products would have to be considered. The preliminary information includes indications about how the products in the market can be restricted. For example, if the protection requirements are aimed solely at availability, the products in the market can be filtered regarding their primary functionality. If the assets to be protected and the risks that have been measured are very low, costly solutions can be left out during the alternative identification.

As shown in Fig. 6.5, the decision making **steps** that will be performed afterwards, i.e. the alternative evaluation and selection of the best alternative, are less influenced by the preliminary information from the decision problem identification. They also depend on this information, but the information has already been considered in the previous steps so that the influence here is rather indirect. Therefore, it must not be explicitly included.

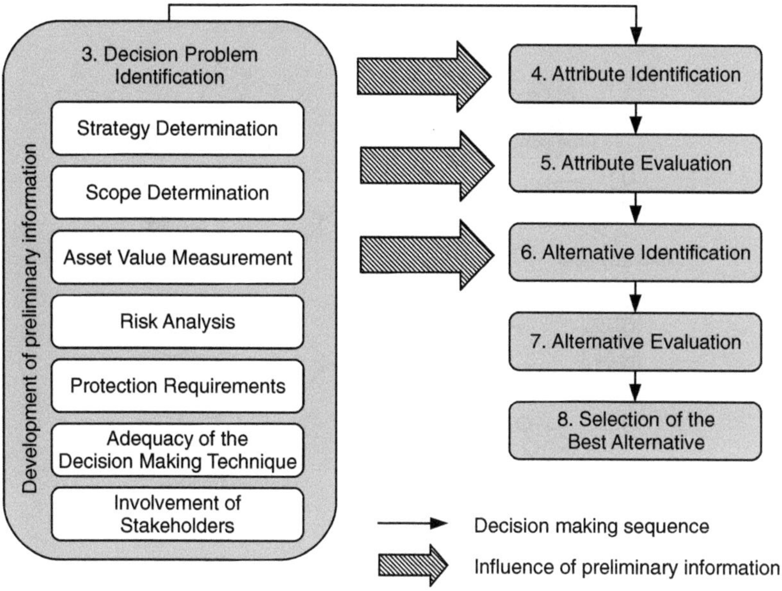

Fig. 6.5 Influence of preliminary information

6.4.1 Strategy Determination

3.1 The strategy for the cybersecurity investment has been determined.

Before determining the specific scope of the decision making process, a **strategy** has to be found. Many companies are characterized by strictly limited resources. Therefore, they are steadily seeking the most efficient options for applying these resources. In addition, some companies might follow a holistic approach in order to consider as much as possible within one investment cycle.

The following phases of the investment lifecycle strongly depend on the chosen strategy. In particular, the **parameters** shown in Fig. 6.6 influence the specific investment decision. Therefore, they should be defined at the beginning.

3.2 The asset to be protected has been identified.

- The **asset** that shall be protected has to be specified at least roughly. At this point, no specific systems or data have to be identified. Moreover, the asset to be protected has to be differentiated on a general level from other company assets. This can be challenging because the number of company assets is often very extensive. Possible assets can be, among other things, business processes that

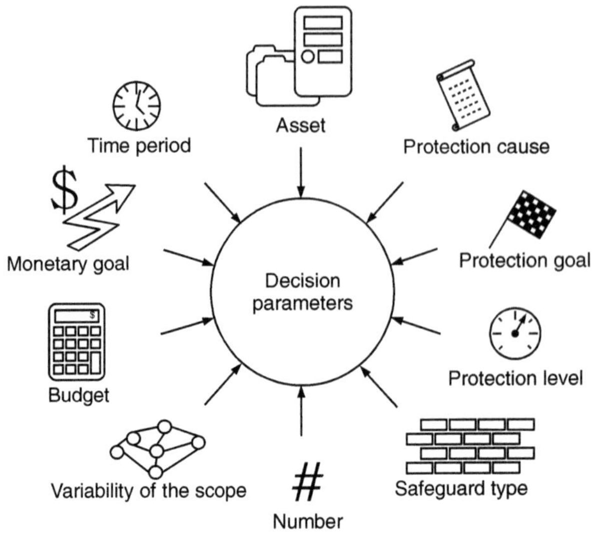

Fig. 6.6 Decision strategy

are vital for the profit generation of the company, data types that are characterized by high threats, like personal or financial data, and highly sensitive systems, e.g. within a critical infrastructure. The general identification of the asset provides an orientation for the further steps. Often, one asset is related to other assets so that a broader approach has to be performed. For example, an important business process is mostly supported by various systems that process, store and transmit the needed data within the process. The exact amount of affected objects is determined in the subsequent phases, primarily in the scope determination.

3.3 The protection cause has been identified.

- The **protection cause** illustrates why the company seeks protection. The cause can be, among other things, a regulatory requirement, contractual obligation, costumer requirement, competitive factor or a previous breach:
- A **regulatory requirement** can be a law, e.g. HIPAA, a general standard, e.g. ISO 27001, or an industry-specific standard, e.g. PCI DSS. While laws are generally binding, standards are only optional but often strongly recommended.
- A **contractual obligation** is based on the business relation of two business partners. The company that engages in a new business can be obligated per contract to fulfill specific security requirements from other companies. Some companies possibly have high protection levels on their own and want to ensure these levels over the whole supply chain by obligating their business partners.

- A **customer requirement** arises due to specific protection needs of customers. Although there is often no legal binding for a company to fulfill the resulting requirements, it is mostly recommended to fulfill them. Otherwise, customers can hardly be tied to the company so that the revenues will probably decrease in the long term.
- Ensuring a high protection level can be also a **competitive factor**. Security can be an important factor to distinguish a company from competitors in the market. It can also be used in advertising for attracting new customers, e.g. by showing security certifications from independent institutions.
- A **previous breach** at other companies or even at the company itself often raises the awareness level. The breach might have demonstrated which possible damages have to be faced by a company with security vulnerabilities. Information regarding a previous breach can give indications about which vulnerabilities should be eliminated and about what protection levels should be implemented. Especially if a well-known company suffers from major losses and reputational damage, the market will be sensitized regarding current threats and the market participants will seek higher protection levels.

3.4 The protection goal has been specified.

- The **protection goal** is needed to specify how the asset shall be protected. The common options are given by the primary and extended cybersecurity principles as described in Sect. 2.2. Often, the protection cause gives a specific direction to one or multiple principles. For example, regulatory requirements often concentrate on the confidentiality and integrity of data while neglecting the availability. Of course, multiple principles can be addressed at the same time. Many safeguards protect multiple protection goals at once. For example, antivirus software prevents the compromising, manipulation and deletion of data by malicious software. Thus, it protects the confidentiality, integrity and availability at the same time.

3.5 The desired protection level has been found appropriate.

- As described in Sect. 2.3, a continuous **protection level** of 100 % is practically impossible. Instead of seeking a maximum protection level, a company should strive for an appropriate protection level. Nevertheless, an indication for the protection level should be given within the decision problem identification. This level should always be related to certain identified objects. It is mostly specified with qualitative terms, e.g. low, medium or high. The protection level correlates to the previously determined protection goal. For example, a specific protection level can address the confidentiality or availability of an object. How the protection level shall be reached and which safeguard can be seen as appropriate, will be analyzed in later steps of the lifecycle.

3.6 An adequate safeguard type has been chosen.

- In order to limit the large amount of possible safeguards, the **safeguard type** should be chosen at the beginning of the decision making, too. As demonstrated in Sect. 3.1, the safeguard type can be characterized by a functional and time perspective:
- The **functional** perspective distinguishes safeguards in administrative and technical safeguards. Administrative safeguards should be chosen if technical means are of minor importance when protecting assets. Technical safeguards should be chosen if technical means are of major importance.
- The **time** perspective clarifies when a safeguard will be activated in relation to a special event. Preventive safeguards can prevent negative effects, because they are activated before an event is even happening, e.g. a firewall that blocks malicious traffic. However, they are often difficult to configure and to implement. Alternatives are detective and corrective safeguards. Detective safeguards are necessary to recognize that a negative event has actually happened. Corrective safeguards are necessary to repair or limit the subsequent damages that were caused by a negative event. Sometimes, a combination of different safeguards can be the preferable solution. Especially, detective and corrective safeguards are often combined.

3.7 The number of desired safeguards has been determined.

- The **number** of safeguards that shall be implemented is a parameter that strongly depends on other preliminary parameters. In particular, the number of necessary safeguards depends on the comprehension of the asset, protection cause, protection goal, protection level and safeguard type. With this information, it can mostly be anticipated if a single safeguard is sufficient or if multiple safeguards are required. For example, the confidentiality of data on a single system can be easily ensured with one safeguard, namely hard disc encryption. However, if the compliance to a security standard for the whole environment of the company is in focus, e.g. ISO 27001, a mix of various safeguards will definitely be required.

3.8 The scope and its variability have been analyzed.

- Another important parameter is the **variability of the scope**. As described in Sect. 2.4, the scope can possibly be limited with network segmentation, point-to-point-encryption, tokenization or outsourcing. Generally, the scope has to be analyzed beforehand in order to decide whether it is unchangeable or variable. Limiting the scope can strongly influence the amount of needed safeguards. For example, if only personal health data shall be protected, the amount of relevant systems can be drastically reduced if these data are stored only on systems that require them definitely for business purposes. Other systems that do not need the data or only require a unique identification of the data, e.g. for counting patients, can be excluded from the scope, for example with tokenization techniques.

3.9 The budget has been estimated.

- The available **budget** is also an important parameter within the decision making process. A tight budget can forbid a costly implementation of sophisticated technical and preventive safeguards. In this case, more affordable administrative safeguards with detective or corrective protection mechanisms would have to be chosen. Even if the specific amount of safeguard costs is mostly not available in this early stage of the lifecycle, at least, the decision maker should find a rough indication. If money is no issue, safeguards that generate more costs than benefits can be chosen. For example, the decision maker can focus on preventive and highly automated safeguards that are, in most cases, more sophisticated and more costly than detective and corrective ones.

3.10 The monetary goal of the cybersecurity investment has been defined.

- The **monetary goal** of the cybersecurity investment is also important to know. With most safeguards, a direct profit, like a profit margin in sales, cannot be achieved. Moreover, certain risks, which can also be viewed monetarily, can be mitigated. Regarding the monetary goal, the company has to consider if the benefits of a safeguard, which can be expressed with the amount of risk mitigation, i.e. prevented losses, must exceed the investment costs or if the cost coverage is insignificant. The company can also value the non-monetary benefits of safeguards, like reputation, so high that the investment costs are of minor importance. In conclusion, a straight monetary goal can result in an unintended exclusion of certain safeguards, which are only reasonable from a non-monetary point of view.

3.11 The time-period for further analyses has been defined.

- Different safeguards often have different lifetimes. Therefore, it can be difficult to compare these safeguards reasonably with indicators that are related to different time-periods. In order to build a common ground for the calculation and comparison of indicators about different safeguards, it is necessary to define a specific **time-period**. Thereby, all needed information about costs, profits, risks and other indicators can be gathered consistently from the perspective of time. The time-period can be specified by a concrete number of years, for example five or ten years. In general, a longer period gives a better indication about the monetary situation in the long term. In contrast, new technical innovations or new threats can make old safeguards unfavorable or even unusable in the future. Therefore, the longer the time-period is, the higher is also the uncertainty. In conclusion, a good balance between a short and a long time-period should be found by the company so that its individual preferences regarding future orientation and certainty can be considered.

The above-mentioned parameters define the overall investment strategy. They influence the subsequent steps of the decision making process by **supporting and guiding** primarily the attribute identification, attribute evaluation and alternative identification:

- The type of **asset** that needs protection influences the identification of appropriate attributes. For example, if the network perimeter of the company has to be protected against attacks from the outside, the response time to suspected attacks will be an important attribute. In contrast, if cryptographic software is needed, the response time to encryption or decryption requests will possibly be neglected from the security view. Moreover, the response time will be considered as a usability factor.
- The **protection cause** influences the identification of appropriate attributes, too. If a specific protection cause exists, details about how to reach and implement the protection can be derived. For example, if the cause is a breach, the vulnerabilities that have been exploited can be identified and analyzed. Thereby, the company knows which vulnerabilities should be eliminated and which assets should be protected. Besides, particular requirements from regulations, contracts and customers mostly include details about how the protection has to be established. These details can be transformed into attributes.
- The **protection goal** influences the identification of appropriate attributes at a more abstract level than the protection cause does. The protection goal gives direction about which safeguards are desired from a general view. Primarily, it influences the alternative identification. If concrete security principles shall be covered, the alternative identification can be directed towards adequate types of safeguards. For example, if the protection goal is to ensure the confidentiality of

data, encryption tools should be considered, while redundancy and backup tools will be irrelevant.

- The **protection level** gives information about the required quality of the protection goal. In particular, the protection level influences the attribute evaluation. Attributes that correlate to a protection goal can be prioritized with information about the relevant protection level. For example, if the desired protection level of the protection goal availability is higher than the protection levels of the goals confidentiality and integrity, the decision maker should assign higher priorities to the attributes that correlate to the goal availability. Furthermore, the protection level helps to restrict the amount of appropriate alternatives during the alternative identification. Especially if all relevant protection levels are very low, costly alternatives can be excluded from the decision making. This is because low protection needs are seldom addressed by costly safeguards.
- The **safeguard type** defines the desired safeguard from the functional and time perspective. Although a specific determination of the safeguard type is seldom done at the early beginning of the decision making process, this parameter will provide very useful information. Even a rough determination of the safeguard type can strongly facilitate the decision making. Based on the safeguard type, exclusion attributes can be defined that filter the safeguards before evaluating them in detail. The decision maker can also use this information during the alternative identification in order to control the identification process more efficiently. Safeguards that do not fit to the desired type can be neglected from the beginning.
- The **number** of safeguards is important for the alternative identification. Especially if multiple safeguards are required, products that include multiple safeguards and product suites can be preferred during the identification. By using only a single vendor for multiple safeguards, the license costs can be reduced and processes for support and maintenance of these safeguards can be simplified, e.g. bug fixing. If a single safeguard is required, the attribute evaluation can be more restrictive. Relevant attributes can be evaluated in a certain way so that the combination of multiple safeguards will be rated lower than single safeguards. Besides, some attributes can be handled as exclusion attributes rather than as comparison attributes. For example, high license costs can lead to an exclusion of alternatives that are expensive because of their comprehensive content. However, when purchasing products that include multiple safeguards or a product suite from a single vendor, the license costs are often reduced or agreed individually.
- The **variability of scope** affects the attribute identification and evaluation. For example, safeguards that are required to cope with hundreds of systems instead of dozens can be problematic to administer, especially regarding configuration, updating and monitoring. In result, appropriate attributes that consider the scope should be added into the decision process. Besides, safeguards should be scalable. If the scope is variable, it can also be changed after the implementation of the safeguard. In this case, the administrators must be able to adjust the safeguard appropriately. A variable scope can also lead to an expansion of the

scope due to new business demands, e.g. an increase in transactions that was initiated by new customers. The safeguard must still be functional in the new scope or it must be adjustable. For example, it must be possible to add more resources to the safeguard. The scalability should be considered as an important attribute if the scope is seen as variable.

- The available **budget** strongly influences the attributes that are related to safeguard costs, i.e. license costs, hardware and software costs, implementation costs and maintenance costs. If the decision maker must meet a tight budget, he should define additional exclusion attributes. For example, the requirement that the license costs must be lower than $20,000 can be used to exclude all alternatives that exceed these costs. If the budget is not so tight, the decision maker can rather focus on a reasonable balance between safeguard benefits and costs.
- The **monetary goal** of the investment influences the attribute evaluation. In general, it can be assumed that monetary attributes are always part of a decision making process under economic aspects. However, the decision maker has to find out how the monetary attributes should be evaluated and weighted. A straight monetary goal is mostly focused on a benefit that exceeds the costs as much as possible. For example, the reduction of expected losses that saves $50,000 and is enabled by an investment in the amount $30,000 would clearly meet this monetary goal. Besides, the investment costs can be limited in order to limit the project risks that are related to the investment. Impacts from these risks will occur if the investment project cannot be completed or if the planning cannot be met, e.g. in case of exploding costs. The decision maker can filter costly safeguards by defining exclusion attributes that address the maximum acceptable costs from the risk perspective.
- The **time-period**, which represents the expected lifetime of the safeguard, is an important baseline for identifying and defining attributes. The calculation of many quantifiable attributes depends on the underlying time. For example, the expected losses that are caused by risks are calculated with consideration of the rate of occurrence. The longer the time-period is, the more often losses can occur. Some financial indicators are also related to a given time-period, e.g. the ROI. A long time-period can lead to big changes in the indicators. Often, safeguards are most costly during the early stages of their lifecycle, i.e. during development and implementation. Normally, the benefits are steady over the whole lifecycle. The longer the time-period of the financial indicators, the more advantageous the investment seems to be. In consequence, a thoughtful definition of the underlying time-period for attributes is important because it can strongly influence the evaluation results of the alternatives.

Case Study

*The **asset** that needed to be protected was the payment card data that were stored, processed and transmitted by the PSP within the processing of chargebacks, retrieval requests, and fraud-related requests.*

- *The payment card data had to be secured by an adequate safeguard. The decision maker remembered to identify primarily the attributes that were relevant for safeguards with the purpose of protecting data. Thereby, he collected preliminary information for the step of attribute identification (see* Sect. 6.5*). In order to find appropriate safeguards, they had to be evaluated with generally suitable attributes.*

The ***protection causes*** *at the PSP were a regulatory requirement and previous breaches: The regulatory requirement was the PCI DSS, which is an industry-specific standard. Although the standard was not legally binding, it was necessary to avoid negative consequences for the PSP, i.e. higher interchange fees, reputational damages and possible breaches. The previous breaches had been occurred at other companies from the payment card industry. Breaches that included the compromise of payment card data was mostly accompanied by high penalties and high reputational damages.*

- *Based on the information about the PCI DSS and previous breaches, the decision maker had to identify related attributes. Among other things, they had to cover the protection of confidentiality, which was derived from the PCI DSS requirement 3 that aimed at protecting stored cardholder data (PCI SSC 2015). The decision maker had to analyze information about the previous breaches, e.g. which vulnerabilities had been exploited. Therefore, he used business contacts between the PSP and business partners that probably had further knowledge about the breaches. However, this information was hard to acquire because companies that had been affected by breaches tended to keep this information strictly confidential.*

The ***protection goal*** *was clearly the confidentiality of the payment card data. The problem that had to be addressed at the PSP was that during and after using payment card data for the processing of chargebacks, retrieval requests and fraud-related requests, the data were still stored on local hard drives. Here, it could possibly be accessed by unauthorized persons that could try to misuse the data. The confidentiality of the data had to be ensured. The integrity of the data was irrelevant because the data were only stored after processing them. A manipulation of the data would have caused no advantage to the hacker. Besides, even the manipulation of answers to chargeback, retrieval and fraud-related requests could not be performed in order to gather any kind of personal benefit. The case that a fraudulent customer decided to hack the PSP for covering a single fraudulent purchase would have been very unlikely. The availability was also irrelevant because the unavailability of data from already processed answers to chargeback, retrieval and fraud-related requests would have caused no interruptions of the business operations at the PSP.*

- *The PSP needed a safeguard that covered the confidentiality. In conclusion, the decision maker aimed at identifying only alternatives that addressed the confidentiality. Here, he concentrated on identifying only encryption tools.*

The **protection level** *of the confidentiality was very high at the PSP. Because other protection goals than the confidentiality had not been identified at the PSP, additional protection levels for prioritizing different goals were not necessary.*

- *In general, the protection levels can be used to restrict the identified alternative by considering only alternatives that are sufficient to fulfill the protection levels regarding different protection goals. At the PSP, only one protection level for the confidentiality was given. Here, the protection level also gave an indication about the importance of the safeguard and, thereby, about the expected budget. The decision maker did not need to exclude costly alternatives because the protection level was very high at the PSP.*

The **safeguard type** *that was needed by the PSP was technical from the perspective of functionality and preventive from the perspective of time. The PSP chose a technical safeguard because it could be used automatically without the risk of human errors. In general, the preventive type will always be preferable if it is possible and reasonable. The confidentiality was supposed to be protected with preventive safeguards. The PSP considered the possibility of data that had been compromised as a serious problem. The detection of a compromise could stop the compromise of other data, but data that had already been compromised could not be secured again. It also could not be corrected.*

- *The decision maker at the PSP focused only on technical, preventive safeguards. Other safeguards, i.e. administrative, detective and corrective safeguards, were not taken into consideration. While identifying the alternatives, which had to be evaluated in subsequent steps, the decision maker searched specifically technical safeguards that were aimed at preventing breaches.*

The **number** *of safeguards needed by the PSP was just one. In order to ensure the confidentiality of stored data, the PSP found one safeguard sufficient. A combination with other safeguards was not planned.*

- *The decision maker did not need to prefer vendors with multiple products or product suites. In addition, he did not have to be reserved to define related attributes for exclusion purposes. There was no risk that a single exclusion attribute would unintentionally have led to an exclusion of a comprehensive product suite that would possibly have included multiple safeguards.*

The **variability of scope** *at the PSP was high. The safeguard was supposed to be used for other confidential data that will be identified in the future, too. Besides payment card data, confidential company data might be moved into the scope, too.*

– *While the decision maker identified and evaluated the attributes, he was supposed to consider the variability of scope, e.g. by including the scalability. Even the possibility to expand the scope from a few workstations from the accounting department to all workstations from the whole company was included. In particular, up to 500 workstations in the company were considered to get equipped with the safeguard. This led to a higher weight of certain attributes, e.g. the operation costs, which would have increased sharply in case of a scope expansion.*

The **budget** *that the PSP had made available for the investment was limited to $30,000. In relation to the small amount of workstations that had to be secured, the budget were not a limiting factor here.*

– *Because the budget could not be viewed as tight for securing a few workstations, the budget did not require special exclusion attributes. However, very costly alternatives still had to be excluded. With this budget, no restriction regarding preventive or technical safeguards that are often more costly was needed. Moreover, the decision maker could concentrate on finding a reasonable balance between safeguard benefits and costs.*

The **monetary goal** *for protecting the payment card data that the PSP processed for chargebacks, retrieval requests and fraud-related requests was low. A compromise of the data would have resulted in financial consequences, i.e. penalties and higher interchange fess. However, the more critical goal here was non-monetary. The high reputational damage could have led to a dramatic decrease of customers. If the PSP's image had stayed poor in the long term, the PSP would probably have gone out of business.*

– *At the PSP, the monetary goal was behind the non-monetary goal of reputation. The financial benefits of the safeguard were supposed not to exceed the costs in the short term. Moreover, the decision maker had to consider qualitative factors, like reputation, more important during the attribute evaluation.*

The PSP had to define the viewed **time-period** *of the safeguard thoughtfully. On the one hand, a very short time-period would have neglected the benefits of the safeguard in the long term. Moreover, the money flow that occurred at the beginning would have been overrated, i.e. the purchasing and implementation costs. On the other hand, a very long time-period would have created a high uncertainty. The safeguard could have become obsolete or inefficient.*

– *The PSP defined a time-period of five years as a basis for the decision making. The decision maker assumed that this was a good balance between considering the benefits in the long term and limiting the uncertainty. An encryption solution was expected to generate high implementation costs at the beginning but also to mitigate the risk of data compromise permanently. However, encryption algorithms can be considered insecure sometimes. In this case, they must be upgraded or replaced. This would have led to major migration costs at the PSP.*

6.4.2 Scope Determination

3.12 The scope for the cybersecurity investment has been determined.

The determination of the scope can be significantly facilitated by analyzing important **business processes** at first. Based on the business processes that are vital for the success of the company, the relevant objects and their protection needs can be derived. The required information to enable the smooth function of business processes gives an indication about relevant data and information systems. Special security requirements of information lead to protection needs of concrete objects. Furthermore, legal obligations can have a high influence on the specific scope. For example, systems that process certain data can be affected by protection and storage requirements. In addition, the applications that support the business processes and the relations between applications, data and systems can give valuable information about the content of the scope.

Documentations about business processes normally provide a good source of information about the relevant objects that are part of the scope. Business processes can be documented by **modeling techniques**, which illustrate a simplified view of the particular business processes. In general, the reality is much too complex as that it can be documented completely. However, the complexity can be reduced by using a higher level of abstraction. Business processes can be described on a high abstraction level in order to bring objects, data or processes in an understandable context. The high abstraction level is a limitation of the modeling object on selected aspects in order to focus on relevant perspectives. Modeling techniques provide a good opportunity to focus on key steps and events without explaining every trivial detail thoroughly. In conclusion, existing documentation about business processes should be viewed critically because particular data and systems might not be explicitly listed.

According to the **Architecture of Integrated Information Systems** (ARIS) Framework, business processes can be described from different perspectives and on different levels, which are shown in Fig. 6.7.

The perspectives help to describe a business process under a specific **view**, in particular the organization, data, control, functions and product view:

- The **organization view** describes the performers of the company. These are the organizational positions and the people who fill these positions. In addition, the individual duties and responsibilities of the people can be described. A tool for the organization view is the organization chart, which helps to model the organizational units and their relations with each other hierarchically.
- Within the **data view,** the data and the thereby represented information that are needed by the company are described. In addition, the sources of the data are taken into account. A common suitable modeling tool is the entity relationship diagram (ERD), which is used to visualize properties and relations with objects.

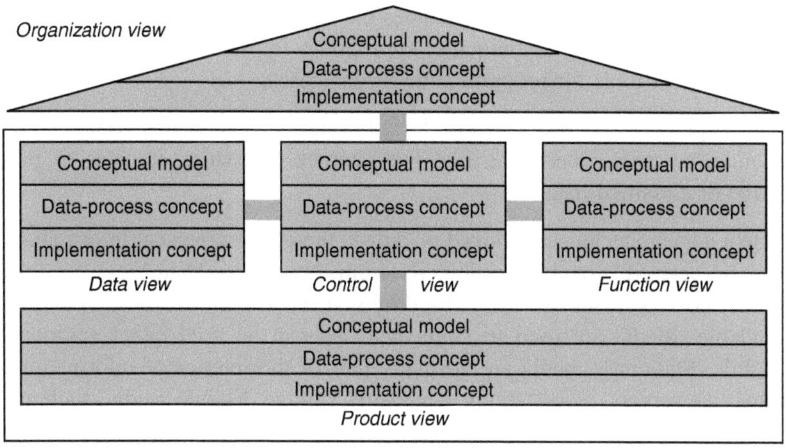

Fig. 6.7 ARIS house

- The **control view** allows the connection between different views by combining different modeling objects. For example, the sequence of events and functions can be modeled with the event-driven process chain (EPC). Besides, the extended EPC allows the combination with organizational, data and product elements. In addition, the Business Process Modeling Notation (BPMN) and flowcharts are adequate techniques for this view.
- Within the **function view**, the operations are described that are performed by the company to carry out or support business activities. A suitable modeling tool is the function tree that makes functions understandable by breaking them down into sub-functions.
- The **product view** is focused on the inputs and outputs of business processes. These can be services or goods. Products of all kind can be modeled with the product tree, which enables the structuring of products, their composition and relations. Hereby, various levels of abstraction can be used, for example the visualization of assemblies and components. The product composition can be viewed in detail and substitution relationships can be shown.

The different **levels** within the ARIS Framework facilitate the concentration on specific aspects when modeling business processes. In particular, these levels are the conceptual model, the data-process concept and the implementation concept:

- With the **conceptual model**, business processes are described regarding the underlying economic problem. In general, the authors are from the departments outside of the IT department. Suitable modeling techniques are, among other things, the ERD, EPC, function tree and organizational chart.
- With the **data-process concept**, the conceptual requirements for the business processes are transferred into technical requirements for data processing. Techniques in this level are, among other things, relations and structure charts.

- The **implementation concept** includes the realization of the business processes with data processing techniques. Appropriate tools are, among other things, development tools for program code or databases.

The scope generally includes all relevant **systems** and attached components that are connected to a cyberspace, like the Internet, and store, transfer or process sensitive or classified data:

- When data are technically **stored** on a disk, these data represent information that can be derived directly or indirectly from these data. Data have the form of binary code, which can be converted by systems, or text data, which are human readable. Media are used to store data that can be used either stationary or mobile. Stationary media are normally part of the interior of information systems like servers, workstations or network storage. Mobile media, such as CD, DVD, tapes and SD cards, are only readable using drives. Other removable media, such as USB hard drives, USB sticks and FireWire hard drives, can be connected directly to system interfaces.
- The **transmission** of information includes the delivery of data from one system to another. For the purpose of transmission, local area networks, e.g. within an office building, and wide area networks, such as the Internet, can be used. The infrastructure of local networks can be wired or wireless. Especially the transmission over the Internet has to be protected regarding the confidentiality and integrity of data.
- The **processing** of data involves the transfer of interpretable data in a different format or structure. For example, data can be merged, distributed, enriched, abstracted or transformed. The processing is often part of a business process or supports it. The processing can be triggered by a user or by a time- or event-related event. Users generally use applications to process data semi-automatically. A time-related event occurs e.g. at a certain day of the week. A case-related event occurs e.g. when a customer orders something. After the triggering, a system begins the semi-automatic or automatic processing.

Systems can be, among other things, any kind of servers, e.g. the ones that provide services for web, database, mail or domain names. They can also be virtual systems, hosts for virtual systems, application systems or security systems, e.g. authentication servers.

Attached **components** are, among other things, network components, like firewalls, switches, routers and wireless access points. Generally, every technical device, like a storage device, can also be an attached component.

Which **data** are seen as sensitive or classified cannot be pre-defined in general. Moreover, the individual preferences and viewpoints of the company that owns the data determine how specific data should be seen and handled. A good way to find out where these data are stored, transferred or processed is to follow the information flow through the business processes.

After the systems and data that are worth to be protected have been identified, the final **scope determination** is still not trivial. It is important to know how the systems are connected to each other and where the perimeters are. A network diagram including the IT systems, communication links and external interfaces should be analyzed. In addition, the spatial conditions should be taken into account. It can be helpful to combine objects with similar protection needs to groups. Afterwards, the groups whose objects exceed a pre-defined level of protection need can be included in the scope.

Case Study

*The **business processes** in focus were processes for chargebacks, retrieval requests and fraud-related requests. Because the payment card data were in focus at the PSP, modeling techniques from the data and control view of ARIS have been used. The PSP created an **ERD**, which is shown in* Fig. 6.8, *to describe the data and its sources.*

*The **entities** that were related to each other were the customer, the order, the payment and the merchant:*

- *The **customer** makes one or more orders and according payments. The customer is defined by the attributes customer number (a unique number given by the merchant), name, address, phone and e-mail.*
- *The **order** is fulfilled by the merchant. It is characterized by a unique order number, date and time of the order, a product description (including name, type, price and quantity of purchased items), the amount of money to be paid, and shipping information.*

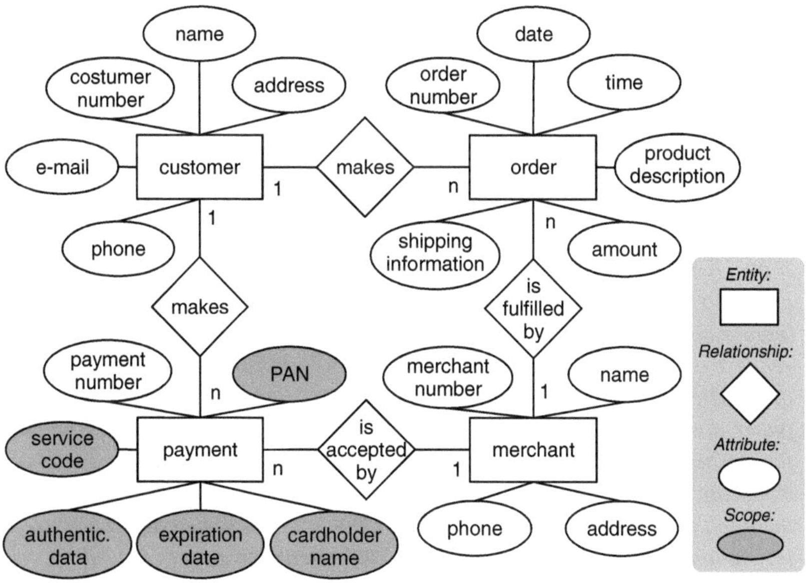

Fig. 6.8 ERD

- *The* ***payment*** *is accepted by the merchant. It is specified mostly by sensitive attributes. Only the payment number (given by the PSP) is of no use for attackers and, thereby, not sensitive. However, the PAN, cardholder name, expiration date, authentication data, and service code are highly sensitive according to the PCI DSS and, thereby, in scope.*
- *The* ***merchant*** *has a unique merchant number at the PSP. The PSP also stored the name, address and phone of the merchant.*

Besides, the PSP created an ***EPC*** *to visualize the control view. It was expanded with data objects so that the connection between events, functions and data was clear. Because the process steps at the PSP were the same regardless of the request type, all requests were covered by one business process at the PSP. The PSP visualized and described the process flow of this business process as shown in* Fig. 6.9.

The ***process*** *starts at the customer or the law enforcement agency. The subsequent process steps are performed by the issuing bank, the PSP and the merchant. The functions and events at the PSP were in scope for the decision making.*

- *The process can start at the* ***customer*** *if the "customer has concerns" about a specific payment. There are many reasons for concerns, mostly returned products, terminated services, errors or fraud. If the customer disputes the payment, he will create a chargeback request. If the costumer just seeks more information about the payment, he will create a retrieval request. For example, he might have lost his copy of the transaction receipt, or he does not remember the payment. Retrieval requests often precede chargebacks.*
- *The process can also start at the* ***law enforcement agency*** *if the "agency has a fraud suspicion". Many forms of fraud can occur in the payment sector. Often, attackers use stolen or lost cards, try to generate false payments with bogus data, intercept and manipulate payment transactions, or create fraudulent claims based on false information. Most agencies do not only wait passively for reports or complaints but also respond to new threats and try to raise the protection levels. In case of fraud that was enabled by a data breach in the payment sector, the amount of affected payment cards is often significant, reaching up to millions of cards.*
- *If the costumer requests a chargeback, the issuing bank will grant a provisional credit to the customer. In all cases, the* ***issuing bank*** *requests a clear and legible copy of the particular sales draft from the PSP. The issuing bank can request a specific form of the copy: a microfilm, original draft or substitute draft. Microfilms are very common because they have smaller storage costs than paper documents. They enable the storage of strongly scaled-down images on films. The original draft is seldom requested. Even if requested, the merchant or PSP can generally substitute it with a microfilm copy. Substitute drafts do not include the signature of the customer or the imprint of the card. They are used for, among other things, mail orders and telephone orders (MOTO), vehicle rentals, airline and passenger railway, and parking lots.*

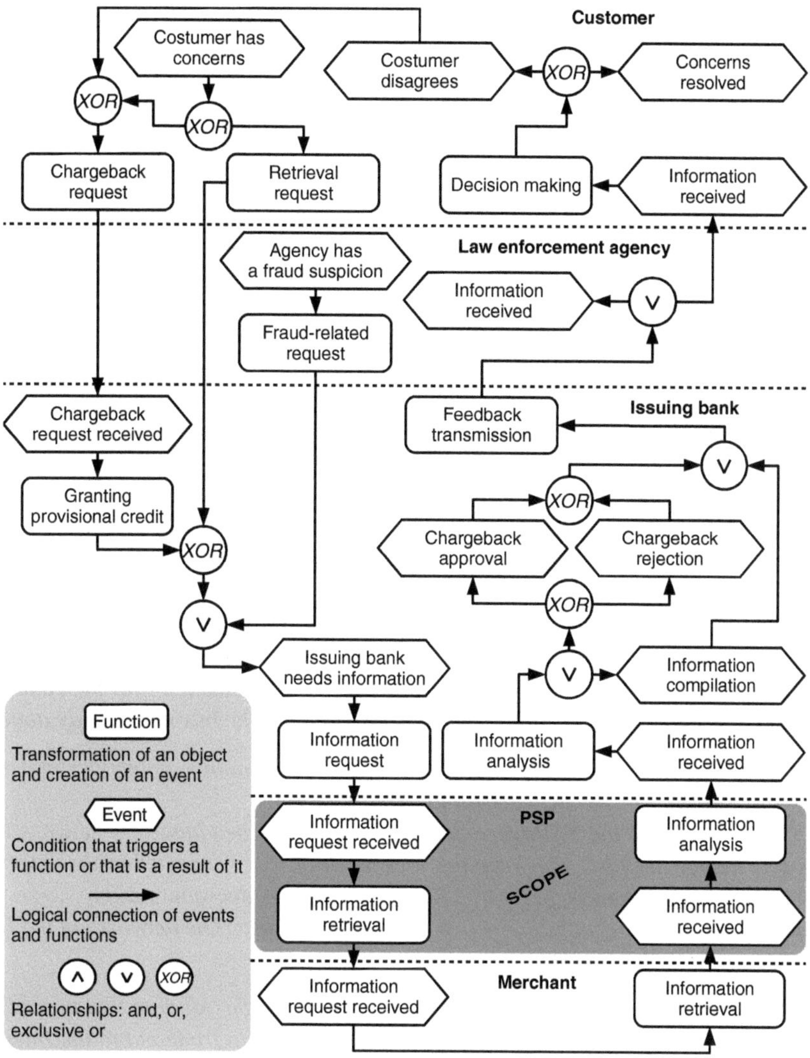

Fig. 6.9 EPC

- *The* ***PSP*** *requests information about the payment from the merchant. Normally, the request from the issuing bank is forwarded. Besides, the PSP might request additional information, e.g. certain supporting documentation, like a translation of documentation.*
- *The* ***merchant*** *must now supply a legible copy of the sales draft and any supporting documentation to the PSP. Requirements regarding timeframes and documentation are given by the credit card organizations. The merchant should respond to retrieval requests in a timely manner. Otherwise, the customer will*

probably create a chargeback request. If the merchant does not respond to a retrieval request, the issuing bank will not offer the chance to the merchant to defend himself against a related chargeback.

- *The **PSP** analyses the received information and enriches it with additional transaction data. Afterwards, the PSP presents the complete information to the issuing bank.*
- *The **issuing bank** now has enough information to find out what has probably happened at the point of sale. If the process has started with a chargeback request, the issuing bank now decides whether the chargeback is valid. If the chargeback is valid, the provisional refund will become final. Otherwise, the chargeback will be rejected and the refund will be withdrawn. If the process has started with a retrieval request, the issuing bank will hand the information over to the customer. If the process has started with a fraud-related request, the issuing bank will hand the information over to the agency.*
- *If the process has started with a fraud-related request, the **law enforcement agency** will now receive the information requested. Now, the agency analyses the information thoroughly. Possibly, the information can be enriched by other information from the private and federal sector. Collaboration can be an important factor for efficiently managing new threats and attacks.*
- *If the process has started with a retrieval or chargeback request, the **costumer** will receive the related information. Either the concerns of the customer regarding the payment are resolved now or he still disagrees with the payment. In the last case, he can now request a chargeback if he has not already done it.*

*The **networks** of the PSP comprised multiple workstations, notebooks and servers as visualized in the network diagram in* Fig. 6.10.

*The **networks** of the PSP were distinguished in the headquarters network and the data center network. The headquarters network was connected to the Internet, merchants, and business partners. In scope for the decision making were the workstations and notebooks in the accounting department. The networks of the PSP comprised the following objects:*

- *The **firewall** controlled the in- and outgoing data traffic. All data that passed the perimeter were analyzed by the firewall. Thereby, data from and to the Internet were monitored and controlled. The firewall was supposed to filter the traffic and block malicious connection attempts.*
- *The **routers** forwarded data packets between networks with different address ranges or architectures. They were needed to connect the headquarters with the data center over a private line. They also connected the internal network and the Internet.*
- *The **switches** forwarded data packets within a network or between network segments. Therefore, they were needed to connect multiple workstations, notebooks and servers with each other.*
- *The **workstations** were computers that were available to the users for local use. They were stand-alone computers that could be operated autonomously. They enabled the use of application software that supported or enabled the fulfillment*

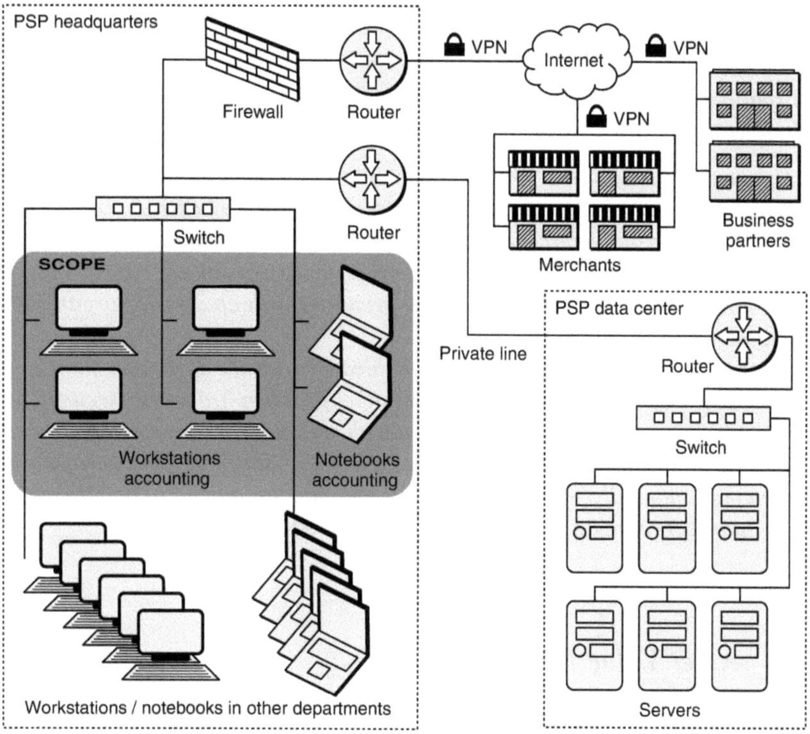

Fig. 6.10 Network diagram and scope

of operational tasks. They had been integrated into the company to provide additional server functions. Peripherals that were connected to workstations provided interfaces for the input and output of data, e.g. mouse, keyboard, monitor, and printer. Confidential payment data were stored on the workstations of the accounting department. These data were at risk because it could be compromised by transferring data over the interfaces of the computer, by stealing the hard drive or the whole computer, and by network-based attacks.

- *The **notebooks** were mobile computers, which did not necessarily require additional peripherals. Important input and output components, like monitor, keyboard and trackpad, were already integrated. Notebooks included a built-in power supply in the form of a rechargeable battery. Therefore, they could be used independently at any location. The notebooks included also confidential payment data that were at risk. Because the notebooks were often used for mobile work, the risk that it could be stolen or lost was even higher than that of workstations.*
- *The **servers** were computers that operated one or more server programs. They offered resources or functions to other computers or users over the network. In general, servers often have a high robustness and reliability. The servers of the PSP used hardware encryption to secure all stored files. Payment data that were*

stored on the file server by a staff member of the accounting department were sufficiently protected with encryption.

*From outside of the network, the following **organizations** were communicating with objects from the PSP network:*

- *The **merchants** sent the payment transactions to the PSP. These highly confidential data were sent over a virtual private network (VPN). A strong encryption prevented the interception, compromise or manipulation of payment data.*
- *The **business partners** sent and received data over an encrypted VPN, too. The PSP exchanged confidential data primarily with credit card organizations, and issuing banks.*
- *The **law enforcement agencies** communicated with the PSP over the Internet. This had been considered as a possible problem from the security view. However, the risk had been eliminated with specific work instructions from both the PSP and the law enforcement agencies. The staff that performed the data exchange manually were instructed to encrypt the data on the file level. No deviations from these instructions had occurred at the PSP.*

6.4.3 Asset Value Measurement

3.13 The value of the assets that need protection has been calculated.

After the scope has been determined and all systems and components that store, transfer or process sensitive data—hereafter called assets—have been identified, their **value** can be measured. The amount of an asset value depends on the profit, which is generated for the company with the support of the asset. The more money a company can earn when operating the asset, the higher is the asset value.

The asset value measurement will be obvious if the profit that is assigned to the asset is clearly **quantifiable**. However, qualitative factors often play an important role for the economic success of a company, too. For example, the outage of a web server might not directly prevent business but can have a negative impact on customer opinion, which might lead to a decrease of orders in the long term.

The calculation of asset values with quantitative impacts can be directly derived by the profit that is generated by selling goods or providing services. In the case of **qualitative** impacts, an estimation by experts must be performed. Mostly, terms like low, medium and high are used and linked to value ranges.

As described in Sect. 4.2, the asset value measurement includes identifying the asset type, considering value-characteristics, choosing the measurement method, determining the measurement precision, and dealing with dependencies. From these steps, a **procedure** for the asset value measurement can be derived as shown in Fig. 6.11.

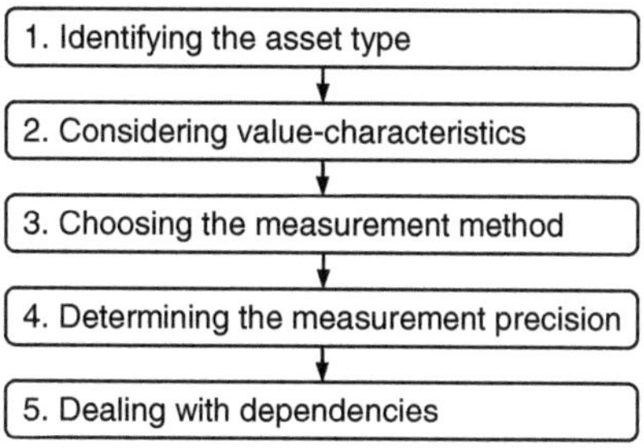

Fig. 6.11 Procedure for asset value measurement

16. The appraisement of assets depends on the **asset type**. Assets can be tangible objects, e.g. information systems, or intangible objects, e.g. information. Besides, they can be distinguished in current assets, e.g. raw material, and fixed assets, e.g. machines or systems.
17. Every asset type has specific **characteristics** that influence the asset value. For example, the value of information can be influenced by its quality, and related business improvements. The decision maker should consider these specific characteristics.
18. The decision maker has to choose a **measurement method** in order to determine how the information that is needed for the value measurement shall be obtained and on which perspective it shall be based. The most common methods are those that base the asset value on the replacement costs, revenue changes or market value.
19. The **measurement precision** will be high if a quantitative measurement is performed, while it will be low if a qualitative one is performed. Therefore, the quantitative measurement should be preferred. However, sometimes the required numbers for a quantitative measurement are missing and practically impossible to acquire. In this case, a qualitative measurement with a non-numerical scale can be used.
20. Besides, the decision maker has to decide if **dependencies** between the asset in focus and other assets shall be considered. The value of other assets must be included if dependencies are taken into account. Especially from the income perspective, assets can depend on another while generating an outcome, like a good that is built with the help of various assets.

Case Study

As determined in Sect. 6.4.1, *the PSP sought protection for* ***information assets****, which belong to the intangible assets. In particular, the asset was payment card data that were stored, processed and transmitted within the processing of chargebacks, retrieval requests and fraud-related requests. In* Sect. 6.4.1, *also the* ***protection goal*** *has been specified. The PSP wanted to ensure the confidentiality of the payment card data. The integrity and availability had been found irrelevant. The* ***value-characteristic*** *that influenced the value of the payment card data most* *was the intrinsic quality. In detail, the data were supposed to be correct and reliable, unbiased, unprejudiced and impartial, regarded as true and credible, and highly regarded in terms of its source or content. The PSP used the revenue as the* ***measurement method*** *for all payment card data in the company. The business of the PSP was based on providing technical infrastructure and processing payments. Therefore, the amount of payment card data directly affected the revenue. If all payment data were in focus, they could be measured quantitatively. However, the PSP restricted the view only on the data that were used for the processing of chargebacks, retrieval requests and fraud-related requests. Therefore, a direct effect on the revenue was not found. Only an indirect effect that was derived from possible reputational damage were measured here in a qualitative way. Even just a few compromised payment cards were expected to lead to negative press and bad customer opinions. In consequence, the value of the data in focus had been found middle. The* **measurement precision**, *which was influenced by the qualitative measurement, was low. There were no* **dependencies** *from the data in focus to other data or any other assets.*

6.4.4 Risk Analysis

3.14 The risks have been analyzed.

In general, the common **risk management** process includes the risk identification, risk assessment, risk treatment and risk monitoring:

- The **risk identification** is fundamental for the subsequent steps. Only if risks have been identified, the assessment, treatment and monitoring of risks can be performed. The relevant assets that can be affected by risks have already been selected in the preceding steps of the lifecycle. Now, exploitable vulnerabilities of these assets—the threats—must be found. Therefore, the decision maker can use scenarios, which represent undesirable situations that can be caused by deviations from the normal state.
- The **risk assessment** is an important task for gathering enough information in order to create a decision template and, thereby, to facilitate a reasonable decision regarding the risk treatment. As shown in Sect. 4.3.4, quantitative and qualitative indicators can be used for assessing the risk. Thereby, values or categories are assigned to the identified risks from the previous step. In this way, the consequence and the likelihood of occurrence for each risk can be illustrated.
- The **risk treatment** depends on the individual preferences of the company. In general, the company can choose to mitigate, transfer, accept or avoid the identified risks:

- **Mitigating** a risk means to select and implement safeguards that are reasonable under economic aspects. This is exactly the procedure that is described in the following chapters.
- The company can also **transfer** a risk by making an agreement with another company that is going to cover the possible financial damages that result from a risk, e.g. with an insurance or outsourcing.
- The **acceptance** of risks means that the risk has been analyzed and that the company decided not to mitigate or transfer the risk. Mostly in the case of acceptance, the safeguard costs are higher than the reduction in expected losses. In other words, the available safeguards are not reasonable from the economic view.
- The **avoidance** of a risk is performed by deciding not to proceed with the activities that led to the existence of a risk. Here, the risk is circumvented by doing business without the risk-related activities or by choosing other activities that can replace the risk-related ones.
- The **risk monitoring** addresses the situation that a risk is often changing over time. Besides, new technologies can lead to more efficient safeguard opportunities that should be considered. Only if risks are monitored continuously and safeguards are regularly compared to new ones, the efficiency of the risk management can be ensured. In the lifecycle, the monitoring can be performed within the operation and maintenance steps.

The **risk analysis** within this step of the lifecycle includes only the risk identification and assessment. The risk treatment is covered by the subsequent steps up to the closing. Hereby, the mitigation of the risk is addressed. The risk transfer or acceptance can be reasonable alternatives, which can be chosen if the lifecycle steps do not lead to the selection of a suitable safeguard. The risk monitoring is integrated into the operation and maintenance of the selected safeguard. In contrast to a separate risk management, the risk analysis within the lifecycle is focused on a single risk. In general, the risk management in a company covers all relevant risks.

Frameworks that give instruction on how to perform a risk management have been described in Sect. 4.3.3. They support the risk management procedure by guiding the risk manager through multiple steps. In general, it cannot be answered which framework is most favorable. Moreover, the individual characteristics of the company, the actual situation and the available resources influence the appropriateness of the frameworks. Therefore, the company should not only select a suitable framework once but also every time an actual risk management shall be performed.

Case Study

*The **risk analysis** at the PSP addressed the risks that were related to the data and processes that were connected to the processing of chargebacks, retrieval requests and fraud-related requests.*

As mentioned above, the **risks** *must be identified before the assessment can start. The PSP identified risks based on various scenarios. Next, it assessed the risks based on qualitative views on losses and probability. The risks had been described as follows:*

- ***Disclosure*** *can occur if the payment data is seen by unauthorized persons. In case of disclosure, the confidentiality will be affected strongly. The probability that disclosure actually occurs will be very high if no safeguards are implemented.*
- ***Loss*** *will be relevant if portable devices, in particular notebooks, get lost. In this case, the confidentiality will be affected strongly, too. The probability that loss actually occurs is seen as high.*
- ***Manipulation*** *can be performed by hackers that aim at altering data in order to achieve a personal benefit. This scenario addresses the integrity, which had been found irrelevant by the PSP as mentioned in* Sect. 6.4.1. *Besides, the probability that a hacker tries to manipulate data of chargebacks, retrieval requests or fraud-related requests is rather low. The hacker can hardly gain a benefit from this manipulation. A benefit can only be gained if the hacker is directly affected by the chargeback, retrieval request or fraud-related request. However, this is highly unlikely. In other words, the probability of occurrence is seen as low.*
- ***Corruption*** *can occur if the data that are needed for chargebacks, retrieval requests and fraud-related requests are damaged by hardware failures or human errors. If essential data are affected, the business process cannot be completed. This scenario also addresses the integrity, which had been found irrelevant. The probability of occurrence is seen as moderate.*
- ***Hardware and infrastructure failures*** *influence the availability of the data. For example, a failure of the power supply unit or the hard drive can occur. Power outages or network connection problems can interrupt the processing of chargebacks, retrieval requests and fraud-related requests. These scenarios address the availability, which had been found irrelevant by the PSP as mentioned in* Sect. 6.4.1. *Considering the situation at the PSP, the probability of occurrence is seen as moderate.*

According to ***CRAMM****, which has been introduced in* Sect. 4.3.3.2, *a table for the risk assessment at the PSP was created (see* Table 6.1*). Here, the asset had been categorized as "confidential" because the confidentiality had been found as the primary protection goal. Thereby, the importance of the confidentiality was set very high. In contrast, the integrity and availability of the data had been categorized as "low", which is the lowest category in CRAMM. The vulnerability includes the likelihood of occurrence and the risk is the product of impact and vulnerability. For medium risk levels, the company focused on an encryption solution. For low risk levels, no safeguard was searched.*

Table 6.1 CRAMM table for the case study

Asset: payment data in chargebacks, retrieval requests and fraud-related requests **Asset owner**: accounting department						
	Confidentiality: public (0), restricted (1–5), confidential (6–9), secure (10)		**Integrity**: low (1–3), moderate (4–7), high (8–9), very high (10)		**Availability**: low (1–3), moderate (4–6), high (7–8), very high (9), mandatory (10)	
Impact	6		1		1	
Threats	Disclosure	Loss	Manipulation	Corruption	Hardware failure	Infrastructure failure
Vulnerability: none (0), low (1–4), moderate (5–7), high (8–9), very high (10)	10	8	1	7	6	6
Risk: impact x vulnerability	60	48	1	7	6	6
Risk level: low (1–33), medium (34–67), high (68–100)	Medium	Medium	Low	Low	Low	Low
Countermeasures	Encryption	Encryption	None	None	None	None

6.4.5 Protection Requirements

3.15 The protection requirements for the assets have been specified.

In this step, all assets that need protection must be analyzed regarding their particular protection requirements. The overall protection goal and level have already been set within the strategy determination in Sect. 6.4.1. Now, these preliminary results are used as the basis for **detailing** the protection requirements. The decision maker has to find out all protection requirements for the company's assets that are in scope. Therefore, every relevant asset has to be analyzed regarding its specific protection needs.

At first, **protection classes** have to be defined. These classes can correspond to the protection levels from Sect. 6.4.1. However, they could also be extended by additional intermediate levels. Besides, the protection classes have to be described in detail so that the assets can be categorized clearly. Scenarios can be helpful for this description, e.g. in the form of situations that are related to damages, laws, regulations, contracts, business disruptions, reputation, or life and health. For example, the protection classes low, middle, high, and very high can be used:

- A **low** protection is chosen for assets that can cause only minor damages to the company. If laws, regulations or contracts are violated because of a security incident at these assets, no consequences will be expected. Business disruptions that are caused by these assets are insignificant. There is no possible reputational damage. A harm to the life and health of individuals is definitely impossible.
- A **middle** protection is chosen for assets that can cause only limited and moderate damages to the company. If laws, regulations or contracts are violated because of a security incident at these assets, only marginal consequences will be expected. Business disruptions that are caused by these assets are tolerable. The possible reputational damage is low. A harm to the life and health of individuals is nearly impossible.
- A **high** protection is chosen for assets that can cause serious damages to the company. If laws, regulations or contracts are violated because of a security incident at these assets, significant consequences will be expected. Business disruptions that are caused by these assets are not tolerable in the view of some involved individuals or companies. The possible reputational damage affects only some business parts that are connected to few costumers. A harm to the life and health of individuals cannot be excluded but is rather improbable.
- A **very high** protection is chosen for assets that can cause damages that threaten the existence of the company. If laws, regulations or contracts are violated because of a security incident at these assets, fundamental consequences will be expected. Business disruptions that are caused by these assets are not tolerable in the view of all involved individuals or companies. The possible reputational

damage affects the whole company and nearly every business part that is connected to costumers. A harm to the life and health of individuals is possible.

The **protection goals** have to be defined, too. The rough determination of protection goals from Sect. 6.4.1 can be kept or extended. The decision maker has the opportunity to select the protection goals that match to the individual company goals. In addition to the protection goals that are derived from the basic cybersecurity principles in Sect. 2.2.1, among other things, the extended cybersecurity principles in Sect. 2.2.2 can be considered.

Then, every **asset** in scope has to be categorized regarding each relevant protection goal. The basics for this categorization are the relevant risks, which have been analyzed in the previous chapter. For example, if the confidentiality, integrity and availability have been selected, and the classes low, middle, high, and very high have been defined, a table with four columns can be used (see Table 6.2).

The **data classification**, which has been described in Sect. 3.2.6, is also a good way for categorizing information assets. It is focused on the confidentiality of information that is represented with data. While performing an analysis of the protection requirements, an existing data classification can be a valuable input for categorizing information assets regarding their confidentiality. Even, if the existing data classes do not correspond to the chosen protection classes, at least, the decision maker will get an indication about the most reasonable categorization.

A **business impact analysis**, which is part of the business continuity management as described in Sect. 3.2.14, includes a determination of the maximal accepted downtime and data loss. Thereby, an important input can be given for evaluating the protection requirements regarding the availability. In general, assets with a low maximal accepted downtime and data loss have higher protection requirements than other assets.

Case Study

For categorizing the assets from the case study regarding their protection requirements, much information from the ***previous chapters*** *is needed. The identification of relevant assets has been described in* Sect. 6.4.2. *After the identification, the value of these assets had been determined as shown in* Sect. 6.4.3. *Based on this information, the risks had been identified and assessed as explained in* Sect. 6.4.4. *Besides, while determining the overall strategy as described in* Sect. 6.4.1, *some first indications had been found for selecting the protection goal.*

Table 6.2 Protection requirements example

Asset	Protection of confidentiality	Protection of integrity	Protection of availability
Workstation	Middle	Middle	Low
File server	High	High	Middle
Online shop server	Middle	High	Very high

The protection classes that were used in the case study were—in accordance to the above example—low, middle, high, and very high.

In the case of the PSP, the **assets** *workstations, notebooks, and payment card data had been identified. Because the overall strategy had been focused on confidentiality, the physical aspects of workstations and notebooks were irrelevant. Moreover, the payment card data had to be protected. The* **value** *of the payment card data had been found middle. From the perspective of* **risks**, *a compromise of payment card data was expected to lead to negative consequences. Because the risk had also been found middle, the* **categorization** *of the asset "payment card data" regarding the protection goal "confidentiality" was "middle".*

6.4.6 Adequacy of the Decision Making Technique

3.16 An adequate decision making technique has been chosen.

Before performing the decision making process in the narrower sense, the decision maker must select an adequate technique so that he can systematically walk through the necessary steps. Multiple individual factors influence the selection of the technique. At first, the decision maker should be aware of the disadvantages of making a decision solely based on **intuition** and the advantages of performing a **reasoning** with a systematic approach:

- The **intuition** is the ability to make a decision without the use of reasons and conscious conclusions. Although using intuition is a subconscious process, it is still based on certain factors, like personal values and previous experiences. The personal perceptions of the decision maker plaid a major role in building these factors. Therefore, intuition is highly subjective and seldom completely understandable. Intuition can be a sufficient approach if very fast decisions must be made without having further information. Besides, intuition can be an indication whether further research should be conducted before completing a reasoning approach.
- The **reasoning**, which is part of a systematic procedure, creates decisions based on transparent facts. In contrast to intuition, reasoning is generally understandable by others. Often, decisions are complex and need a clear structure in order to consider every important factor. A systematic procedure, like provided by the SAW and AHP, helps to perform the decision in an understandable way so that stakeholders can reconstruct the decision. However, intuition should not be completely neglected because it could indicate that something might not be considered sufficiently. Although intuition should not replace reasoning, it can be used to improve the reasoning process, e.g. by identifying areas of concern that should be analyzed deeper.

Assuming the company prefers reasoning with a systematic procedure, a technique for handling multiple attributes and alternatives should be used for selecting the preferable cybersecurity investment. If the decision maker focuses on the SAW and AHP, which are relatively easy to understand and use as described in Sects. 5.2 and 5.3, he will still be challenged to **choose** the more appropriate of these two techniques:

- The **SAW** should be chosen if the selected attributes are very understandable and if they can be evaluated directly without the need for more sophisticated pairwise comparisons as used in the AHP. The direct evaluation is easier for quantitative attribute values than for qualitative ones. The drawbacks of the SAW (see Sect. 5.2) should be known and accepted.
- The **AHP** will be the better choice if the decision maker accepts more complexity in the decision making process in order to achieve a higher quality. Especially if many qualitative attribute values are present, pairwise comparisons will be easier to conduct. The AHP facilitates more thoughtful and consistent evaluations (see Sect. 5.3), but the understandability by non-experts is often lower. Besides, the aggregation of the evaluation results will be more complex, especially if no dedicated AHP software is used.

Case Study

*The PSP decided to perform both decision making techniques—the SAW and AHP—**concurrently**. Thereby, possible weaknesses of one particular technique were supposed to become clear. Especially if the application of these techniques had led to different alternative rankings, the decision making would have been questioned. The additional labor for using two techniques in parallel was consciously taken into account.*

6.4.7 Involvement of Stakeholders

3.17 Relevant stakeholders have been identified and involved.

In order to consider different views and perspectives without overlooking the interests of influential people and organizations, the **involvement** of relevant stakeholders can be crucial. Stakeholders from different areas can address specific factors that can easily be overlooked by a single decision maker. The most important questions to be answered regarding the involvement of stakeholders are which stakeholders should be involved and how should they be involved.

The **stakeholder analysis**, which has been described in Sect. 2.5, includes a procedure that can be used perfectly for addressing these questions. By orienting this procedure to a cybersecurity investment, the **goal** is obvious. The stakeholders that can support or block the selection of an adequate safeguard shall be identified. The **scope** and **granularity** depend on the risks that shall be mitigated with the safeguard. The probability and impact of the threat in focus give an indication about the scope of stakeholders that should be considered, e.g. internal or external stakeholders. Subsequently, the number of analyzed stakeholders can be determined. Thereby, a granularity that gives a balance between a good level of detail and a limited work effort can be chosen. The **identification** of stakeholders should not solely performed by the analyst. Moreover, the stakeholders should be enabled to participate. A transparent communication, which includes, among other things, a kick-off meeting, helps to raise the knowledge and awareness at potential stakeholders. The analyst should perform the **selection** of stakeholders in accordance to their impact on the successful selection and implementation of the safeguard. The **prioritization** of stakeholders illustrates the influence of stakeholders on the cybersecurity investment. The identification of stakeholder **interests** is necessary for determining the opinion of stakeholders regarding the cybersecurity investment. While positive opinions can improve the investment success, negative opinions can cause serious obstacles. The **stakeholder map** allows the visualization of the findings from the stakeholder analysis regarding the intended cybersecurity investment.

During the stakeholder analysis, the decision maker needs to gather much **information**, which can be difficult to obtain. Common techniques that can be used for this purpose are the same techniques that can be used within the qualitative risk analyses (see Sect. 4.3.4.2). **Interviews** allow questioning experienced stakeholders and experts about relevant cybersecurity topics directly. **Surveys** are often used when the participants are very numerous. They can be quick and simple, but it is almost impossible to create an exhaustive survey. **Brainstorming** helps to obtain a comprehensive list of ideas that can be anything from highly relevant to irrelevant. The **Delphi technique** reaches a consensus of experts that can participate anonymously. Here, the responses regarding the cybersecurity investment are summarized and sent back to the experts for further comment.

Case Study

The PSP decided to include only internal stakeholders in the ***scope****. As described in* Sect. 6.4.4, *the relevant risk levels had been found medium so that a group of internal experts was assumed sufficient to manage the investment. The PSP performed a kick-off meeting and invited all department heads to this meeting. Thereby, the awareness about cybersecurity was raised and the department heads had the opportunity to participate or recommend particular department members for participation. By voicing their thoughts and concerns in the meeting, indications about their type of interest were collected. From the perspective of the departments, the PSP selected the following* ***stakeholders****, which had a high impact on the investment lifecycle:*

- *The* ***senior management*** *had a rather big influence on the outcome of the investment project. Important steps from the lifecycle fully depended on the decisions from senior management, in particular the sponsoring and approval.*
- *The* ***accounting department*** *included the actual users of the new safeguard that was supposed to be the outcome from the investment.*
- *The* ***chief information security officer*** *sponsored the investment and was responsible for ensuring an appropriate protection level.*
- *The members of the* ***IT operations*** *were responsible for the technical implementation, the administration and the maintenance of the safeguard.*
- *The members of the* ***IT architecture*** *helped designing the solution or finding requirements for it. Hereby, the compatibility and suitability regarding the current IT environment were considered.*
- *The members of the* ***HR department*** *managed the available staff and assigned individual workers to specific departments or project groups.*

The analysts also conducted a series of ***interviews*** *with the selected stakeholders. They asked about the stakeholder's vision for the future and specific details. They also asked about concerns and alternative ideas. Thereby, the impact and opinion of every selected stakeholder were determined. While senior management, the chief information security officer and the IT architecture generally supported the investment, the accounting department, IT operations and HR department disapproved it. Although the most members of the accounting department disapproved it, some members actually supported the investment. The disapproval was caused by the impression that the security improvement would not justify the additional effort for the implementation and operation of the safeguard. The* ***stakeholder map*** *for the cybersecurity investment at the PSP had been visualized as shown in* Fig. 6.12.

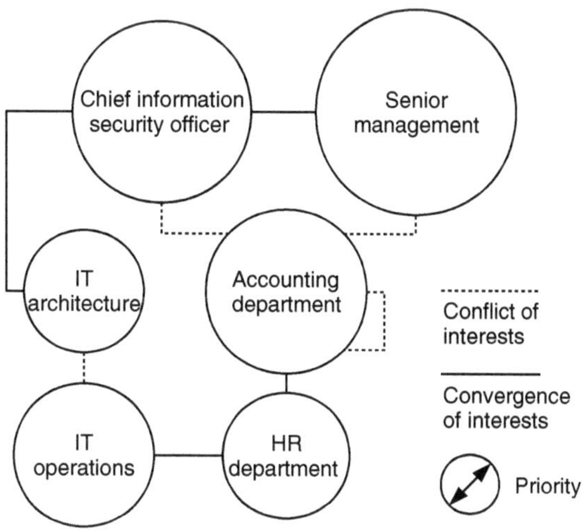

Fig. 6.12 Stakeholder map from the case study

6.5 Attribute Identification

4.1 Attributes that address company requirements have been identified.

The **attributes** that can be considered by the decision maker can be distinguished in attributes for product quality, quality in use, and economic evaluation. Attributes for product quality and quality in use are defined in ISO 25010, which addresses systems and software quality requirements. Thereby, cybersecurity investments in systems and software are also addressed. In 2011, ISO 25010 replaced the preceding ISO 9126. In ISO 25010, the attributes are distinguished in main- and sub-attributes. In addition, economic attributes should also be considered. They include indicators that give information about the actual or future financial situation related to the cybersecurity investment. Primarily, costs, benefits and risks are in focus here.

The attributes for **product quality** address the quality of the product, in particular the software or information system that can be used as a safeguard. The related attributes (see Fig. 6.13) cover static and dynamic properties of software or a system.

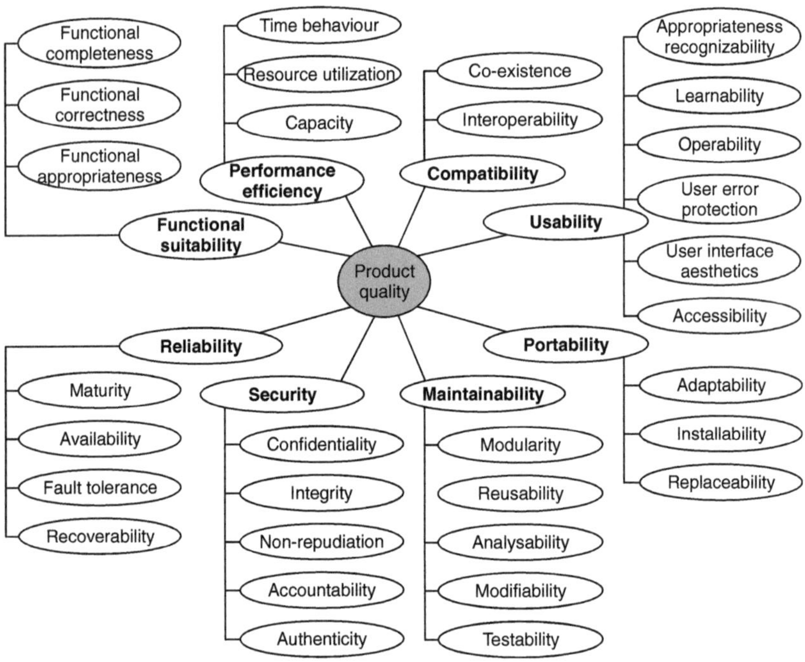

Fig. 6.13 Product quality attributes

According to ISO 25010 (2011), the eight main-attributes of product quality (bold printed in Fig. 6.13) are:

- The **functional suitability** is the degree to which a product or system provides functions that meet stated and implied needs when used under specified conditions. In the context of cybersecurity, the functionality is related to the availability of functions that address cybersecurity goals, e.g. the identification of malicious code, or encryption of files.
- The **performance efficiency** is the performance relative to the amount of resources used under stated conditions. A safeguard that requires many resources, e.g. CPU time and RAM, would be seen critical from the view of performance efficiency.
- The **compatibility** is the degree to which a product, system or component can exchange information with other products, systems or components, and/or perform its required functions, while sharing the same hardware or software environment. The compatibility of a safeguard should be considered in order to assure that it could be used in the whole company. For example, Linux computers cannot be protected with software that can only be used with Windows.
- The **usability** is the degree to which a product or system can be used by specified users to achieve specified goals with effectiveness, efficiency and satisfaction in a specified context of use. A safeguard is often integrated into the daily user activity, e.g. in the form of authentication. Besides, employees have to configure and operate the safeguards. Among other things, an interface that can be easily understood and used can be an important usability factor.
- The **reliability** is the degree to which a system, product or component performs specified functions under specified conditions for a specified time-period. If a safeguard were not reliable, the risk of a breach would increase during the time of unavailability or errors.
- The **security** is the degree to which a product or system protects information and data so that persons or other products or systems have the degree of data access appropriate to their types and levels of authorization. From the view of this attribute, every product, even a safeguard, should be analyzed regarding its built-in security. For example, a firewall can be an essential improvement to the security at the network parameter, but also the security of the administration interface must be sufficient.
- The **maintainability** is the degree of effectiveness and efficiency with which a product or system can be modified by the intended maintainers. In cybersecurity, handling modifications can be crucial. New threats or technological changes can lead to high risks that can be addressed with modification.
- The **portability** is the degree of effectiveness and efficiency with which a system, product or component can be transferred from one hardware, software or other operational or usage environment to another. A safeguard that has been selected after thorough analysis should be runnable on all relevant systems of the company. When analyzing the portability, it should be considered that most company environments are heterogeneous.

The attributes for **quality in use** address the use of the product and the needs of the user that are fulfilled during this use. Thereby, the outcome of the interaction that occurs during the use within a specific context is in focus. Quality in use cannot be analyzed generally. Moreover, the context is an important parameter here. A product can be evaluated completely different from before if the context of the product use changes. The attributes that are related to this field are shown in Fig. 6.14.

According to ISO 25010 (2011), the five main-attributes of quality in use (bold printed in Fig. 6.14) are:

- The **effectiveness** is the accuracy and completeness with which users achieve specified goals. For example, an evaluation of antivirus software can include the accuracy and completeness of the virus detection after a user starts a complete scan of his computer.
- The **efficiency** is measured by the resources expended in relation to the accuracy and completeness with which users achieve goals. Again, the context plays a major role in the evaluation. The above-mentioned antivirus software can be analyzed regarding its resource utilization during the virus scan.
- The **satisfaction** is the degree to which user needs are satisfied when a product or system is used in a specified context of use. For example, the satisfaction of the user after the antivirus software scanned his computer can be evaluated here.
- The **freedom from risk** is the degree to which a product or system mitigates the potential risk to economic status, human life, health, or the environment. The risk mitigation is the most important aspect of selecting a safeguard. For the purpose of the safeguard selection, the risk mitigation should get a high emphasis. Therefore, a separate risk inspection as described below is mostly recommendable.

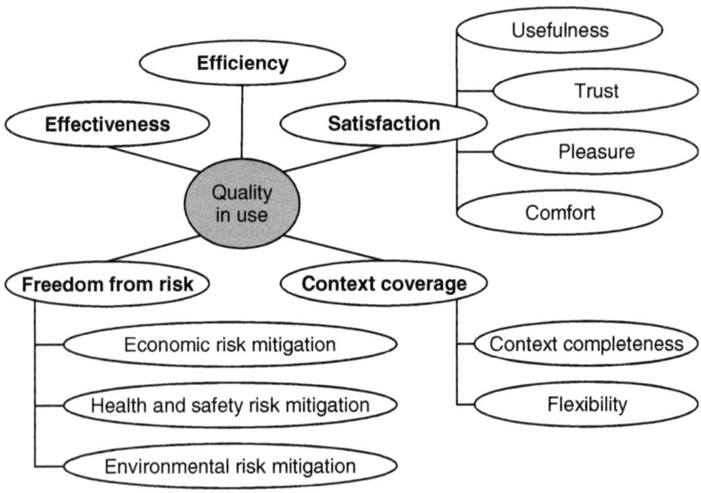

Fig. 6.14 Quality in use attributes

- The **context coverage** is the degree to which a product or system can be used with effectiveness, efficiency, freedom from risk and satisfaction in both specified contexts of use and in contexts beyond those initially explicitly identified. In other words, the operation in different contexts and the flexibility to adapt to specified situations are in focus here. For example, data leakage prevention at a laptop that works as intended regardless of whether it is used within the company, at home and at other locations covers many contexts.

The attributes for **economic evaluation** (see Fig. 6.15) can address the costs, benefits and risks, which are mutually overlapping or, at least, related. Costs depend not only on the safeguard but also on the occurrence of a breach. Benefits can often be found in the form of cost reduction and risk mitigation. Risks represent negative events that occur with a given probability and lead to subsequent costs and losses. Besides, many indicators include multiple aspects that compare, among other things, costs and benefits.

When seen separately, the terms can be described as follows:

- The **costs** can be connected to the safeguard itself, as described in Sect. 4.4.1, or to the costs that occur during or after a breach, as described in Sect. 4.4.2. Besides, the costs of the business operation can be reduced if the safeguards are connected to functional benefits, e.g. benefits from a more convenient authentication method.
- As described in Sect. 4.5, **benefits** are any improvements that are seen positive or worthwhile by a stakeholder. The benefits of a safeguard are mostly the result of a risk mitigation or elimination. In other words, the costs that are expected from a possible breach can be reduced. A profit gain will be rather unlikely if a safeguard is implemented. However, this can be possible in some scenarios. For example, if the safeguard raises the security level of the company in such a way that a competitive advantage is created. In particular, a safeguard that is the last piece for obtaining a certification can have a significant impact on the revenues of the company.

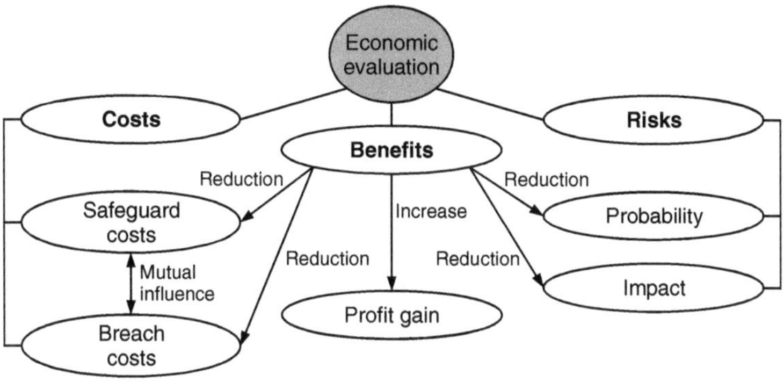

Fig. 6.15 Basics for economic attributes

- Generally, every company tries to mitigate **risks**. The mitigation can be measured by calculating the expected loss before and after the implementation of the safeguard. As described in Sect. 4.3.4, the expected loss depends on the impact and the probability of a negative event. Beside quantitative measures, qualitative terms can be used for unspecific losses that are difficult to quantify.

The **attributes** that are often selected to cover the economic evaluation have been described in Chap. 4, which includes various financial indicators, risk attributes, and details about costs and benefits.

Besides identifying the attributes, the **value ranges** of these attributes must be determined. By making the possible values transparent, the evaluation of alternatives regarding the attributes will be facilitated. For example, it must be clear if a cost attribute can have negative values, which can stand for earnings. Besides, if qualitative values like "low" and "high" are used, it must be clear which other values are allowed and how they can be ordered.

Then, these values must be assigned to **scores**, which can be used to perform the actual evaluation of the alternatives. This step is important because a high value can be positive regarding one attribute (e.g. availability) and negative regarding another one (e.g. hardware costs). In addition, the distances between values can be different for each attribute. For example, an availability of 99 % can be very good, while 90 % can be average and 80 % can be bad. Therefore, an equal distribution of scores and values is not natural. While the scores are directly used within the SAW calculation, they are only an indirect support for the pairwise comparisons within the AHP.

The **granularity** of the attribute identification is variable and depends on the preferences of the decision maker. Available resources, desired flexibility, and the required transparency play a decisive role for choosing between generic or specific attributes.

- If the attributes are more **generic**, the decision making process can be simplified. Fewer attributes and evaluations must be handled and fewer calculations must be made. However, the quality of the decision can be negatively affected. Generic attributes, e.g. maintainability, can be difficult to understand. Especially if multiple decision makers participate in the process, different opinions about the specific meaning of generic attributes will arise. Important sub-attributes might be overlooked by the decision makers. Besides, single sub-attributes can compensate very good or very bad evaluations of other sub-attributes. In the case of maintainability, the sub-attributes modularity, reusability, analyzability, modifiability and testability can compensate each other. In particular, the product might not be modifiable but still have a good evaluation regarding the overall maintainability. For example, the bad evaluation of the sub-attribute modifiability might be fully compensated by a very good testability. In the overall evaluation, the generic attributes can obscure the sub-attributes and impair the transparency for outside parties. This can be very problematic for the practical use of the product.

- If very **specific** attributes are considered, the decision making process will be more time-consuming and laborious. More effort is required before and after attribute identification. Before, more research must be performed in order to consider all relevant attributes. Because the granularity is high, the attributes do not allow room for interpretation that can be used later for adding newly discovered sub-attributes. All attributes must be very clear from the beginning. Afterwards, the data collection and calculations are more complex because more attributes lead to a more extensive process. In contrast to generic attributes, specific attributes raise the transparency and understandability. In particular, if a team of decision makers performs the evaluation, high differences in the interpretation of the chosen attributes can be prevented.

A distinction of attributes in **exclusion and comparison** attributes should always be considered. The standard decision making procedure includes just comparison attributes. Using exclusion attributes is an additional preliminary step before the alternatives are actually compared. By using this step, the decision maker can prevent the substitutability of attributes. If only comparison attributes are used, one alternative can get a good overall score without fulfilling certain important attributes. The bad sub scores regarding these attributes can be compensated by very good sub scores regarding other attributes. In conclusion, the alternative with the best overall score might not fulfill certain attributes that are seen as crucial. Therefore, crucial attributes that should be fulfilled by the alternatives in any case should be used as exclusion attributes. Only alternatives that fulfill the exclusion attributes are taken into account within the second step, the actual comparison of alternatives. Thus, alternatives that do not fulfill the exclusion attributes are filtered out. Examples for exclusion attributes can be the compatibility, language of user interfaces, and delivery time. With these exclusion attributes, a company can exclude incompatible alternatives that do not support the employees' native language and are not available in the short term.

Case Study

*The PSP used **ISO 25010** in order to identify attributes that can be used for evaluating the product quality and quality in use. Every main-attribute from the standard was analyzed regarding the relevance for the company's decision making. Sub-attributes were not considered. As a result, it had been clarified for every single attribute if the attribute was relevant and if the attribute was supposed to be used as an exclusion or comparison attribute. The decision maker decided to choose generic attributes because he performed the process solely so that problems in understanding and interpretation were not expected. Besides, he did not have enough resources and prior knowledge for considering and defining all relevant sub-attributes at the beginning. For the attributes in **product quality**, the following had been found:*

- ***Functional suitability:** The function of encryption with a secure algorithm had to be delivered by the software. Therefore, the attribute was used as an exclusion attribute.*

- ***Performance efficiency:*** *Because only particular files had to be encrypted, the amount of needed resources was secondary. The attribute was not used here.*
- ***Compatibility:*** *The compatibility was important regarding the workstations and notebooks in the accounting department. This attribute was defined as an exclusion attribute because if the compatibility had not been given, the software would have been unusable.*
- ***Usability:*** *Although the times when the company expected to use the software were few, this attribute was relevant. If the usability of the software had been extremely bad, the users would have tried to avoid using the software. Then, the sensitive data would have not been encrypted. The attribute was used as a comparison attribute.*
- ***Reliability:*** *The reliability was not important because the encryption software were not required to be available and error-free at all times. If the software had not been available, the encryption task would have been repeated later. If the software had produced errors occasionally, the user would have started the task again. Therefore, the attribute was not used here.*
- ***Security:*** *This attribute was important because the security of the encrypted data had to be ensured. Unauthorized users had to be prevented from decrypting the cypher text. A strong algorithm and key were needed. The decision maker decided to use this attribute as an exclusion attribute so that the security was mandatory.*
- ***Maintainability:*** *The software was supposed to handle specific tasks—the encryption and decryption of files. No changes in the functioning of the software were expected. Besides, the algorithm that was used by the software was assumed being secure for many years. Therefore, maintenance was not seen as important here, and the attribute was not used.*
- ***Portability:*** *The normal operation of the PSP did not include the transfer of the encrypted files to other internal or external devices. Therefore, the portability was not relevant here, and the attribute was not used.*

For the attributes that address the **quality in use**, *the following had been found:*

- ***Effectiveness:*** *The accuracy and completeness of the software had already been considered under the attribute functional suitability. In the context of the PSP, no further functions had to be included. Therefore, the attribute was not used.*
- ***Efficiency:*** *Performance efficiency, which is the more general attribute, had not been included. Therefore, the efficiency in the specific context of usage was also irrelevant.*
- ***Satisfaction:*** *The satisfaction of the user while using the software had been seen as important regarding the intensity of which the user actually used the software. Therefore, the attribute was used for comparison.*
- ***Freedom from risk:*** *The mitigation of risks was an important attribute for the evaluation. However, the attributes for the economic evaluation were also aimed to consider this aspect. Therefore, the attribute was irrelevant at this point.*

- ***Context coverage:*** *The software was intended only for encryption and decryption of files. Further usage contexts or other areas of application were not taken into account. Therefore, the attribute was not used.*

The ***economic evaluation*** *was based on the following attributes, which addressed the safeguard costs, the risk mitigation, and an overall dynamic indicator that combined costs and benefits. The used attributes allowed being broken down to further sub-attributes, e.g. software and infrastructure costs. However, in the actual case with not very complex solutions, a too detailed breakdown of the attributes would have led to unnecessary efforts within the decision making.*

- *The* ***initial investment costs*** *were used as a comparison attribute. They included expenses regarding hardware, software, infrastructure, labor (e.g. trainings) and organizational changes.*
- *The* ***operation costs*** *included costs for administration, support and changes. This attribute was used for comparison.*
- *The* ***risk mitigation*** *was measured with the reduction in expected losses. These losses were used as a comparison attribute, too.*
- *The* ***net present value*** *(NPV) was used to combine the costs and benefits while taking into account different payment flows. The inflows and outflows were correlated to the present day. The NPV was used for comparison, too. The NPV covered the lifetime of a particular safeguard. In order to make different safeguards fully comparable, their lifetimes were supposed to be defined with the same length if possible.*

The ***value ranges*** *for the attributes usability and satisfaction had been set to {very low; low; middle; high; very high}. The value ranges for the attributes initial investment costs, operation costs, risk mitigation, and NPV had not yet been determined at this time because they were assumed to depend on the received information about the alternatives. For example, the maximum value for the operation costs was set according to the alternative with the highest operation costs.*

The ***scores*** *for every attribute were set to the range from zero to four. For the attributes usability and satisfaction, zero meant very low and four meant very high with equal distances between the other values. For the attributes initial investment costs, operation costs, risk mitigation and NPV, the lowest identified value for each attribute was represented by the score zero and the highest one by the score four. Intermediate values were assigned to a corresponding score.*

For the ***exclusion attributes*** *functional suitability, compatibility and security, value ranges were just {yes; no}. Scores were irrelevant. It only had to be determined whether an alternative fulfilled the requirements regarding an exclusion attribute. The requirement regarding functional suitability was that file encryption and decryption were provided. The compatibility requirement was fulfilled only by the solutions that supported the hardware and software in the accounting department. Regarding security, an adequate encryption algorithm and key handling had to be supported.*

6.6 Attribute Evaluation

5.1 The identified attributes have been evaluated.

The attribute evaluation will be relevant if the comparison attributes are not all equally **important** in the decision making. In most cases, some attributes are more important than others are. For example, the NPV is mostly more important than a single cost attribute because the NPV combines all payment flows within one indicator. The decision maker can assign individual weights to every comparison attribute. An attribute with a high weight is considered more influential than an attribute with a low weight.

The method of **weight assignment** depends on the decision making technique.

- When using **SAW**, the weights are individually assigned to each attribute. Next, the weights are normed so that their sum is 100 %.
- When using **AHP**, the attributes are compared in pairs so that it can be determined if some attributes are more important than others are. If a certain attribute is more important than another one is, the decision maker can use a suitable value to specify the difference between the attributes regarding their importance. The resulting attribute weights are normed in AHP, too.

The weight assignment strongly depends on the **individual preferences** of the decision maker's company. This step is very vulnerable to manipulation. If the decision maker has any conflict of interests, he can easily adjust the attribute evaluation so that his personal favorite alternative will get the first place within the subsequent ranking. Therefore, an objective and responsible execution of this step is crucial for the quality of the decision making results.

Manipulation within the decision making process is a fraudulent activity. Reasons for fraud can be derived from the **fraud triangle** (Nimwegen 2009, pp. 18 ff.), which is visualized in Fig. 6.16.

- **Motivation** is based on a need that a person tries to satisfy with fraud. On the one hand, he might try to avoid negative consequences. For example, he might

Fig. 6.16 Fraud triangle

be under pressure to fulfill high expectations and failure might be connected to disciplinary penalties. On the other hand, he might desire positive consequences, which are based on incentives. For example, he might try to achieve appreciation or a financial award. The fraudulent activity is seen as reasonable in order to meet the expectations or the requirements for an incentive. The motivation can also be amplified by external conditions, e.g. financial problems, or internal factors, e.g. desire for recognition. Although fraud motivation cannot be controlled by the company completely, some aspects should be considered, e.g. background checks for decision makers, and conflict-free incentives.
- A person that considers fraud seeks **justification** beforehand. Justification for fraud is mostly based on a wrong sense of justice or on a denial of laws or responsibilities. The person thinks that his acting is actually accepted, justifiable or admissible. The characteristics of justification are related to the position and attitude of the person and loosely connected to the specifics of the fraudulent activity. A company can influence the sense for justice by communicating appropriate expectations and values.
- **Opportunity** is the chance to perform a fraudulent activity unnoticed with a low risk that it would be discovered afterwards. In order to assess the situation properly, a person must have knowledge about internal processes and circumstances within the company. Among other things, he must know how he can take advantage within his scope of action. Besides, technical knowledge is important for discovering fraud opportunities. With the help of control measures, fraud opportunities can be reduced and fraudulent activities can be discovered and traced properly. Skilled fraudsters often focus on weaknesses in control measures as entry points for fraud.

Case Study

For both decision techniques—the SAW and AHP, the PSP conducted the evaluation of the comparison attributes.

While using the ***SAW****, the attributes were evaluated separately by assigning a value that represented the importance of the attribute regarding the decision making.*

- ***Usability*** *was important in order to facilitate the understanding and efficient usage of the solution by the users. Usability was influencing the acceptance by the users. Safeguards that were hard to use, e.g. because of complex menus, were expected to be hardly accepted and possibly avoided by the users. In result, sensitive data would not have been encrypted. The importance value for usability was 10 points.*
- ***Satisfaction*** *was seen as a condition that can be achieved by the user if he is actually satisfied with the functions and the operation of the safeguard. Satisfaction also influences the acceptance. A low satisfaction was expected to lead to a willful neglecting of the safeguard and related security requirements. However, a safeguard was seen as primarily focused on security. It put business*

functionality, which can lead to high user satisfaction, in the background. Therefore, the satisfaction got a value of 4 points.

- *The* ***initial investment costs*** *were an important economic factor. They showed how much liquid funds were needed in order to handle the implementation of the safeguard. Although the investment costs were also included in the NPV, a separate consideration was helpful for matching the investment costs to the funds that were available at most. This attribute got 5 points.*
- *The* ***operation costs*** *were also economically relevant. Because these costs had to be covered steadily, a separate consideration was helpful for the financial planning. These costs were also included in the calculation of the NPV. Therefore, the attribute was as important as the previous one and got 5 points.*
- *The* ***risk mitigation*** *was the most important reason for selecting a safeguard. Therefore, it was very important. By addressing the reduction in expected losses, it also influenced the payment flows during the investment lifecycle. Because the NPV included all payment flows, the risk mitigation was covered by this attribute, too. Overall, the risk mitigation got 15 points.*
- *The* ***net present value*** *(NPV) was an accumulation of all payment flows starting at the initial planning and ending at the termination of the safeguard. By expressing the security impact financially, it also covered the primary reason for selecting a safeguard. Therefore, this attribute was most important from the economical view and got 20 points. However, it did not substitute other economic attributes. A separate consideration of payment flows with certain characteristics, e.g. with an early payment date, was helpful for the financial planning of the company.*

In order to determine the attribute weights, the values of importance had to be ***normalized*** *so that their sum was 100 %. Therefore, every value was divided by the sum of the initial importance values, i.e. 59 (Due to the rounding, the percentages in* Table 6.3 *summed up to 99 %).*

AHP *required a different approach for determining the weights of the attributes. With pairwise comparisons, the decision maker had to decide which of two attributes was more or less important than the other one was. Besides, it was possible to find the attributes as equally important to each other. An evaluation matrix had to be completed with the results from the pairwise comparisons. At first, all values along the main diagonal were set to one. Next, the actual comparisons had to be conducted for all values above the main diagonal in the matrix. Afterwards, the*

Table 6.3 Attribute evaluation with SAW

Attribute	Importance	Weight (normalized) (%)
Usability	10	17
Satisfaction	4	7
Initial investment	5	8
Operation costs	5	8
Risk mitigation	15	25
NPV	20	34

values below the main diagonal were set to the reciprocal values of the values that were above the main diagonal.

The ***pairwise comparisons*** *by the PSP were based on the following considerations:*

- ***Usability*** *was strongly more important (5) than* ***satisfaction*** *because usability was related to an efficient usage and the acceptance by the users, while satisfaction was only loosely related to the acceptance.*
- ***Usability*** *was strongly more important (5) than the* ***initial investment*** *because problems in usage or missing acceptance could make the safeguard fail, while the initial investment was only one of multiple economic factors.*
- ***Usability*** *was strongly more important (5) than the* ***operation costs*** *because usability was related to an efficient usage and the acceptance by the users, while the operation costs were only one of multiple economic factors.*
- ***Usability*** *was moderately less important (1/3) than the* ***risk mitigation****. Usability was important in order to avoid problems in the context of usage, but the risk mitigation was the primary reason for implementing a safeguard.*
- ***Usability*** *was strongly less important (1/5) than the* ***NPV****. Although usability could be crucial from the perspective of usage, the NPV combined all economic factors, including the risk mitigation.*
- ***Satisfaction*** *is slightly less important (1/2) than the* ***initial investment****, in other words the importance is between equally and moderately less important. Satisfaction is a small factor for a safeguard. In contrast, the economic consideration is more important, even if only one special factor like the initial investment is considered.*
- ***Satisfaction*** *is slightly less important (1/2) than the* ***operation costs****. While satisfaction is only loosely related to the acceptance, and, thereby, could influence the success of the safeguard, the operating costs are an economic factor, which could be important but must be seen in context with other factors.*
- ***Satisfaction*** *was very strongly less important (1/7) than the* ***risk mitigation****. Although satisfaction could influence the success of the safeguard, the risk mitigation was much more important because it was the main reason for safeguard selection.*
- ***Satisfaction*** *was extremely less important (1/9) than the* ***NPV****. As described above, satisfaction could influence the success. In contrast, the NPV combined all economic factors, including the risk mitigation, and was the most important attribute.*
- ***Initial investment*** *and the* ***operation costs*** *were equally important (1) because both attributes were economic factors that were supposed to be considered within the decision making.*
- ***Initial investment*** *was very strongly less important (1/7) than the* ***risk mitigation****. While initial investment could be an important economic factor, the risk mitigation was the main reason for a safeguard and, thereby, much more important.*

- ***Initial investment costs*** *were extremely less important (1/9) than the* ***NPV****. Initial investment costs could be an important economic factor, but the NPV combined all economic factors and was, therefore, the most important attribute.*
- ***Operation costs*** *were very strongly less important (1/7) than the* ***risk mitigation****. The operation costs were a single economic factor while the risk mitigation was essential for the safeguard selection.*
- ***Operation costs*** *were extremely less important (1/9) than the* ***NPV****. The operating costs were not be as important as the NPV, because the NPV combined all economic factors, including operating costs.*
- ***Risk mitigation*** *was moderately less important (1/3) than the* ***NPV****. Although the risk mitigation was fundamental for the safeguard selection, only cost-efficient safeguards were supposed to be considered. In conclusion, the NPV was more important.*

In accordance to the possible ***evaluation results*** *from* Table 5.1 *in* Sect. 5.3, *the PSP expressed the results from the pairwise comparisons of the attributes with the values in* Table 6.4. *In addition, the sum of every column was calculated in order to allow the subsequent normalization.*

The ***normalization*** *of the matrix was performed by dividing every value with its column sum, as shown in* Table 6.5.

Next, the line sums of the normalized evaluation matrix from Table 6.5 *were calculated. From these line sums, which are shown in* Table 6.6, *the* ***impacts*** *were calculated by dividing the line sums by the number of attributes. The impacts were expressed in percentage. Their sum was approximately 100 % because they were already normalized. Due to the rounding of the calculated values, the actual sum was 101 %. The impacts were used as weights within the alternative evaluation.*

The results were ***approximations*** *that were used for completing the decision making. However, they were not as precise as results from dedicated AHP*

Table 6.4 Attribute comparison with AHP

	Usability	Satisfaction	Initial investment	Operation costs	Risk mitigation	NPV
Usability	1	5	5	5	1/3	1/5
Satisfaction	1/5	1	1/2	1/2	1/7	1/9
Initial investment	1/5	2	1	1	1/7	1/9
Operation costs	1/5	2	1	1	1/7	1/9
Risk mitigation	3	7	7	7	1	1/3
NPV	5	9	9	9	3	1
Sum	9.6	26	23.5	23.5	4.76	1.87

Table 6.5 Normalized evaluation matrix

	Usability	Satisfaction	Initial investment	Operation costs	Risk mitigation	NPV
Usability	0.10	0.19	0.21	0.21	0.07	0.11
Satisfaction	0.02	0.04	0.02	0.02	0.03	0.06
Initial investment	0.02	0.08	0.04	0.04	0.03	0.06
Operation costs	0.02	0.08	0.04	0.04	0.03	0.06
Risk mitigation	0.31	0.27	0.30	0.30	0.21	0.18
NPV	0.52	0.35	0.38	0.38	0.63	0.54

Table 6.6 Attribute prioritization with AHP

Attribute	Line sum from Table 6.5	Impact (normalized) (%)
Usability	0.89	15
Satisfaction	0.19	3
Initial investment	0.27	5
Operation costs	0.27	5
Risk mitigation	1.57	26
NPV	2.80	47

software, which would have provided iterative calculations. Besides, a consistency check that also would have been provided by AHP software would have helped to assure the quality of the results from the attribute evaluation.

6.7 Alternative Identification

6.1 Alternatives have been identified after collecting relevant knowledge.

The alternative identification is an essential step that should not be rushed through. Only alternatives that have been identified within this step can be considered during the subsequent steps. Therefore, a diligent **market analysis** should be performed. This market analysis can be based on external knowledge and own research. Thereby, not only a general overview about possible solutions but also as much relevant information as possible should be gathered in order to facilitate the subsequent alternative evaluation.

By acquiring **external knowledge**, the decision maker can get wide and well-founded knowledge in a short time. Besides, no additional staff have to be allocated for the market analysis. The knowledge has already been or will be collected and organized by external consultants. The drawbacks of this type of knowledge acquisition are the high costs that will be charged by consultants or information providers. The acquisition of external knowledge can be performed with the following approaches:

- Engaging **external consultants** is the easiest way to receive the desired knowledge. At the same time, it is the most expensive way. Consultants can be instructed to collect knowledge that matches completely to the expectations and underlying conditions of the company that plans to implement the safeguard. Many consultant companies provide services around decision making regularly. Often, the consultants have much experience and skills that can be used to perform an efficient analysis. Besides, the subsequent steps of the decision making can be performed by the consultants, too. After communicating the expectations and conditions, the consultants can be instructed to perform all relevant steps until a ranking of adequate safeguards can be provided to the customer.
- **Expert studies** can provide a good overview about cybersecurity solutions. Because these studies are independent from vendors, they can include a critical comparison without biases. Purchasing expert studies can even be faster than engaging consultants, but it is rare that a study exists that matches exactly the expectations of the company. Mostly, the available studies are based on scenarios or general questions. The specifics of the company are not considered. Therefore, an expert study can be a good start. However, the knowledge that can be gathered from the study would have to be adapted to the individual expectations and conditions of the company. Because most studies are sold to multiple customers, they are often less expensive than an individual assignment to external consultants.
- Attending **fairs, exhibitions or conferences** can be very useful if the decision maker has already created an overview about possible solutions. In general, many vendors participate here. They provide information, answer questions, and perform live demonstrations. The decision maker can ask specific details about the solutions and test the actual usage. However, fairs, exhibitions or conferences are hold at fixed dates so that the decision maker might not be able to attend within a tight schedule.

In contrast to the acquisition of external knowledge, **own research** is much more time-consuming and laboriously. Especially if the factors to be considered are comprehensive and the existing knowledge is low, the research can require extensive resources. Relevant information can be found in multiple places, but the unstructured and heterogeneous presentation makes it difficult to extract and understand the needed information. The effort that is needed to collect and unify the available information should not be underestimated. Good sources for information when conducting own research are journals and websites:

- In **journals**, various reviews can be found. Because they are independent from vendors, they can be very helpful. Hardware or software products are compared critically and evaluated based on multiple attributes. Although these attributes mostly do not match the individual preferences and conditions of the company, these reviews include valuable information and can be a basis for further individual evaluation. While using journals, it is important to ensure that they are up to date. New product versions that have been released after a certain review can include new functions and improvements. Besides, reports about single products can be useful. For example, new major releases or completely new products can be in focus here. Journal articles deliver much information about different products and their functionality. This information must be adapted to the company in order to allow a well-founded alternative identification and evaluation.
- **Websites** can also include valuable details about relevant products. However, because of the different structures of websites, finding comparable information on multiple websites can be very time-consuming. In general, websites can be distinguished in vendor websites and independent websites:
- **Vendor websites** will be most useful if the decision maker has already created an overview about relevant products. He can use the information from these websites in order to get more details about the products, i.e. functionalities and technical specifications. Besides, free test or demonstration versions, and product manuals are often available. Contact details on the websites allow the decision maker to address open questions. Sometimes, the vendor also lists references on his website. The number of references and the reputation of the referenced companies can be important indicators for the product and support quality. A communication with referenced companies or others that use relevant products can also lead to helpful insights into the products.
- **Independent websites** include articles from journalists and professional authors, who mostly publish unbiased descriptions, reviews and comparisons of products. Among other information, some websites provide listings of products that address specific security needs, e.g. antivirus software. Therefore, these kind of websites cannot only be used for a first overview of relevant products but also for a more detailed analysis of the products. Although the independence from product vendors implies a high objectivity, the content quality can vary strongly. Because the content quality of a particular website can be unclear for the decision maker, he should not rely on only one single article from an unknown author.

In the previous chapter, the possibility of fraud in the decision making process has been described with the fraud triangle. Besides fraud in the form of manipulation by the decision maker, fraud can also originate from **vendors**. Especially information that has been particularly prepared by the vendor for the decision making should be questioned. The higher the scope of the cybersecurity investment and the potential order volume from the company are, the higher is the risk that the vendor might have manipulated the information in order to outrank competitors.

Case Study

Based on the ***preliminary information*** *that has been described in* Sect. 6.4.1, *products for encryption had to be identified. In addition, the PSP decided to focus on products for file encryption. In case of an attack, file encryption provided higher security against logical access on running systems. In contrast, hard drive encryption would have only protected against hackers that tried to steal a system or a hard drive.*

The PSP decided to collect all relevant information about adequate alternatives with ***own research****. The decision maker focused on a combination of vendor websites and independent websites for his research. Thereby, the following alternatives including relevant information had been collected:*

- ***Alpha*** *was a dedicated file encryption tool, which was available for Windows 7, 8, 10 as well as OS X, and Linux. For encryption, it used the Advanced Encryption Standard (AES) with 128-bit keys. It included a command line and a graphical interface. The tool also offered additional functions in form of a file shredder and password generator. The cost for an unlimited license per computer was $99.95 ($1999 for 20 computers). The tool was accompanied by FAQs, online manuals and tutorials. In addition, the vendor provided a toll-free technical support hotline. For the initial installation, $12,000 had been calculated (12 person-days with $1000 each). This amount covered the purchasing (1 person-day), packaging (2 person-days), documentation (1 person-day), testing (2 person-days), rollout (5 person-days) and training (1 person-day). The initial investment costs summed up to $13,999. If credit card data had been misused after it had been compromised at the PSP, there normally would have been no direct damages for the PSP because most fraudulent transactions would have been canceled. Moreover, the reputation of the company probably would have been damaged. The PSP estimated that one compromised credit card would have led to a revenue loss of $500. Assuming that in total 500 cards were processed over a year, the expected loss without encryption would have been $25,000. Under consideration of the characteristics of the encryption tool, the PSP assumed that 18 of 20 employees would have used this tool. Therefore, the risk mitigation were 90 % of $25,000, in other words $22,500. The NPV had been calculated with the formula from* Sect. 4.1.2.1:

$$NPV = \sum_{t=1}^{n} (R_t \times d_t - T_t \times d_t) - T_i + L_n \times d_n$$

The PSP used a discounting interest rate (i) of 2 %. As the revenue, the yearly risk mitigation, in other words the reduction in expected losses, had been used. Like the risk mitigation, the operation costs were equally distributed over 5 years. In the case of Alpha, low operation costs of $625 (1 h per year) were *expected because support, monitoring, and change management were fully covered by the already existing processes in the company. Besides, the support hotline were used for problems that are more complicated. The initial investment costs were given and the liquidation yield was set to \$0. In result, the NPV was calculated with the following numbers (Intermediate values had been calculated with two decimal places):*

$$d_1 = \left(\frac{1}{1+0.02}\right)^1 = 0.98, d_2 = \left(\frac{1}{1+0.02}\right)^2 = 0.96, d_3 = \left(\frac{1}{1+0.02}\right)^3 = 0.94,$$
$$d_4 = \left(\frac{1}{1+0.02}\right)^4 = 0.92, d_5 = \left(\frac{1}{1+0.02}\right)^5 = 0.91$$
$$R_1 = R_2 = R_3 = R_4 = R_5 = \$4500$$
$$T_1 = T_2 = T_3 = T_4 = T_5 = \$125$$
$$T_i = \$13{,}999$$
$$L_n = \$0$$

The calculation for Alpha resulted in a NPV of \$6607 (rounded).

- ***Beta** was another dedicated file encryption tool. It was executable without installation, and useable under Windows 7 and 8. For encryption, it used Blowfish with 128-bit keys. The tool was simple to use and easy to understand, but it was lacking a good-looking interface. It did not offer any additional functions. The license was priced at \$26, for 20 computers \$520. In contrast to Alpha, the packaging needed just 1 person-day and the training just 0.5 person-days. In sum, \$11,020 (10.5 person-days or \$10,500 plus \$520) were needed for covering the initial investment costs. The technical support hotline was charged with \$0.25 per minute. Assuming that a telephone support of 10 min per week over 5 years would have been necessary, the total operation costs were \$650. With this encryption tool, the PSP expected a use by 80 % of the employees. This resulted in a risk mitigation of \$20,000. The NPV had been calculated in the same way as above. In the case of Beta and the other alternatives, the liquidation yield was also set to \$0 because the software was free to use or the PSP did not expect to gain a notable yield by selling the software licenses. Only the following variables had to be changed:*

$$R_1 = R_2 = R_3 = R_4 = R_5 = \$4000$$
$$T_1 = T_2 = T_3 = T_4 = T_5 = \$130$$
$$T_i = \$11{,}020$$

The calculation for Beta resulted in a NPV of \$7208 (rounded).

- ***Gamma*** *was a free, open source encryption tool that was GNU GPL-licensed. This license model allows everybody to run, study, share, and modify the software. This tool was available for Windows 7, 8, 10 as well as OS X and Linux. It used AES with 256-bit keys. It provided a very convenient file handling: Files could be decrypted or kept encrypted while they were in use. When they were modified or closed, they were automatically re-encrypted. Out-of-the-box, no additional functions were provided, but due to the openness of the source code, additional functions could be built in by internal developers. The tool caused no license costs. Because of the open source code, it was possible to expand the testing to the source code. Especially, efforts for rollout and documentation were reduced. 5.5 person-days or $5500 were needed for covering the initial investment costs, in particular 0 for purchasing, 1 for packaging, 3 for testing, 0.5 for documentation, 0.5 for rollout and 0.5 for training. For support and changes, internal work effort had been estimated with operation costs of $2167 per year or $10,835 over 5 years (20 min per week). With this highly customizable tool, the PSP expected a use by 85 % of the employees. This resulted in a risk mitigation of $21,250. The NPV had been calculated in the same way as above. Only the following variables had to be changed:*

$$R_1 = R_2 = R_3 = R_4 = R_5 = \$4250$$
$$T_1 = T_2 = T_3 = T_4 = T_5 = \$2167$$
$$T_i = \$5500$$

The calculation for Gamma resulted in a NPV of $4311 (rounded).

- ***Delta*** *was primarily a compression tool, but it came with an integrated encryption algorithm. It was freeware and runnable on Windows 7, 8 and 10 as well as OS X, and Linux. It used AES with 128-bit keys. It was very lightweight with less than 1 MB file size of the tool. It integrated well into the file manager menus of the operating systems. It also provided an own user interface, which was, however, very simple. As freeware, no license costs were charged. This tool was already in use at the PSP so that no installation was needed. Only effort of 2.5 person-days or initial investment costs of $2500 were needed for additional documentation (0.5 person-days), testing (1 person-day) and training (1 person-day) regarding the encryption functions. The PSP planned to perform the support internally. Due to low documentation, the internal work effort had been estimated with operation costs of $3250 per year or $16,250 over 5 years (30 min per week or 16.25 person-days). With this encryption tool, which was executable from the file manager, the PSP expected also a use by 85 % of the employees. This resulted in a risk mitigation of $21,250. The NPV had been calculated in the same way as above. Only the following variables had to be changed:*

$$R_1 = R_2 = R_3 = R_4 = R_5 = \$4250$$
$$T_1 = T_2 = T_3 = T_4 = T_5 = \$3250$$
$$T_i = \$2500$$

The calculation for Gamma resulted in a NPV of $2210.

6.8 Alternative Evaluation

7.1 The identified alternatives have been evaluated.

In this step, the **information** that has already been collected can be used for evaluating the identified alternatives regarding the relevant attributes. After the evaluation, the results are aggregated with the weights, which have been determined during the attribute evaluation in Sect. 6.6.

In case that not enough information is available for evaluating every alternative regarding every attribute, the decision maker should select an appropriate approach that makes alternatives with **missing information** comparable to other alternatives. As described in Sect. 4.1, three different approaches can be used in these situations: the optimistic, pessimistic and mean approach. Based on the risk tolerance of the company, the decision maker can select the approach that matches the decision risks that are acceptable to the company. The optimistic approach can lead to overrated alternatives, the pessimistic approach to underrated ones, and the mean approach to both ones. If the pessimistic approach is chosen, the alternatives with missing information will rather be underestimated and placed further down in the ranking. Thereby, the best alternative in the ranking will be rarely accompanied by negative surprises when discovering unclear characteristics of the alternative during the practical use.

The distinction between **exclusion and comparison** attributes is a reasonable step that fulfills a common evaluation requirement: Alternatives with certain characteristics that are inacceptable for the decision maker's company shall be sorted out reliably. By using exclusion attributes, inacceptable characteristics can be defined and used as a filter. Every alternative must be analyzed regarding these attributes. Thereby, inappropriate alternatives can be identified and sorted out easily. Otherwise, these inacceptable characteristics would have to be evaluated with comparison attributes. Then, they might be compensated with other characteristics so that the particular alternative would not be sorted out. Actually, an alternative with inacceptable characteristics might even reach a high position in the final ranking.

The evaluation depends on the decision maker. Although a structured process is used, **subjectivity** can never be fully eliminated. The decision maker has his own experiences and attitudes that constantly influence his decisions consciously or unconsciously. In general, it should be avoided that the decision maker has a bias towards single alternatives that is not based on objective reasons. Another problem can be the **response biases**, which are systematic deviations of the evaluation results. These biases are caused by the reaction of the decision maker. Common forms of response biases are:

- **Consistency bias**: Similar information about alternatives will also be evaluated similarly, even if the alternatives are actually very different.
- **Recall bias**: Information that has been collected and analyzed in the past, e.g. a few days or weeks before the evaluation, might be evaluated more positive or negative. In the memory of the decision maker, the information is biased.
- **Recency effect**: Information that has been collected recently have a greater weight than information that has been collected a longer time ago. This is caused by the short-term memory of the decision maker, which often has a stronger effect on the evaluation than his long-term memory.
- **Hindsight bias**: The memory of the decision maker is systematically inaccurate. Information that the decision maker analyzed in the past is not correctly recalled from his memory.
- **Error of central tendency**: This tendency of a decision maker is shown by his personal preference to select middle values on the evaluation scales. Thereby, the actual variance in the evaluation results is limited. Therefore, the results will not provide as much information as results that use the full variance will do.
- **Error of extreme tendency**: Similar to the error of central tendency, the decision maker prefers only certain values on the evaluation scales. In this case, he focusses on extrema instead of middle values. He uses only very good or very bad evaluation values. This tendency also limits the variance in the evaluation results and, thereby, reduces their information value.

Usually, it is very difficult to avoid subjectivity and biases of a single decision maker. However, by setting up a **team** of decision makers with different backgrounds, the impacts of the subjectivity and biases of a single decision maker can be reduced.

Another crucial aspect within the alternative evaluation is the prevention and handling of **conflicts of interests**. They will occur if the decision maker jeopardizes the primary interests of his company by considering personal interests within the alternative evaluation. Reasons for conflicts of interests are, among other things:

- A vendor delivers **voluntary contributions, gifts or donations** to the decision maker.
- The vendor does already have a **business relation** to the decision maker. For example, the decision maker might hold shares of the vendor's company.
- The decision maker has a **personal relation** to particular representatives or employees from the vendor.

In order to avoid conflicts of interests, the following **measures** can be implemented:

- The decision maker can be bound to **ethical standards**, which include rules for handling and disclosing potential conflicts of interests.
- The decision making process can be **controlled**, e.g. by implementing quality checks, which should also include the discovery of conflicts of interests.
- Dedicated **trainings** can be provided in order to make rules and expectations regarding conflicts of interests transparent to the decision maker.

If a conflict of interests cannot be avoided, it must be **disclosed** to the sponsor of the cybersecurity investment. Based on detailed information, the sponsor can decide if the conflict of interests can be accepted or if certain countermeasures, e.g. the replacement of the decision maker, have to be implemented.

The result of the alternative evaluation is a full **ranking** of all alternatives regarding their suitability to the expectations and needs of the company. At the top of the ranking, at least on alternative can be found that is more adequate than all other considered alternatives. This ranking is the basis for the actual alternative selection in the next step of the process.

Another point that can be considered before the ranking will be used further is the stability of the evaluation results in the case that minor adjustments are conducted. By performing a **sensitivity analysis**, the consequences of varying single attributes or weights can be analyzed.

6.8.1 Exclusion Attributes Analysis

7.2 The identified alternatives have been evaluated with exclusion attributes.

The exclusion attributes are used to **filter** the identified alternatives so that fundamentally unsuitable alternatives can be found and excluded early. On the one hand, the effort for the subsequent steps can be reduced because no more evaluations are needed for the excluded alternatives. On the other hand, the risk that the finally selected alternative might be actually unsuitable can be eliminated. Without exclusion attributes, low sub scores for single attributes might be compensated by high sub scores for other attributes. Therefore, it would be difficult to ensure that actually unsuitable alternatives will not have high overall scores and appear on high positions in the final ranking.

Attributes that can be crucial for the **suitability** of the alternatives are related to, among other things, the quality, cost or time aspects of the alternatives:

- **Quality aspects** can play an important role for the company if certain limitations or conditions regarding the selected alternative have to be avoided. For example, if the compatibility requirements are not fulfilled, an alternative can actually be unusable. Therefore, its acquisition would have no benefit for the company. Besides, particular functions can be seen as necessary. For example, if the company searches an antivirus software, alternatives that do not offer full system scans or real time protection can be seen as unsuitable.

- **Costs aspects** must be seen in context to the financial resources of the company. If the company can invest at most $10,000 for a new safeguard, every alternative that is more expensive should be excluded. The investment costs are a good example for an attribute that can be used as both an exclusion and comparison attribute. For the exclusion, it will only be checked if an alternative exceeds a certain threshold, e.g. $10,000. For the comparison, the attribute will be used to assign an evaluation score for alternatives that cause investment costs lower than the threshold value. Thus, alternatives with different investment costs can be compared.
- **Time aspects** can be significant in cybersecurity, too. If high risks have been identified, the solution for mitigating or eliminating these risks will mostly have to be available as fast as possible. Solutions that will only be available after a long waiting time can lead to inacceptable risks, which would endanger the whole company. The company can use the exclusion attributes for limiting the considered alternatives to those that are available fast enough. For example, solutions with a release date in the distant future can be excluded. Besides, individually developed solutions can be filtered according to their anticipated development time. In addition, response times from the technical support of the vendor in case of problems and the processing times for the implementation of changes can be important aspects, too.

Case Study

The decision maker at the PSP had collected sufficient information to evaluate the alternatives regarding the specified exclusion attributes. Any alternative that did not fulfill at least one exclusion attribute was excluded from the further evaluations. During the evaluation, the following statements had been found:

- ***Functional suitability:*** *All alternatives provided file encryption and decryption. None of the identified alternatives was fundamentally unsuitable for securing sensitive files. Therefore, this attribute had been fulfilled by all alternatives.*
- ***Compatibility:*** *The alternatives had to be usable on every workstation and notebook in the accounting department. Since these computers had been deployed with mostly Windows 7 and rarely Windows 10, these two operating systems had to be supported by the alternatives. Although Windows 10 was only used on two pilot systems for gathering first user experiences in the company, it was supposed to replace Windows 7 in the long term. In this case, the compatibility to Windows 10 will be crucial. All alternatives supported Windows 7, but only Alpha, Gamma and Delta supported Windows 10. Therefore, Beta did not fulfill this attribute.*
- ***Security:*** *The PSP decided to accept only encryption algorithms that were approved by NIST (Barker* et al. *2012, p. 36). Alpha, Gamma and Delta used AES with at least 128-bit keys. Beta used Blowfish with 128-bit keys. AES was*

Table 6.7 Alternative evaluation with exclusion attributes

Attributes	Alternatives			
	Alpha	Beta	Gamma	Delta
Functional suitability	Yes	Yes	Yes	Yes
Compatibility	Yes	No	Yes	Yes
Security	Yes	No	Yes	Yes
Exclusion	**No**	**Yes**	**No**	**No**

approved by NITS, but Blowfish was not. Besides, AES had a 128-bit block size, but Blowfish had only a 64-bit block size. The block size was also an important security factor, because the smaller the block size was, the higher was the probability of a repeated block in the cipher text. Generally, repeated blocks are very helpful in cryptanalysis. In conclusion, only Alpha, Gamma and Delta fulfilled the attribute, but Beta did not (Table 6.7).

Only the alternatives that fulfilled the exclusion attributes completely were considered in the subsequent steps of the decision making process. Alternatives that did not fulfill at least one attribute had been excluded. Particularly, Alpha, Gamma and Delta had been accepted for further consideration, and Beta had been excluded.

6.8.2 Comparison Attributes Analysis

7.3 The identified alternatives have been evaluated with comparison attributes.

After excluding alternatives that have been found fundamentally unsuitable, the remaining alternatives have to be **compared**. Therefore, an overall score has to be assigned to every alternative. This overall score is based on the sum of sub scores for single evaluations that are based on the comparison attributes.

As described in Sects. 5.2 and 5.3, the use of comparison attributes can be accompanied by possible **disadvantages** in both techniques—the SAW and AHP:

- **Dependencies** between attributes that can lead to the over- or undervaluation of single alternatives.
- **Manipulation** during the evaluation of the alternatives can lead to falsified results.
- **Substitutability** of the attributes can lead to a compensation of very high or very low sub scores for single attributes. Although the use of exclusion attributes can reduce the substitutability, it cannot be avoided completely. Otherwise, only exclusion attributes have to be used, but this would forbid a detailed comparison of the alternatives.

- **Leveling** can occur if many attributes are used. In consequence, the results are more likely to be in the middle region. Alternatives with high weaknesses or strengths might not be recognizable anymore.

However, these disadvantages can hardly by avoided so that it is important to **understand** and accept them. Otherwise, possible biases in the results can remain unnoticed. If the decision maker understands how the results have probably been biased, he can consider this knowledge while selecting the best alternative. For example, if the best and second best alternatives are close together, the decision maker can perform further analyses before choosing one alternative.

With AHP, an additional **consistency check** can be performed. Hereby, specific variables, which are named consistency index and consistency ratio, are calculated. If certain thresholds are exceeded by these variables, the results from the pairwise comparisons should be revised. Dedicated AHP software, like Expert Choice, includes the calculation procedures for automatically checking the consistency. Details about the required calculations can be found e.g. in publications from Saaty (2000, pp. 47 ff.; 2001, pp. 80 ff.), and Zelewski and Peters (2002, p. 12).

Case Study

In order to find proper scores during the evaluation of the alternatives at the PSP, the existing information had to be considered. For the ***qualitative attributes*** *usability and satisfaction, the value ranges {very low; low; middle; high; very high} had been assigned to numbers from zero to four* (see Table 6.8).

Based on the information about the alternatives in Sect. 6.7, *the value ranges for the* ***quantitative attributes*** *initial investment costs, operation costs, risk mitigation, and NPV had been determined. By an equal assignment of evaluation scores, the value distribution in* Table 6.9 *had been created.*

- *The* ***initial investment costs*** *that had been identified in the alternative analysis had been between $0 and $13,999. Therefore, the assignment of scores to values had been performed in $2800 steps backwards from $14,000 to $0.*
- *The* ***operation costs*** *were limited by $625 at the lowest and $16,250 at the highest point. Here, the assignment of scores to values had been performed in $4000 steps backwards from $20,000 to $0.*
- *As described in* Sect. 6.7, *it was determined that 500 cards were processed over 5 years in the accounting department. Assuming that one compromised credit card could lead to a revenue loss of $500, the expected loss without encryption was limited to $25,000. The* ***risk mitigation*** *values had been defined in a way that they covered the whole value range from $0 to $25,000.*
- *As a combination of all payment flows, the* ***NPV*** *was influenced by the above-mentioned three attributes. The sums of the according values, which had been found during the alternative analysis and properly discounted or compounded, were at least $2210 and at most $7208. Hereby, the different payment times, in other words the interests, had been taken into account. The value assignment was based on an equally distributed range from $0 to $8000.*

While using the ***SAW*** *technique, each alternative that had not been excluded got a sub score for each comparison attribute. These* **sub scores** *were based on the following considerations:*

- ***Alpha:***

– *Because the tool offered necessary interfaces without any special features, the* ***usability*** *was middle. According to* Table 6.8, *this was represented with 2 points.*
– *Because of the additional functionality, in particular the file shredder and password generator, the* ***satisfaction*** *was high. According to* Table 6.8, *this was represented with 3 points.*
– *The* ***initial investment costs*** *were relatively high with $13,999. According to* Table 6.9, *this was represented with 0 points.*
– *The* ***operation costs*** *were very low with $625. According to* Table 6.9, *this was represented with 4 points.*
– *The* ***risk mitigation*** *had been measured with $22,500. According to* Table 6.9, *this was represented with 4 points.*
– *The* ***NPV*** *was $6607. According to* Table 6.9, *this was represented with 4 points.*

- ***Gamma:***

– *Because of the good handling of encrypted files, the* ***usability*** *was very high. According to* Table 6.8, *this was represented with 4 points.*
– *Assuming that the desired functionality could be built-in by the developers as needed, the* ***satisfaction*** *was very high. According to* Table 6.8, *this was represented with 4 points.*

Table 6.8 Value assignments for qualitative attributes

Attributes	Value assignments				
	0	1	2	3	4
Usability	Very low	Low	Middle	High	Very high
Satisfaction	Very low	Low	Middle	High	Very high

Table 6.9 Value assignments for quantitative attributes

Attributes	Value assignments				
	0	1	2	3	4
Initial investment costs	$11,200–$14,000	$8400–$11,199	$5600–$8399	$2800–$5599	$0–$2799
Operation costs	$16,000–$20,000	$12,000–$15,999	$8000–$11,999	$4000–$7999	$0–$3999
Risk mitigation	$0–$4999	$5000–$9999	$10,000–$14,999	$15,000–$19,999	$20,000–$25,000
NPV	$0–$1599	$1600–$3199	$3200–$4799	$4800–$6399	$6400–$8000

– *The* ***initial investment costs*** *were $5500. According to* Table 6.9, *this was represented with 3 points.*
– *The* ***operation costs*** *were $10,835. According to* Table 6.9, *this was represented with 2 points.*
– *The* ***risk mitigation*** *had been measured with $21,250. According to* Table 6.9, *this was represented with 4 points.*
– *The* ***NPV*** *was $4311. According to* Table 6.9, *this was represented with 2 points.*

– ***Delta:***
– *Because of its integration into the file manager, the* ***usability*** *was high. According to* Table 6.8, *this was represented with 3 points.*
– *Because the tool also offered a good compression, but no more additional functions, the* ***satisfaction*** *was middle. According to* Table 6.8, *this was represented with 2 points.*
– *The* ***initial investment costs*** *were $2500. According to* Table 6.9, *this was represented with 4 points.*
– *With internal support that was based on low vendor documentation and closed source, the* ***operation costs*** *were high with $16,250. According to* Table 6.9, *this was represented with 0 points.*
– *The* ***risk mitigation*** *had been measured with $21,250. According to* Table 6.9, *this was represented with 4 points.*
– *The* ***NPV*** *was $2210. According to* Table 6.9, *this was represented with 1 point.*

After finding the required sub scores, one table had been used (see Table 6.10*) for collecting these sub scores and for* ***calculating*** *the weighted sub scores (product of sub score and weight) and the overall scores (sum of weighted sub scores). The weights had been determined during the attribute evaluation (see* Table 6.3*)*

With ***AHP****, the alternatives were compared pairwise from the aspect of each comparison attribute. The evaluation values that were used as results from the comparisons are described in* Table 5.1 *in* Sect. 5.3. *In each matrix, only the values above the main diagonal were given. As described in* Sect. 5.3, *all values along the main diagonal were set to one. Below the main diagonal, the values were set to the reciprocal values of the values that were above the main diagonal. The normalization of each matrix was also based on the description in* Sect. 5.3. *In simpler terms, every value in the matrix had to be divided by the according column sum. By calculating the line sums of the normalized matrix and dividing the results by the number of alternatives, the impacts, in other words the sub scores, were found.*

The evaluation values that had been found by the PSP from the aspect of ***usability*** *were based on the following considerations:*

- ***Alpha*** *was strongly less important (1/5) than* ***Gamma*** *because Alpha offered necessary interfaces without any special features, while Gamma allowed a good handling of encrypted files.*
- ***Alpha*** *was moderately less important (1/3) than* ***Delta*** *because Delta offered a slightly better usability due to its integration into the file manager.*

Table 6.10 SAW results

Alternative	Attribute	Sub score	Weight (%)	Weighted sub score	Overall score
Alpha	Usability	2	17	0.34	3.23
	Satisfaction	3	7	0.21	
	Initial investment costs	0	8	0.00	
	Operation costs	4	8	0.32	
	Risk mitigation	4	25	1.00	
	NPV	4	34	1.36	
Gamma	Usability	4	17	0.68	3.04
	Satisfaction	4	7	0.28	
	Initial investment costs	3	8	0.24	
	Operation costs	2	8	0.16	
	Risk mitigation	4	25	1.00	
	NPV	2	34	0.68	
Delta	Usability	3	17	0.51	2.31
	Satisfaction	2	7	0.14	
	Initial investment costs	4	8	0.32	
	Operation costs	0	8	0.00	
	Risk mitigation	4	25	1.00	
	NPV	1	34	0.34	

- ***Gamma** was moderately more important (3) than **Delta** because Gamma allowed a good handling of encrypted files, which generated a slightly higher usability than Delta's integration into the file manager* (Tables 6.11 and 6.12).

*The evaluation values that had been found from the aspect of **satisfaction** were based on the following considerations:*

- ***Alpha** was moderately less important (1/3) than **Gamma** because Alpha had some additional functionality, in particular the file shredder and password generator, while the PSP planned to built-in all desired functionality into Gamma.*

Table 6.11 Matrix for usability

	Alpha	Gamma	Delta
Alpha	1.00	**0.20**	**0.33**
Gamma	5.00	1.00	**3.00**
Delta	3.00	0.33	1.00
Sum	9.00	1.53	4.33

Table 6.12 Normalized matrix for usability

	A.	G.	D.	Sum	Imp.
A.	0.11	0.13	0.08	0.32	0.11
G.	0.56	0.65	0.69	1.90	0.63
D.	0.33	0.22	0.23	0.78	0.26

- ***Alpha*** *was moderately more important (3) than* **Delta** *because Alpha led with its additional functionality to a slightly higher satisfaction than Delta, which just offered the additional compression.*
- ***Gamma*** *was strongly more important (5) than* **Delta** *because Gamma was assumed to offer all needed functionality and Delta just offered the additional compression* (Tables 6.13 and 6.14).

The evaluation values that had been found from the aspect of ***initial investment costs*** *were based on the following considerations:*

- ***Alpha*** *was very strongly less important (1/7) than* **Gamma** *because Alpha's initial investment costs were relatively high with $13,999 and those of Gamma were just $5500.*
- ***Alpha*** *was extremely less important (1/9) than* **Delta** *because Alpha could not compete against Delta with initial investment costs of $2500.*
- ***Gamma*** *was moderately less important (1/3) than* **Delta** *because Gamma's initial investment costs were not very high. However, they were not as low as those of Delta were* (Tables 6.15 and 6.16).

The evaluation values that had been found from the aspect of ***operation costs*** *were based on the following considerations:*

- ***Alpha*** *was strongly more important (5) than* **Gamma** *because the operation costs of Alpha were very low with $625. In contrast, Gamma had operation costs of $10,835, which were rather in the middle range.*

Table 6.13 Matrix for satisfaction

	Alpha	Gamma	Delta
Alpha	1.00	**0.33**	**3.00**
Gamma	3.00	1.00	**5.00**
Delta	0.33	0.20	1.00
Sum	4.33	1.53	9.00

Table 6.14 Normalized matrix for satisfaction

	A.	G.	D.	Sum	Imp.
A.	0.23	0.22	0.33	0.78	0.26
G.	0.69	0.65	0.56	1.90	0.63
D.	0.08	0.13	0.11	0.32	0.11

Table 6.15 Matrix for initial investment costs

	Alpha	Gamma	Delta
Alpha	1.00	**0.14**	**0.11**
Gamma	7.00	1.00	**0.33**
Delta	9.00	3.00	1.00
Sum	17.00	4.14	1.44

Table 6.16 Normalized matrix for initial investment costs

	A.	G.	D.	Sum	Imp.
A.	0.06	0.03	0.08	0.17	0.06
G.	0.41	0.24	0.23	0.88	0.29
D.	0.53	0.72	0.69	1.94	0.65

- ***Alpha*** *was extremely more important (9) than* ***Delta*** *because Alpha with operation costs of $625 clearly won against Delta, which had with $16,250 the highest operation costs.*
- ***Gamma*** *was strongly more important (5) than* ***Delta*** *because Gamma had with $10,835 much lower operating costs than Delta with $16,250* (Tables 6.17 and 6.18).

The evaluation values that had been found from the aspect of ***risk mitigation*** *were based on the following considerations:*

- ***Alpha*** *and* ***Gamma*** *were equally important (1) because, from the view of the PSP, they both provided a sufficient risk mitigation with nearly the same reduction in expected losses.*
- ***Alpha*** *and* ***Delta*** *were equally important (1) because, from the view of the PSP, they both provided a similar risk mitigation.*
- ***Gamma*** *and* ***Delta*** *were equally important (1) because, from the view of the PSP, they both provided a similar risk mitigation* (Tables 6.19 and 6.20).

Table 6.17 Matrix for operation costs

	Alpha	Gamma	Delta
Alpha	1.00	**5.00**	**9.00**
Gamma	0.20	1.00	**5.00**
Delta	0.11	0.20	1.00
Sum	1.31	6.20	15.00

Table 6.18 Normalized matrix for operation costs

	A.	G.	D.	Sum	Imp.
A.	0.76	0.81	0.60	2.17	0.72
G.	0.15	0.16	0.33	0.64	0.21
D.	0.08	0.03	0.07	0.18	0.06

Table 6.19 Matrix for risk mitigation

	Alpha	Gamma	Delta
Alpha	1.00	**1.00**	**1.00**
Gamma	1.00	1.00	**1.00**
Delta	1.00	1.00	1.00
Sum	3.00	3.00	3.00

The evaluation values that had been found from the aspect of ***NPV*** *were based on the following considerations:*

- ***Alpha*** *was strongly more important (5) than* ***Gamma*** *because Alpha's NPV was $6607, while Gamma's was just $4311.*
- ***Alpha*** *was very strongly more important (7) than* ***Delta*** *because Delta came with a relatively low number of $2210. Therefore, it could not compete with Alpha's NPV of $6607.*
- ***Gamma*** *was moderately more important (3) than* ***Delta*** *because Gamma's NPV was with $4311 slightly better than Delta's with $2210* (Tables 6.21 and 6.22).

By aggregating the numbers, the ***overall score*** *of every alternative was found. From* Tables 6.12, 6.14, 6.16, 6.18, 6.20 and 6.22, *the impact scores were transferred as sub scores to* Table 6.23. *The weights were transferred from the attribute evaluation in* Sect. 6.6 *(see* Table 6.6*). The product of weights and sub scores delivered the weighted sub scores (rounded), which summed up to the overall scores.*

In order to understand and accept the potential ***disadvantages*** *in the decision making, the PSP took a close look into the following aspects:*

- ***Dependencies*** *were found between the attribute NPV and each of the attributes initial investment costs, operation costs and risk mitigation. This was caused by the comprehensiveness of the NPV, which covered all payment flows. Because the NPV was a very important attribute, from the view of the PSP, a possible overvaluation of attributes that were connected to payment flows had been accepted.*

Table 6.20 Normalized matrix for risk mitigation

	A.	G.	D.	Sum	Imp.
A.	0.33	0.33	0.33	0.99	0.33
G.	0.33	0.33	0.33	0.99	0.33
D.	0.33	0.33	0.33	0.99	0.33

Table 6.21 Matrix for the NPV

	Alpha	Gamma	Delta
Alpha	1.00	**5.00**	**7.00**
Gamma	0.20	1.00	**3.00**
Delta	0.14	0.33	1.00
Sum	1.34	6.33	11.00

Table 6.22 Normalized matrix for the NPV

	A.	G.	D.	Sum	Imp.
A.	0.75	0.79	0.64	2.18	0.73
G.	0.15	0.16	0.27	0.58	0.19
D.	0.10	0.05	0.09	0.24	0.08

Table 6.23 AHP results

Alternative	Attribute	Sub score	Weight (%)	Weighted sub score	Overall score
Alpha	Usability	0.11	15	0.02	0.5
	Satisfaction	0.26	3	0.01	
	Initial investment costs	0.06	5	0.00	
	Operation costs	0.72	5	0.04	
	Risk mitigation	0.33	26	0.09	
	NPV	0.73	47	0.34	
Gamma	Usability	0.63	15	0.09	0.31
	Satisfaction	0.63	3	0.02	
	Initial investment costs	0.29	5	0.01	
	Operation costs	0.21	5	0.01	
	Risk mitigation	0.33	26	0.09	
	NPV	0.19	47	0.09	
Delta	Usability	0.26	15	0.04	0.2
	Satisfaction	0.11	3	0.00	
	Initial investment costs	0.65	5	0.03	
	Operation costs	0.06	5	0.00	
	Risk mitigation	0.33	26	0.09	
	NPV	0.08	47	0.04	

- ***Manipulation*** *can lead to falsified evaluation results. Therefore, the decision maker and his assistants had been questioned regarding possible biases and conflicts of interests. The residual risk that potential reasons for manipulation had been overlooked despite the questioning had been accepted.*
- ***Substitutability*** *of the attributes could not be avoided completely. However, the use of exclusion attributes reduced the substitutability to a satisfactory level. Therefore, the PSP accepted the remaining substitutability.*
- ***Leveling*** *primarily occurs with many attributes. It can complicate the decision making because the evaluation results can move to the middle region. With six attributes in the decision making, leveling was unlikely in the case of the PSP.*

6.8.3 *Sensitivity Analysis*

7.4 The effects of changes in the evaluation have been analyzed.

After the evaluation results have been created, the decision maker should analyze the effect of **changes** in the set of attributes and alternatives. Even minor changes can lead to significant changes in the results.

Generally, **robust** results that are not affected by minor changes testify a higher quality. However, if the results will change after certain modifications, it can also be reasonable. For example, the elimination of a substantial attribute can lead to a new ranking that is fully appropriate.

Generally, two **analysis attempts** are of a major concern when the most influential parts, in other words the most critical parts, of the decision making shall be searched. Hereby, most critical should not be confused with most important. The most important weight or evaluation is the one with the highest value, while the most critical ones are those that cause changes in the ranking with the lowest adjustment. One analysis attempt is focused on finding the most critical attribute and the other one is focused on finding the most critical evaluation:

- The most critical **attribute** can be found by looking after the attribute that causes a change in the alternative ranking after this attribute has been removed. However, often more than one attribute can cause a change in the alternative ranking. In this case, the attribute that causes a change in the alternative ranking with the lowest adjustment of the attribute weight is most critical. At first, for every attribute, the minimum weight adjustment that causes a change in the alternative ranking has to be found. Next, the attribute with the lowest minimum weight adjustment has to be identified. This attribute is the most critical attribute. In order to assure the quality of the decision results, this attribute and the related evaluations should be checked regarding correctness and consistency.
- The most critical **evaluation** is the evaluation that causes a change in the current alternative ranking with the lowest adjustment of the sub score (in SAW) or evaluation value (in AHP). For every evaluation, the minimum adjustment that causes a change in the ranking has to be determined. By sorting the results, the evaluation with the lowest minimum adjustment will be visible. This evaluation is the most critical evaluation. Like the most critical attribute, the most critical evaluation should be checked closely. In particular, any possible errors, biases and conflicts should be disclosed.

In addition, the decision maker should be aware of an **AHP specific** situation: If a certain alternative is removed, the ranking can also change. This type of change is unreasonable because the ranking of other alternatives should not be changed because of the inclusion or exclusion of a single alternative. This weakness of the AHP technique is caused by the high linkage of alternatives with the pairwise comparisons. In contrast, the SAW technique is not affected by this problem because the decision maker determines the SAW scores of each alternative autonomously from other alternatives.

Case Study

The results from the case study had been analyzed regarding the ***most critical*** *parts in order to facilitate a targeted quality check.*

The most critical attribute from the ***SAW*** *results had been searched, at first, by removing each attribute separately from the evaluation one after another and looking for changes in the ranking (see* Table 6.24*).*

By removing each attribute separately, while the other attributes were still within the calculation, the attributes that caused a ranking change could be identified. In the case study, the ***NPV*** *was the only attribute that caused a ranking change. Therefore, the NPV was the most critical attribute. If more than one attribute had caused a ranking change, further comparisons would have been necessary: For every removed attribute that had caused a change, the lowest weight adjustment of this attribute that also had caused a change would have been found. By comparing the weight adjustments, the most critical attribute would have been found: the one with the lowest weight adjustments (in percent).*

The most critical evaluation from the ***SAW*** *results was also searched in multiple phases: At first, every single sub score was increased by one point. Then, every single sub score was decreased by one point. If no ranking change had occurred, the increase and decrease would have been made by two points and so on. The adjustments of the sub scores that are shown in* Table 6.25 *caused a ranking change.*

Table 6.24 Ranking change after attribute removal

Alternatives	Ranking without the attribute					
	Usability	Satisfaction	Initial investment costs	Operation costs	Risk mitigation	NPV
Alpha	1	1	1	1	1	3
Gamma	2	2	2	2	2	1
Delta	3	3	3	3	3	2
Ranking change	No	No	No	No	No	**Yes**

Table 6.25 Ranking changes after score adjustments

Alternative	Attribute	Sub score adjustment	New ranking
Gamma	Risk mitigation	+1	Gamma, Alpha, Delta
Gamma	NPV	+1	Gamma, Alpha, Delta
Alpha	Risk mitigation	−1	Gamma, Alpha, Delta
Alpha	NPV	−1	Gamma, Alpha, Delta

Table 6.26 Ranking change after attribute removal

Alternatives	Ranking without the attribute					
	Usability	Satisfaction	Initial investment costs	Operation costs	Risk mitigation	NPV
Alpha	1	1	1	1	1	3
Gamma	2	2	2	2	2	1
Delta	3	3	3	3	3	2
Ranking change	No	No	No	No	No	**Yes**

Because the sub scores could only be given in ***whole numbers****, the four identified sub scores could not be differentiated further. Therefore, all four evaluations that led to these sub scores were most critical here.*

Next, the most critical attribute and evaluation from the ***AHP*** *results had been identified. As with the SAW results, each attribute was removed in order to identify the ones that caused a ranking change (see* Table 6.26*).*

As with the SAW results, the ***NPV*** *was the most critical attribute because only the removal of this attribute caused a ranking change.*

The most critical evaluation in the ***AHP*** *results was searched similarly to the one in the SAW results: Every result from the evaluations—in AHP the pairwise comparisons—was increased by one step on the scale from* Table 5.1 *in* Sect. 5.3. *Then, it was decreased by one step. Afterwards, the results were increased and decreased by two steps. By calculating the aggregated AHP results with the adjusted comparisons, ranking changes were found. In particular, the ranking was changed when the pairwise comparison between Alpha and Gamma under the attribute NPV was adjusted by two steps. The result of the pairwise comparison was changed from "Alpha is strongly more important (5) than Gamma" to "Alpha and Gamma are equally important (1)". The ranking was changed from Alpha, Gamma, Delta to Gamma, Alpha, Delta.*

6.9 Selection of the Best Alternative

8.1 The strategy for the cybersecurity investment has been determined.

With the ranking of alternatives, the decision maker can easily understand which alternative is the most appropriate one, in other words the best solution from the company's perspective. Next, he can **select** this alternative, which is on the top of the ranking.

However, the selection is not always as trivial as it might look. If more than one alternative is on the top of the ranking, the decision maker cannot just select the alternative with the highest overall score because there will be multiple alternatives with the **same overall score**. In this case, the decision maker should collect more information until he can distinguish the appropriateness of these alternatives in a higher detail. For example, many kinds of interaction with the vendor can lead to information that supports the final selection:

- If a high number of licenses are required or an individual product has been ordered, **contract negotiations** will be recommendable or even mandatory. By starting these negotiations before the final selection, additional information about the product and vendor can be collected. Besides, reductions in license or implementation costs would also lead to a reduction of the initial investment costs. Therefore, a single alternative can stand out from the other alternatives after starting the contract negotiations.
- If it has not already been requested before, a **live demo** will be an efficient way for checking certain functions that were just known from paper. In addition, a clearer impression about the usability of the alternatives can be found. For example, some aspects, like response times in the graphical interface, might have been overlooked before. Shortcomings regarding these aspects can hardly be overlooked in a live version.
- The decision maker can also request a **test version** from the vendor. In the case of freeware or open source software, he can test the full version directly. The actual test of the alternatives must not be neglected. However, the test is mostly performed after the final selection was made. The test can be moved before the final selection if multiple alternatives have the highest overall score. Then, the test has to be conducted with multiple alternatives so that the required effort will also be multiplied. Although a conscientious test of multiple alternatives is one of the most laborious ways to collect more information, this information would be very suitable and valuable.
- While **communicating** with the vendor, the decision maker can get an impression about the competence and reliability of the vendor. For example, precise and accurate responses usually indicate a high professionalism that would probably influence a possible business relation and the quality of the alternative positively in the long term.
- The more the investment is important for the decision maker's company, the higher the consequences can be if major problems occur at the business partner. Therefore, a thorough **background check** of the vendor can be appropriate. For example, information about the financial stability or pending trials can provide some significant indications about the reliability of the business relationship in the long term.

If multiple alternatives with the same overall score are on the top of the ranking, an additional improvement or advantage that becomes visible during interaction with the vendor can help to **differentiate** the truly best alternative from the others. An update and repetition of the evaluation process must not be performed necessarily. However, if the additional information is too complex to interpret straightaway, a new evaluation can be the best choice. Hereby, new attributes have to be identified and evaluated. Next, the alternatives have to be evaluated again based on the new information. These steps are the same as described in Sects. 6.5–6.8. Mostly, the additional information is not as comprehensive as the initial information from the previous research. Therefore, the repeated process generally requires less effort.

Case Study

In the case study, the ranking of the three alternatives did not include any alternatives with the same overall score. Therefore, the ***final selection*** *of the alternative Alpha was obvious.*

6.10 Approval

9.1 The decision has been approved by senior management.

The selection of an alternative by the decision maker does not necessarily lead to an actual acquisition or implementation of this alternative. Mostly, senior management has to **approve** the decision beforehand. This allows an additional quality check. In particular, changes, errors and manipulations can be recognized in the approval process.

The approval is initiated with the delivery of a **decision paper** to senior management by the decision maker. This paper should at least include the following sections:

- The **cover and preface** of the paper should include general Meta information about the paper. The version number and the date of the finalization will be important if multiple versions exist and senior management has to be sure that it actually has the right version and that all parties communicate about the same paper. A listing of all changes to the previous version simplify the examination of the paper by senior management. If a complete list of changes is given and if senior management already examined the previous version, only the changed chapters will have to be examined. This procedure is much less laborious than the repeated examination of the whole paper. Details about prior approval attempts include the date, names of involved managers, response type (approved/rejected) and possibly the concrete reason for rejection. These details help senior management to assess the decision paper in context to previous requests and responses. The revision and repeated delivery for approval are not only limited to rejected decision papers. Also already approved decision papers can be revised, e.g. in case of major changes that occurred in the time-period between the initial approval and the actual acquisition or implementation of the selected alternative.

- The **management summary** provides a short description of the essential contents. Generally, all minor details are excluded from the summary. Therefore, the summary is a proper way to present the central idea and the rough decision result to senior management. Especially, too many details about the problem should not be included into the summary. Moreover, the recommended solution and significant consequences should be in focus here. The summary should be completely understandable without knowledge from the rest of the decision paper. Technical terms should be avoided, unless they are well known by senior management. The summary should be targeted to the addressees from senior management. Besides, meaningful figures will fit in the summary very well if they improve the understanding by the reader. Because available time at senior management level is often short, a management summary can help to get a prompt attention and to accelerate the understanding and the subsequent approval process. Without a management summary, the approval can take a much longer time.
- On the following pages of the paper, all **details** about the decision should be documented. Primarily, these details include a clear problem description, which explains facts or assumptions about internal and external conditions, and insights from the decision making, which include reasons for all evaluations. Senior management should be able to understand every step from the process. Among other things, it should not be questionable why a certain weight or score has been assigned by the decision maker.
- At the end of the paper, an **attachment** should be added. The primary reasons for an attachment are the delivery of evidences, e.g. price offers from vendors, and the increase of the readability of the previous sections. Otherwise, too specific details in the running text of the previous sections would impair the readability. After transferring these details into the attachment, the reader can still access the information. However, it would not be in the way while reading the main chapters of the paper.

Not only the decision paper but also the written **response** by senior management are important pieces of documentation. Both the approvals and the rejections should be traceable. Therefore, they should be documented in writing. Rejections should be complemented with the reasons that led to these rejections. If the decision paper is revised, the reason for the rejection should be used as a crucial influence factor. For example, if the decision paper is rejected because of low cash liquidity, adding new attributes into the decision making will probably not lead to a less expensive solution. Moreover, the attributes that address the initial investment costs should be evaluated in another way.

The approval is a reasonable quality control that should not be taken lightly. **Rejections** are an important measure that helps to prevent major problems after inappropriate or questionable decisions. The reasons for rejections can be manifold. Among other things, the following reasons should lead to a rejection:

- The **decision problem** has changed afterwards or it was not analyzed sufficiently from the beginning. In conclusion, senior management has to assume that the decision in the decision paper does not completely meet the underlying problem. In particular, the following points can lead to changes in the decision problem:

- Change of **strategy**, e.g. the protection goal or scope has been adjusted.
- Change of **protection scope**, e.g. new business processes have been developed.
- Change of **asset values**, e.g. a new market situation can require a revised measurement of asset values.
- Change of **protection requirements** for the identified assets, e.g. some data have become fundamentally important after a business change.
- Change of **risks**, e.g. new threats have been evolved.
- Change of **adequacy of the decision technique**, e.g. new members of senior management do not understand or accept a certain technique.
- Change of **involvement of stakeholders**, e.g. certain stakeholders have changed their interests and should be involved more or less.

• **Internal conditions** have been overlooked or changed so that the recommended solution would actually not be the best solution. Besides, unfavorable conditions can lead to major problems in the implementation. Among other things, the following internal conditions can be of major concern:

- The available **resources** have been limited after the project was initiated. For example, an economic downturn or problems in primary business processes might have significantly affected the financial resources of the company. The availability of human resources might also be affected, e.g. because of a flu outbreak.
- New **conflicts of interests** between companies can occur after the business relationship has been changed. For example, a company for IT security consulting that joined a holding can be required to provide services to all members of the holding. However, the holding members might not think that this company would actually be the best choice for providing the services.
- The **time schedule** might not be seen as appropriate anymore. For example, changes in business strategy might have caused a reservation of internal staff for new projects. Therefore, the decision making would have to be revised with a planning that includes more external staff.

• **External conditions** have changed so that the initial decision making is not accurate anymore. For example, certain environmental factors can lead to new requirements in the planning phase or potential problems in the implementation and operation phase. Some examples for possible changes of external conditions are:

- Relevant **laws or standards** can be changed. Even minor updates can lead to major changes in the requirements. Especially, new requirements must be fulfilled if the company is suddenly in scope for a law or standard that binds the

company to certain security measures. For example, the PCI DSS requires security measures for information systems that process payment card data.
- The **market** can change because of new events or trends that are related to cybersecurity. For example, customers can change their expectations about an appropriate protection level after a new major breach has occurred. Besides, the demand for companies that meet certain standards, e.g. ISO 27001 or COBIT, might increase over time.
- New **threats** and subsequent risks from the environment can fundamentally influence the company's strategy. For example, natural disasters can affect the location choice and protection needs.

- The **decision making** was incorrect or incomplete. Errors within the decision making process can significantly influence the evaluation results. If an error happens to be related to a critical attribute or evaluation, the ranking of the alternatives can even be changed. In this case, the selected alternative would not be the truly best alternative. Among other things, the following problems can affect the decision making:

- The decision making had not been properly **sponsored** by senior management. If senior management did not have the opportunity to participate in the initiation of the process, the purpose of the project might be questioned or the whole project might be canceled. Even if senior management did not impede the project, it would be possibly threatened by other opponents that might also pull senior management on their side.
- Plausible **reasons** do not exist that would explain certain evaluations and weightings. The problem of missing plausible reasons often occurs when the decision maker acts intuitively. Intuitive approaches are not generally wrong. Moreover, the problem lies in the missing transparency for others. A decision that is based only on intuitions will hardly be understood and approved by others.
- Obvious **errors**, e.g. calculation errors in the aggregation of scores, can affect the subsequent reasoning, including the ranking. On the one hand, these errors can actually falsify the recommended decision. On the other hand, senior management might lose confidence in the decision paper if it is characterized by obvious errors.
- Besides, neglecting relevant opinions and experiences of **experts and peers** in the company can be a crucial mistake. Although this does not necessarily makes the decision paper incorrect, the paper would probably be inappropriate. Mostly, experts and peers have valuable knowledge that can strongly improve the outcome of the decision making. In addition, they facilitate the consideration of many company-specific facts. When neglecting this, the decision might get too general so that the selected alternative might be inappropriate for an integration into the company.
- Mostly, a **market analysis** is an important task in the step of alternative identification. The results influence all subsequent steps, including the

alternative ranking and the final selection. If the market analysis were too restricted or even inaccurate, the results would be strongly affected. The non-consideration of certain vendors or product types would result in the situation that the truly best alternative would not even been considered. For example, the decision maker might only consider firewall software, while a firewall appliance would have been a better choice.
- Overlooked **information** can also lead to strong concerns and often to rejections. Relevant information that is known by senior management but has not been mentioned or considered in the decision paper makes it appear incomplete or even unprofessional. This information can be related to, among other things, important alternatives or new technologies.
- Strong **conflicts** between the recommended solution and the senior management's strategy, e.g. a planned outsourcing, can make the solution inadequate. Ideally, the senior management's strategy had already been considered in the early stages of the process. However, certain strategies are hold secret or created in the short term. The risk that these conflicts impede the approval can hardly be eliminated.
- The **sensitivity analysis** can provide important information about the robustness of the results. If the sensitivity analysis is missing or obviously incomplete, senior management might question the results and, possibly, reject the decision paper. Especially if the overall scores of the alternatives are very close, it will be difficult to understand why the recommended alternative will truly be the best alternative. Only by identifying and checking critical attributes and evaluations, the reliability of the results can be ensured.

• The **documentation** of the decision making should be sufficient regarding its scope and quality. If the documentation were insufficient or not included in the decision paper, senior management might reject the recommendation in the paper. The following points affect the sufficiency of the documentation:

- A clear description of the **decision problem**, including relevant objectives and requirements, is missing.
- The decision paper is not fully **understandable**. For example, details that explain major aspects of the decision are missing, or the reasons for assigning certain scores and weights are unclear.
- Significant **conflicts of interests** are not named in the decision paper. Although the initial disclosure of these conflicts should be performed as early as possible, they must also be described in the decision paper. If any significant conflict of interests that came to the attention of senior management is not descripted in the paper or has even not been disclosed, a rejection will be very likely.

• **Fraud** in the decision making process is caused by motivation, justification and opportunity, as described with the fraud triangle in Sect. 6.6. The attribute evaluation is one of various opportunities that might have been exploited by fraudsters. Senior management should be aware of potential weaknesses or missing control measures in the decision making process. Indications for fraud should be taken serious. If fraud seems to have a high impact on the decision, senior management should reject it. Common indications for fraud are (derived from audit fraud according to AICPA 2002, pp. 1742 ff.):

- Discrepancies in **records**—For example, the data from certain evidences do not match to the data that were considered in the evaluation.
- Conflicting or missing **evidence**—For example, evidence for substantial characteristics of the alternatives has not been attached to the decision paper.
- Problematic or unusual **relationships** between involved parties—For example, team members of the decision making team had multiple problems during the process.

Case Study

The ***decision paper*** *at the PSP included a management summary, details about the decision, and an attachment. The management summary is shown below. The details about the decision were an aggregation of the case study information from all previous sub-chapters. The attachment provided additional background information, primarily from the market analysis.*

The ***management summary*** *addressed the subject matter (selection of a safeguard for confidentiality), decision making techniques (SAW and AHP) and findings (evaluation scores), conclusions (Alpha as the best choice), and recommendations (implementation of Alpha): "This decision paper describes the selection of a cybersecurity investment in order to protect sensitive data that are related to chargebacks, retrieval requests and fraud. In an internal audit, these data had been found unencrypted on several systems in the accounting department. From an insufficient protection of the data confidentiality, compliance issues with the PCI DSS and risks of reputational damages arise. In particular, the actual risk level regarding disclosure and loss has been assessed as medium. A market analysis delivered information about technical, preventive safeguards for securing these data with encryption. The decision making techniques SAW and AHP have been used for evaluating these alternatives based on a time-period of five years. Thereby, various attributes have been selected and weighted. Relevant background information can be found in this paper. The calculation of the overall scores from the evaluation is also described in this paper. From the alternatives Alpha, Beta, Gamma and Delta, Beta has been excluded because of compatibility issues. The evaluation results from the comparison attributes analyses with SAW resulted in 3.23 points for Alpha, 3.04 points for Gamma and 2.31 points for Delta. With AHP, Alpha got 0.5 points, Gamma 0.31 and Delta 0.2. In conclusion, both evaluation rankings are headed by Alpha, which is, in consequence, the best choice. It is recommended that the dedicated file encryption tool Alpha should be implemented on all systems from the accounting department."*

The senior management ***approved*** *the recommendation from the decision paper because the paper was understandable and no relevant reasons for a rejection were found.*

6.11 Planning

10.1 The implementation of the selected safeguard has been planned.

In the **planning** step, all activities shall be performed that are needed to define the objectives and course of action in order to acquire and implement the selected safeguard sufficiently. After the successful planning, a documentation should be available that can be used during the subsequent implementation and closing step. The planning can be a repetitive process because changes in the internal or external environment often occur during the implementation so that the planning has to be adjusted.

The **plan**, which is the output from the planning step, should include the following subjects. Depending on the specific subject, relevant stakeholders should be involved.

- On the most important parts of planning are the identification and arrangement of **work packages** that are required for the implementation. These packages often include the purchasing or development of the solution, installation, configuration, test, and quality assurance. The development of a work breakdown structure is a very suitable technique in this process. However, the work breakdown structure does not consider the time management of the work. It only illustrates what work is needed, not when it must be done. The development can be performed with a top-down or bottom-up approach:

– With the **top-down** approach, the general tasks are decomposed into more specific work packages. By starting at a rather abstract level, the overall work can be understood more easily. Next, the rough descriptions are broken down in very specific packages. Finally, every package should have been planned so detailed that every package is assigned to only one processor.

– With the **bottom-up** approach, the planning starts at the most detailed level. At first, all work packages have to be found. Next, they are aggregated to tasks that are more general. This approach should only be preferred against the top-down approach if the implementation is characterized by very innovative work and if it must be ensured that every known detail is covered by the final work breakdown structure.

- The **implementation time** is also an important aspect that should be covered sufficiently. In order to provide resources as needed and minimize idle times, the previously identified work packages should be put in a chronological sequence. Besides, critical parts of this sequence that can lead to a delay of the whole implementation should be identified. A common tool for time management is the critical path method. Hereby, the single tasks are connected to each other so that dependencies are visible. Multiple visualization techniques can be used here. For example, in network plans, the tasks can be visualized as nodes or arrows. When nodes are used, the graphical visualization can look as shown in Fig. 6.17.

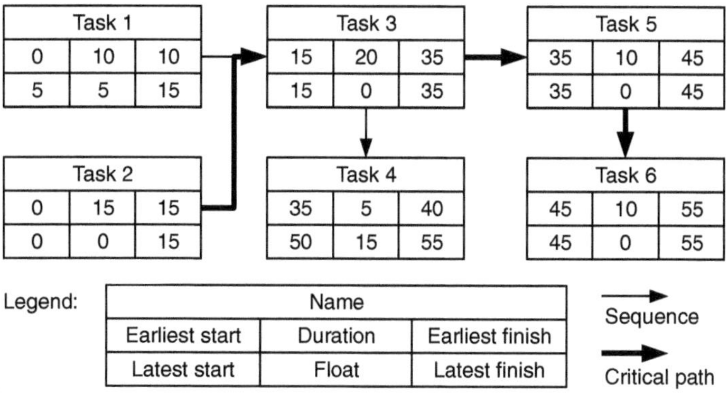

Fig. 6.17 Network plan example

The **network plan** is created in multiple steps:

1. At first, **preliminary information** about the tasks has to be collected, in particular about the durations and dependencies. Table 6.27 includes the information for the example in Fig. 6.17.
2. With the above information, the **nodes** are drawn. Beginning with all nodes without predecessors, the nodes are added systematically and connected with arrows to the specified predecessors. Name and duration of each task can be added directly from the given information.
3. With the **forward calculation**, the earliest start and finish for each task are calculated. For all tasks without a predecessor, the earliest start is zero and the earliest finish equals the duration. For all tasks with a predecessor, the earliest start equals the earliest finish of the predecessor. The earliest finish is calculated by summing up the earliest start and the duration.
4. With the **backward calculation**, the latest start, latest finish, and float for each task are calculated. The calculation starts at the end of the sequence, in other words at the nodes without successors. For all tasks without a successor, the latest finish equals the earliest finish. For all tasks with a successor, the latest finish equals the latest start of the earliest successor. For all tasks, the latest start is equal to the latest finish less the duration. The float is equal to the latest start less the earliest start.

Table 6.27 Preliminary information for the network plan

Task	Duration (days)	Predecessor
Task 1	10	None
Task 2	15	None
Task 3	20	1, 2
Task 4	5	3
Task 5	10	3
Task 6	10	5

5. Now, every box in every node has been filled. The **critical path** can be found on the way of the tasks that have zero float. In Fig. 6.17, the critical path is the sequence of the tasks 2, 3, 5 and 6 (with bold arrows).

   - The **implementation costs** have already been determined in the decision making process. However, it is not sufficient to estimate only the amount of money needed. In addition, it must be anticipated when the money is needed and how the budget should be limited. Especially at high amounts, it will be very advantageous if the liquidity can be adjusted as needed. In contrast, if liquidity is unused, possible interest earnings from other financial investments will be lost. The budget should not only cover the estimated costs but also an additional amount that can be used to handle possible risks. These risks can occur during the implementation or development of the safeguard. If something goes wrong, additional time or money will be needed to complete the investment project. For example, major errors in a security software can lead to costly programming revisions.
   - Another important planning aspect is **human resources**. The availability of appropriately trained professionals must be ensured. Based on the resource requirements of the planned tasks, a human resource plan should be created. This plan should consider the availability of human resources in the company and available support by external parties. If the planned tasks require more human resources than those that can be released from other duties in the company, the tasks can only be performed with external support or with another schedule.
   - In addition, **policies** should be created so that project members are bound to important rules, e.g. regarding communication, and escalation procedures. Thereby, it can be ensured that the right people are addressed at the right time. For example, the management can impose on the project members an obligation to escalate delays of more than two days to the project manager as soon as they will be recognized.

Case Study

For the implementation, the PSP identified multiple ***work packages****, which were further broken down with a work breakdown structure. On the highest level, the following tasks were defined. Subsequently, particular work packages had been derived from these tasks (see* Fig. 6.18*).*

- ***Purchasing:*** *In this task, the licenses for the product Alpha were acquired from the vendor. Therefore, a purchase order was created. Besides, the PSP had to check the terms and conditions, which accompanied the software product. The vendor delivered the product and the PSP recorded the delivery. Afterwards, an invoice was sent by the vendor and checked by the PSP. Finally, the PSP made the payment.*
- ***Packaging:*** *The packaging of the product was done with a package manager in order to automate the subsequent installation and configuration of the product on all relevant computers. This simplified the rollout, which was automated and*

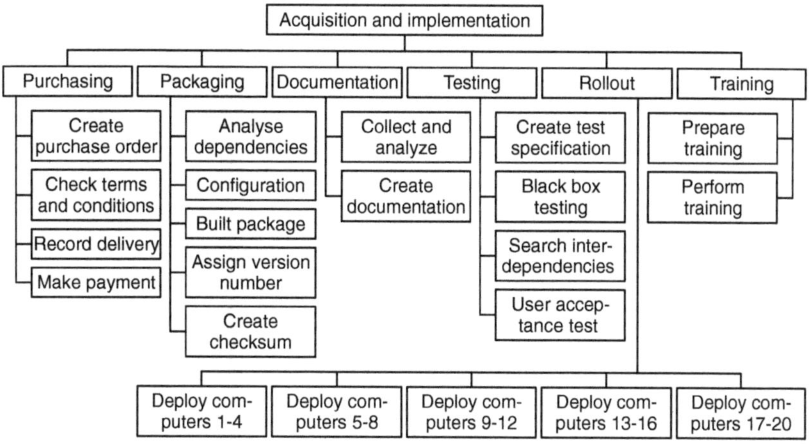

Fig. 6.18 Case study work breakdown structure

monitored more easily. The packaging included the analysis of dependencies, the determination of appropriate configuration parameters, and the actual built of the package. Besides, a version number had to be assigned to the package in order to ensure that the right package was used after performing updates or adjustments. The creation of checksums was also recommended. They were used to ensure that the distributed packages were correct and complete.

- ***Documentation:*** *Because the product Alpha had been purchased from a vendor, some documentation already existed. Therefore, the first step was to collect and analyze available documentation, e.g. user manuals. Next, additional documentation had to be created. In particular, the functional requirements from the company, additional technical information, e.g. regarding software packaging, and user guidance for handling payment card data had to be described.*
- ***Testing:*** *The source code of the software had not been published by the vendor. Therefore, the PSP was not able to perform white box testing, which would have included an analysis of the source code. Instead, the PSP performed black box testing, which focused on the analysis of the outputs from the software. Besides, a search for mutual interdependencies with other software and a user acceptance test had to be performed. All tests were preceded by a test specification. Specifications and results from the testing were also documented.*
- ***Rollout:*** *The rollout was supposed to be performed stepwise. On one business day, at most four of the 20 computers were deployed with the new product. Thereby, the PSP was able to monitor the computers thoroughly. Besides, it was avoided that possible problems by the product would have affected the whole accounting department at once.*
- ***Training:*** *The PSP planned to perform the training in the accounting department after the rollout so that the staff were able to use the product concurrently to the training. Before the training was performed, it had to be prepared by the trainers.*

The PSP collected the following preliminary information about the tasks on the highest level of the work breakdown structure in order to determine the ***implementation time****: The sequence of the task started with the purchasing of the product. Next, the administrators began the packaging. Afterwards the documentation and testing were performed. The stepwise rollout started after the testing. The training was allowed to start only after the rollout and documentation were completed. Here, the duration equaled the effort in person-days. Optionally, more staff could have been assigned to the tasks so that the duration would have been reduced. Besides, the staff could have been assigned in parallel to other tasks, e.g. for upholding the daily operations, so that the duration would have been increased.*

Based on the information from Table 6.28, *the* ***network plan*** *in* Fig. 6.19 *was created for visualizing the sequence. Hereby, the critical path can be found in the sequence of the tasks Purchasing, Packaging, Testing, Rollout and Training (with bold arrows).*

The ***implementation costs*** *were based on the initial investment costs of \$13,999. This money was needed to cover the license costs (external payment) and the efforts for the initial installation (internal billing). Furthermore, a risk-based addition of 50 % of the rollout costs, in other words \$2500, was made. In sum, a budget of \$16,499 was granted. It was completely available from the beginning.*

From the aspect of ***human resources,*** *professionals were needed for all tasks of the implementation and acquisition. In particular, professionals with the following skills were needed:*

Table 6.28 Preliminary information for the case study network plan

No.	Task	Duration (days)	Predecessor
1	Purchasing	1	None
2	Packaging	2	1
3	Documentation	1	2
4	Testing	2	2
5	Rollout	5	4
6	Training	1	3, 5

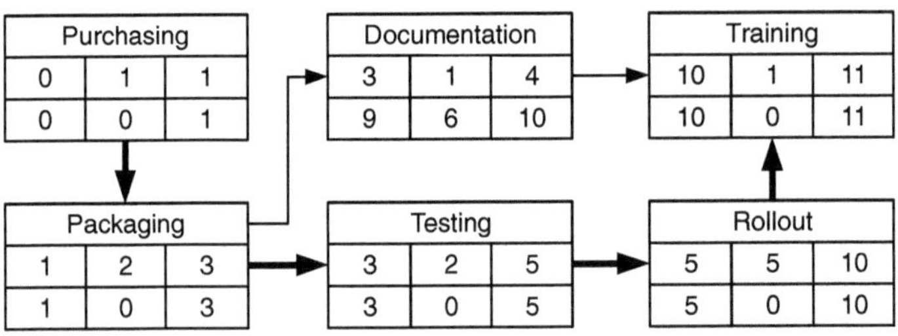

Fig. 6.19 Case study network plan

- *Performing the company's purchase procedures and standards*
- *Building software packages under consideration of quality and security aspects*
- *Creating sufficient documentation that covered the needs of the company*
- *Specifying and performing software tests in order to assure the quality of the software*
- *Planning and conducting a software rollout without jeopardizing business operations*
- *Properly preparing and performing a training under consideration of the individual backgrounds, learning styles, and abilities of the users*

All skills were covered by internal staff of the company so that no external support was necessary. With the network plan, a schedule was created that ensured the availability of the needed professionals on time. Because of the modest effort that was required for the tasks, the professionals were assigned to the new tasks without problems.

The ***policies*** *that were created for controlling the implementation were focused on the communication and escalation during the project. In particular, the policies bound the project members to participate in a status meeting at least once a week. Besides, they had been required to escalate possible problems to the project manager if delays of more than two days would have been occurred, costs would have been more than 10 % higher as planned or exceeded the available budget, or the amount of errors in testing would have been higher than 10. If the project manager had not resolved the problem within three days, an escalation to senior management would have been performed.*

6.12 Implementation

11.1 The implementation of the safeguard has been performed and controlled.

During implementation, all tasks and work packages shall be performed according to the plan from the previous step. Management is challenged to recognize and handle possible **deviations** from the plan. Deviations can occur in different areas:

- The **costs** of the project might dramatically increase. Even if the budget is not yet exceeded, cost increases can indicate an alarming trend. For example, a budget that has been almost fully spent before even the half of the planned tasks have been completed makes it unlikely that the project will be finished with the available financial resources.
- The **schedule** that has been planned might be affected by delays of work packages. If the float of the delayed work packages is low, the planned completion time of the whole project can be endangered. Especially, delays of work

packages with zero float, in other words delays on the critical path, will always affect the whole project.

- The **quality** of the outcomes might decrease. A low quality level leads to more rework and, thereby, to loops within business processes. In consequence, the effort and processing times increase. This also influences the costs and schedules of the project. Besides, if the customer or user receives a low quality outcome, it might not be accepted so that project cannot be closed.

The **reasons** for deviations in costs, schedule or quality are manifold. Everything can happen from unexpected errors to unavailable resources. Besides, internal and external factors might change. Among other things, the scope of the project might change. For example, a data leakage prevention can be implemented while senior management publishes a new bring your own device policy. This strongly expands the previous scope. Besides, changes in laws or standards might influence the project. For example, new requirements might arise from a new version of an important industry standard.

Generally, the company should not seek to prevent all possible deviations because this would be much too costly. Moreover, it should **recognize** possible deviations so that targeted countermeasures can be applied if they are really needed. A common technique to support an early detection of deviations and subsequent problems is the trend analysis, which can be used for time, cost and quality aspects.

- With the **milestone trend analysis**, changes in the milestone dates can be detected and visualized. If certain milestones are shifted repeatedly to later dates, general problems might exist. Typically, the visualization is based on a triangle, as shown in Fig. 6.20.

On the horizontal axis, the reporting period can be read. On the vertical axis, the planning period can be read. Both axes have the same scale. Multiple milestones can be distinguished with different symbols or colors. On every reporting date, the new planned dates for the milestone are inserted into the triangle. If the pattern of

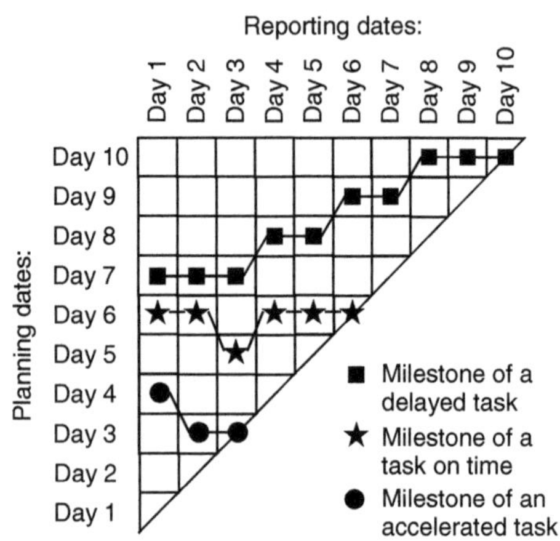

Fig. 6.20 Milestone trend analysis

milestones does not stay horizontal, the initial plan will not be met. If the course of milestones goes up, the completion of particular tasks will be delayed. If it goes down, these tasks will be completed even sooner than planned.

- The **cost trend analysis**, which can be visualized as shown in Fig. 6.21, helps to track the pattern of costs in order to understand possible trends. The planned costs are used as a baseline. The actual costs can be compared to this baseline so that deviations can be detected. Based on these deviations, trends can be anticipated and the necessity for appropriate countermeasures can be seen. In the visualization, the horizontal axis is used to represent the course of time and the vertical one to represent the amount of costs. Optionally, a second vertical axis can be added on the right side in order to represent the percentage of cost increases. Here, the value at the first data record is always 100 % because the cost increases are based on the comparison of the actual separate cost with the actual cumulated cost. At the first data record, both costs are equal.

If the actual cumulated cost significantly exceeds the baseline of the planned cumulated cost, major problems might have occurred. By analyzing the cost curve, it can be anticipated when the cost exceeds the budget. It will be particularly alarming if this is assumed to happen on a date way before the project is supposed to be completed. Besides, high cost increases can also be alarming, especially if they are connected with deviations between the actual and planned cumulated cost.

- In general, also the **quality** can be tracked with a trend analysis. Hereby, parameters that represent quality aspects must be identified. For example, the amount of errors during a software development project can be used as a

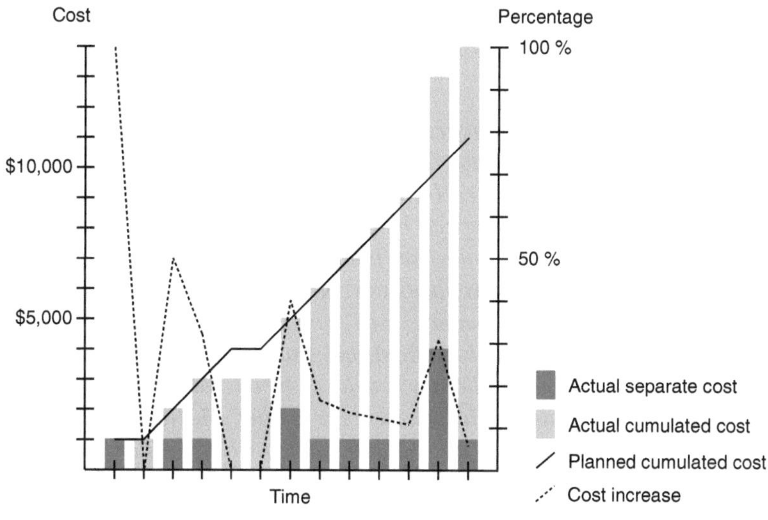

Fig. 6.21 Cost trend analysis

parameter. If the parameter values exceed or fall below certain threshold values, quality problems can be detected or anticipated. However, finding representative quality parameters can be very challenging. In contrast to the quality, the milestones and costs mostly provide very significant and clear indications.

Possible deviations from the plan should be **handled** systematically. Especially, the following points should be considering:

- At first, a deviation should be clearly **identified**. Thereby, the type of deviation, i.e. time, cost or quality issues, and the significance, i.e. the effect on the company, should be determined.
- Then, the handling of the deviation should be **organized**. For this, relevant stakeholders should be found and involved. For example, if the deviation is caused by cost increases, the involvement of an additional financial expert might be advantageous.
- With **short-term countermeasures**, further deviations from the plan can be avoided or, at least, tracked closely. For example, new expenses can be questioned and denied until further analysis. Workarounds, e.g. a new arrangement of tasks, can be used to avoid that a problem in certain tasks influences the whole implementation.
- With **long-term countermeasures**, the effect of actual deviations can be mitigated. Adjustments in plans or rules can improve the progress of the implementation. In the best case, not only further deviations are avoided, but also the remaining tasks can be performed more efficiently so that the overall deviation will not be as significant as assumed.
- By recording **lessons learned**, the experiences that were made during the handling of deviations can be documented. Thereby, the knowledge will not only be useable by the involved project members but also be saved in documents or databases that can be accessed by the whole company.

Case Study

The PSP performed the ***milestone trend analysis*** *at every business day during the implementation in order to monitor the project schedule.* Figure 6.22 *visualizes the milestones and their changes over 14 business days.*

The milestones were characterized by the following situations: The purchasing and documentation were performed as planned. The packaging was completed sooner as planned. However, problems during testing led to a delay of one day. Even the time saved in packaging was not sufficient to cover the delay. Consequently, the depended tasks rollout and training were also affected by the delay of one day. Besides, the rollout was delayed by one additional day because of suspected errors. The training started after the rollout. The training itself needed one more day because of two absent users due to illness. In sum, the whole implementation finished three days later than planned.

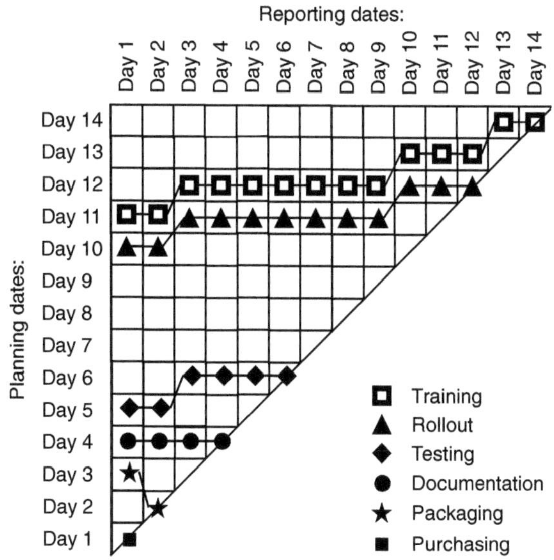

Fig. 6.22 Case study milestone trend analysis

The ***cost trend analysis*** *was conducted in order to monitor the cost behavior. As shown in* Fig. 6.23, *the actual and planned cost were compared over the 14 business days.*

As described in the milestone trend analysis, the packaging was completed sooner. It also led to a cost decrease of $1000 because the effort of one person-day was saved. However, the problems in testing incurred additional effort of $2000 because, on day 6, two additional person-days were used. The delay in training on day 13 was not accompanied by additional costs. In comparison to the planned cost, the final actual cumulated cost was $1000 higher. Several delays in scheduling also caused a later incurrence of cost. If only the cost curve had been considered, the problems in testing, which caused a delay at day 6, would not have been recognized until day 12. The packaging cost had been limited to $1000 instead of $2000. However, more effort in testing led to additional $2000 on day 6. Therefore, from day 4 to day 5, the actual cumulated cost was below the planned cumulated cost. Because of rollout delays, the cost was lower than planned from day 8 until day 12. The training on day 13 was postponed to day 14. In the case study, the cost trend analysis was not very useful because deviations were not seen until day 14—the last day of the implementation.

The ***deviation*** *in testing caused $2000 additional expenses and two more person-days of work for testing. Although the saved expenses and time in packaging partially reduced the overall impact on the implementation result, the problems in testing were handled seriously. They had been identified on the first day of testing. The problems had been addressed by assigning an additional senior test manager to the task. The subsequent short-term measures included a daily reporting to*

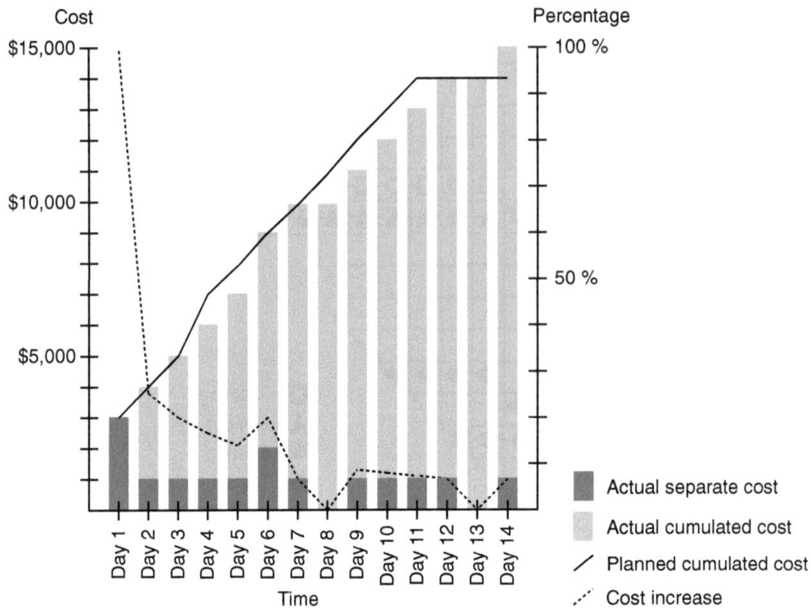

Fig. 6.23 Case study cost trend analysis

senior management and a new approval process for further expenses. In the long term, options for saving time or money were searched. Unfortunately, no options had been found. Therefore, the deviation had to be accepted. The lessons learned from testing were stored in the internal knowledge database of the company.

6.13 Closing

12.1 The successful implementation has been formally closed.

The **closing** comprises all activities to close the implementation of the selected safeguard formally. During the closing, the project manager will review the collected information about the implementation phase in order to check if the objectives have been met sufficiently. Thereby, he uses information from the planning step.

Important **information** from the implementation step has to be stored in the company. For example, documentation about packaging, testing etc. should be kept accessible by the company. Besides, valuable knowledge from the project progress and occurred problems, i.e. lessons learned, should be stored centrally in the company. Otherwise, this information would only be kept in the mind of the involved project members. In future projects with other members, collecting and sharing this information would be very time-consuming. Furthermore, knowledge in the mind of external or terminated employees can actually be lost from the view of the company.

In addition, relevant information should be kept in the **asset and configuration databases** of the company. New software or hardware that were purchased during the implementation of the safeguard should be recorded in appropriate databases. Only if the company has current inventory information, various questions, e.g. regarding capacity, security and dependencies, can be answered reliably. The configuration database also includes useful information that should be up-to-date. Thereby, the company infrastructure can be standardized and maintained more easily. Different configurations and subsequent operational problems can be avoided.

After the project manager ensured the success of the implementation and relevant information was updated, the outcome, e.g. the safeguard, has to be officially **accepted** by the sponsor of the project. Then, the implementation has been formally completed.

Case Study

Relevant information at the PSP that was stored during the closing included:

- ***Documentation**: The documentation that was stored and kept accessible in the long term was a combination of vendor documentation (user manual, administration manual) and internal documentation (package information, configuration, and usage policies).*
- ***Lessons learned**: The results of the performed trend analyses were stored. Especially, the milestone trend analysis combined with recorded deviations and selected countermeasures can be valuable for similar projects. In addition, details about handling the occurred deviations were recorded. The impact of related decisions was transparent for interested members of future projects.*
- *Update of the **asset database**: The new licenses for the software Alpha were recorded. Besides, others assets, in particular workstations and notebooks, that were related to the new software were marked.*
- *Update of the **configuration database**: The workstations and notebooks that were deployed with the new software were updated in the database. If certain parameters in the operating system or other software had been adjusted in order to make the new software ready for operation, details about this adjustment would have been stored in the database, too.*
- *Formal **acceptance**: The CIO took over the sponsorship. Therefore, he checked all relevant information from the preceding phases and, finally, accepted the completion of the project and its outcome in writing.*

6.14 Operation

13.1 The operation of the safeguard has been performed conscientiously.

The **operation** is important to detect, correct and eliminate possible disruptions that are related to or caused by the safeguard. The major tasks in the operation are the support of users in technical and functional topics, the monitoring of relevant events that indicate actual or future problems, and a proper change management.

- The **support** includes all kind of consulting services that help to improve the use or eliminate any problems. The supporter can be on-site at the user's location or off-site. In the latter case, he will communicate with different media, e.g. phone, e-mail or remote sessions. Mostly, tickets are used by the supporter for tracking and processing multiple user requests. Hereby, different priorities indicate how urgent the user needs help or how much the problem affects the company: The highest priority will be assigned if multiple users are affected by the problem and the effect on the value chain of the company is significant. The lowest priority will be assigned if a single user is just partially affected, but he can continue his work. The assigned priority influences the reaction and processing time of a ticket. Besides, these times can also be specified in service level agreements, which will be often used if the support is performed by an external service provider. Because different problems require different types of professionals, the support team can be divided into multiple sub-teams. Often, three levels of support are used: The first level support provides a first point of contact and records user requests. With a knowledge database, the supporters try to solve as many known problems as possible. The second level support is able to process more sophisticated requests or problems. New solutions are stored in the knowledge database. If the second level support does not find a solution, the third level support will search a solution. The third level is performed by highly skilled experts, e.g. software developers from the vendor of the related software or hardware. The primary goal of the support is the recovery of the affected business processes. Therefore, the fastest solution is often preferred. This solution can also be a workaround, which does not eliminate the source of the problem but helps to avoid its consequences. For example, problems with a web browser can be avoided by switching to an alternate software. The actual problem can be solved calmly without the pressure of disrupted business processes.
- The **monitoring** is based on comprehensive information from various databases and files in the company. If certain indicators are derived from the information, a problem possibly have been occurred or will occur in the future. Indicators represent information in a compressed and quantitative way. They can only show a limited aspect of the reality. Therefore, some indicators can only lead to assumptions that have to be proven or disproven after further analyses. If indicators exceed or fall below defined thresholds, countermeasures can be

initiated. With a continued monitoring, a change in indicators can prove if a countermeasure has been successful. Most companies use comprehensive collections of multiple indicators. In order to handle the indicators efficiently, a system of indicators should be established. This system helps to organize multiple indicators and to find relations between them.

- If changes are necessary, e.g. after user requests, a proper **change management** will be essential in order to avoid subsequent problems or misunderstandings. For example, chaotic changes can lead to inconsistent configurations, confused versions and unexpected problems from ignored interdependencies. A proper change management must exclude negative consequences to the business that are caused by changes. Therefore, new change requests must be evaluated and approved before implementation. Besides, a thoughtful planning should be conducted so that problems are avoided and crucial resources are available. After the implementation, the change should be reviewed and documented.

Case Study
At the PSP, the ***support*** *was implemented at two levels. The first level was provided by the internal IT department, which also was the first point of contact for problems with other products. Here, the supporters were skilled IT professionals, who were able to solve many user problems directly. They also used an issue tracking system in order to facilitate the systematic processing and documentation of issues. At the second level, the vendor provided a free technical support hotline. Problems that could not be solved internally were transmitted to the vendor.*

The ***monitoring*** *was performed by analyzing the windows event logs. Because errors, warnings and information from the software Alpha were stored in the logs, the company was also able to use a previously implemented central log system that automatically correlated and evaluated logs from multiple systems.*

Even before the new software was implemented, the company already used a systematic procedure to handle ***changes****. This procedure was derived from the change management process that is part of the ITIL (Information Technology Infrastructure Library) domain "service transition". All changes in the company, including possible changes of Alpha, were managed strictly after this procedure. Thereby, changes were properly evaluated and approved, and the occurrence of potential problems and misunderstandings were minimized.*

6.15 Maintenance

14.1 The safeguard has been maintained regularly.

Under **maintenance**, the adjustment of objects or safeguards that are already in operation can be understood. Maintenance is especially important in cybersecurity because, without maintenance, safeguards that have been implemented as part of a cybersecurity investment are often affected by a decrease in their protection level. For example, a firewall will be vulnerable if it is no longer supplied with updates that address new cyber threats. The reasons for maintenance are primarily eliminating errors, raising performance or achieving other improvements, and considering new environmental factors. In conclusion, maintenance can be distinguished in four types, which are also part of ISO/IEC 14764 (ISO 2006, p. 25). Although this standard is focused on software, the **maintenance types** can applied to other objects, too.

- **Corrective** maintenance will be performed if actual errors are identified and shall be eliminated. If an unscheduled modification is needed in order to keep a system operational until the corrective maintenance, this modification will be called emergency modification.
- **Preventive** maintenance aims at the elimination of potential errors that can possibly occur in the future. Although these errors are currently not an issue, they might influence the business processes in the future. Based on the evaluation of the risks that these errors will actually occur, the preventive maintenance can be focused on the highest risks first.
- **Perfective** maintenance is performed in order to achieve improvements regarding the performance or maintainability of the object. For example, the source code of a software can be adjusted in order to reduce processing times, or a hardware can be adjusted so that components can be installed or removed more easily.
- **Adaptive** maintenance is oriented on changed environmental factors. Mostly, certain new requirements shall be covered, e.g. related to new or updated laws and standards.

Regardless of the type of maintenance, all activities must not negatively affect the actual **stability**. Therefore, maintenance activities that disrupt the uptime of a system or service should only be conducted on redundant systems or during previously agreed maintenance windows. Besides, possible side effects of maintenance should be considered. Adjustments of programs, data and documentation can cause subsequent problems:

- If **programs** and related source code are adjusted, failures can significantly affect the future use. For example, the unintentional removal of essential code, changes in important execution parameters, and undesired behavior can be very problematic. Especially if these failures are not recognized in testing, major problems in vital business processes might occur.
- The **data** can also be very critical for the actual business. If overall database configurations or Meta data are adjusted imprudently, data might be deleted, corrupted or made inaccessible. For example, the adjustment of data ranges can lead to a removal of all values that do not fit into the new data ranges.

- Failures in **documentation** might not affect the operation immediately, but they will possibly cause major problems in the future. If documentation is not updated after the adjustment, users that need up-to-date user manuals, developers that work with code documentation, and database administrators that manage the databases under consideration of the documented dependencies might cause unintentional problems or outages. They would rely on documentation that does not reflect the current situation anymore.

Maintenance can be performed by internal or external **professionals**. Standard solutions that cannot be altered by the customer, e.g. closed source software, are mostly maintained directly by the vendor. At least, the vendor publishes updates that can be installed by the customer. In contrast, individual solutions can be maintained internally. If skilled employees are involved, sophisticated maintenance can be performed. For example, changes in source code or electronic devices can be very challenging. If maintenance is performed internally, the employees can be **organized** in a department or virtual team:

- A **department** is a permanent element of the organization with permanently assigned department members and dedicated budgets and objectives.
- A **virtual team** consists of members from various departments and teams, e.g. administrators, developers and testers. The members of the virtual team will only come together if obvious maintenance tasks are necessary. Primarily, they hold other positions in the company. Therefore, they are mostly busy performing their regular tasks. For a virtual team, maintenance is rather an additional activity that often has to stand back behind other tasks.

The steps of maintenance and **operation** are normally performed in an alternating way. After a certain operation time, maintenance starts. After a successful maintenance, the safeguard goes back into operation until the next maintenance activity will be needed.

Case Study

*The maintenance for the software Alpha was performed only externally by the **vendor**. Due to the closed source, maintenance would had been difficult to perform internally. The vendor covered the corrective, preventive, perfective and adaptive maintenance. He published new updates and releases to improve the software under different aspects, primarily security and functionality.*

*The software Alpha itself was not related to core processes of the PSP's value chain. Therefore, the **stability** was not obviously important. However, the software was installed on computers that were connected to significant systems, e.g. the online transaction processing (OLTP) system. Negative side effects would had disrupted or damaged the connected systems that were actually important. In order to prevent side effects, an internal testing and a systematic deployment of updates and releases were performed by the PSP.*

6.16 Termination

15.1 The safeguard has been terminated upon reasonable grounds.

In general, cybersecurity investments should be **terminated** if they do not deliver an appropriate protection level now or in the near future, or if they cause inacceptable costs. If the investment object is physical, it can be sold or scrapped. Besides, some virtual objects can also be sold, e.g. software licenses. The reasons that can lead to the termination of **technical safeguards** include, among other things, the following:

- Hardware can be affected by **ageing and wear-out**. Therefore, after a certain time, hardware should be replaced. If the hardware is used longer than the mean time to failure that was given from the vendor, the risk that major failures occur will increase exponentially. Occasionally, vendors also reduce the expected lifetime of products on purpose, e.g. by building in inferior parts. This is called planned obsolescence. Hereby, vendors try to induce the customers to purchase new products. This shall lead to higher sales numbers in the long term. Common failures in hardware can be found in:
- Wear-out of **rotating parts**: For example, cooling fans and hard drives are often stressed by environmental factors, like temperatures, vibrations or dust. Besides, if they are switched on and off frequently, the lifetime will strongly decrease.
- Normally, mainboards consist of multilayer **circuit boards**. If the mechanical stress while installing components, like random access memory, is too high, micro-fissures can occur. In addition, head causes mainboards to expand and cold causes them to shrink. Therefore, frequent switch-on and switch-off processes can also result in micro-fissures.
- Faulty electrolytic **capacitors**: On many electronic devices, a high amount of electrolytic capacitors has been installed. If they are inferior, under- or oversized, a failure will become very probable.
- Because of the increasing miniaturization of **integrated circuits**, the current density also increases. Therefore, the probability of electro migration becomes a high concern. Especially in central and graphical processing units, conductor tracks are very thin so that the temperature can increase over time. Possibly, conductor tracks can even blow.
- Externally purchased hardware and software that is no longer **supported** by the vendor can become unsuitable for business use. These products will no longer be supported even if potential problems or vulnerabilities arise. If they actually arise, the company that uses the products can find a workaround or alternative. However, it will not be able to react in a sufficient time so that business processes will be jeopardized. After the mainstream support ends, some vendors also offer an extended support, which might be restricted, e.g. to security related support. In addition, a customer-specific support is also provided by some

vendors. Here, only certain companies are supported after negotiating a dedicated support contract. This provides more flexibility to the costumers, but it is mostly accompanied by high support fees.

- All types of safeguards, even administrative ones, can be affected by significant changes of internal or external **requirements**. For example, organizational changes can lead to the elimination or outsourcing of departments or business processes. In result, related safeguards can become obsolete. Among other things, policies for the separation of duties within a business process that is no longer performed will be no longer needed. From outside the company, influences from customers or standardization bodies might lead to the situation that new or fundamentally changed safeguards are required.

Case Study

Because the safeguard in the case study happened to be a software, hardware-specific problems, i.e. ***ageing and wear-out****, were excluded. Of course, the computers that were needed to run the software were subject to these problems. However, in a narrower view, only software-specific problems were considered.*

The mainstream ***support*** *cycle from the vendor was regularly watched. Thereby, the PSP was able to notice possible decisions from the vendor regarding the continuation or discontinuation of the support. By taking into account these decisions, migrations to new releases or even an alternate software were considered reasonably. If the vendor had decided to discontinue the support and further development completely, replacing the software would have been the only acceptable way. Otherwise, the company would have faced severe problems in the software. For example, the encryption would have become useless if new efficient hacking approaches had been released.*

Besides, the ***requirements*** *for the software were possibly subject to change. If internal or external requirements had changed severely, the PSP would have depended on software modifications. For example, laws or standards could have been changed, e.g. the encryption requirements for payment card data according to PCI DSS. In result, the PSP would have been bound to new requirements that would have been supposed to be met by the software. Besides, internal conditions could have been changed. For example, the migration of all computers to another operating system, like a special Linux distribution, would have caused new compatibility requirements. Although the software Alpha generally supported Linux, it could have been incompatible with the selected distribution. If external or internal requirements had been changed and the vendor had not adjusted the software accordingly, the PSP would have requested a change at the vendor. Possibly, the vendor would have initiated the change on his own. Especially new requirements that had been valid for the whole market or industry sector would have already been considered by the vendor, who wanted to stay competitive.*

Chapter 7
Summary

7.1 Prerequisite Knowledge

A company that seeks an adequate protection in cyberspace must face the question which safeguard is the most appropriate to meet the individual profile of the company. Although performing a systematic approach is strongly recommended, it is not sufficient to focus only on this approach. Furthermore, a thorough understanding about cybersecurity should be obtained. If this **prerequisite knowledge** is combined with a systematic approach, the process of finding a safeguard will be strongly facilitated. Much effort can be saved by focusing on exactly the type of safeguard needed. Besides, the protection scope and decision problem should be specified in order to address the company's needs instead of chasing potential benefits that do not really fit to the company's profile.

In the following, the above-mentioned prerequisite knowledge from the previous chapters is summarized. **Figures** allow a quick overview of important key aspects. Here, also references to the previous chapters are given.

Before actually preparing a decision process for finding the most appropriate safeguard in which the company should invest, the **fundamentals** of cybersecurity should be understood—the principles, protection, stakeholders and safeguards.

The cybersecurity **principles** (see Fig. 7.1) describe the possible protection goals that a company might have. Knowing the principles is important for considering various aspects of protection and being able to specify the company's needs in cybersecurity protection. The principles are distinguished in basic and extended principles. Especially the **basic principles** should always be considered and understood by the decision maker:

- Confidentiality—the prevention that unauthorized persons or systems read sensitive information
- Integrity—the protection of information against damages and manipulations
- Availability—the assurance that functions are always provided as needed

S. Beissel, *Cybersecurity Investments*, Progress in IS,
DOI 10.1007/978-3-319-30460-1_7

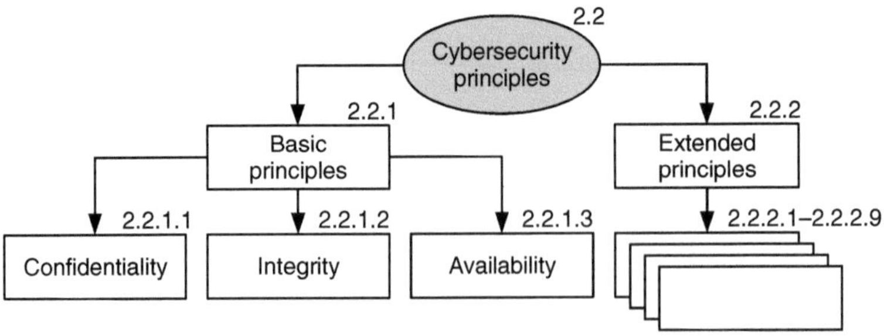

Fig. 7.1 Overview of cybersecurity principles (with chapter references)

The **extended principles** can be derived from the basic principles. Instead of being a steady consideration, they are rather defined when needed. Depending on the used sources, different collections and interpretations of extended principles can be found. Therefore, they should be precisely selected and defined if the company's expectations cannot be covered only with the basic principles.

Understanding the principles is also crucial for recognizing possible mutual **interferences**. Especially, the principles confidentiality and availability are mostly interfering. The more the confidentiality of data is protected, the higher is the risk that even authorized persons cannot access the data. For example, encrypting the data protects their confidentiality, but the key management is accompanied with additional risks to the availability. Losing the decryption key would block also authorized access attempts. Besides, the principle of integrity is often implemented with safeguards that create additional copies of the data in order to prevent uncorrectable damages. However, more copies mean more attack possibilities for hackers that want to read the data. Therefore, the confidentiality can be impaired.

From the various safeguards that can be purchased or developed, only a subset is actually useful for a specific company—the safeguards that provide an adequate **protection level** (see Fig. 7.2). In order to evaluate the usefulness properly within the decision making process, two basic perspectives must be covered: the

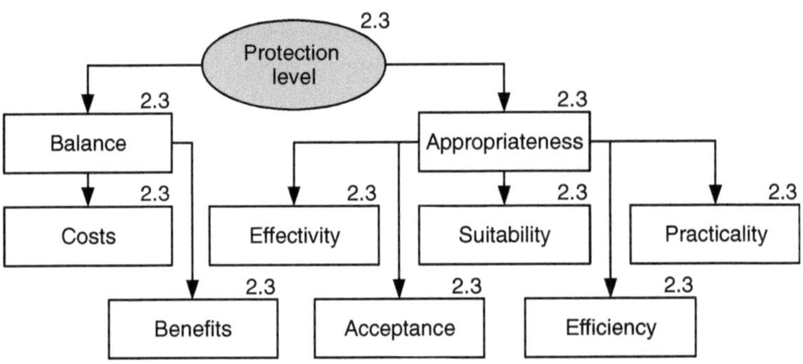

Fig. 7.2 Overview of protection level (with chapter references)

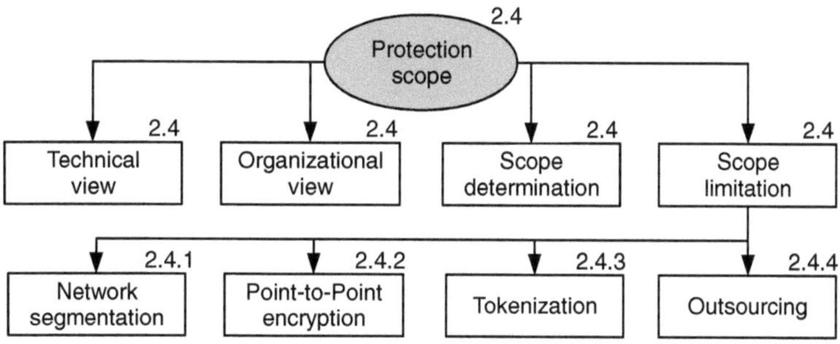

Fig. 7.3 Overview of protection scope (with chapter references)

cost-benefit balance and the appropriateness. If the costs of a safeguard are higher than the expected damages without this safeguard, the investment will make no sense. Besides, some safeguards might be inappropriate, e.g. because the users would not accept them.

The importance of the **protection scope** (see Fig. 7.3) should not be underestimated. On the hand, it must be **determined** and understood from the technical and organizational view before a safeguard can even be evaluated. Otherwise, crucial parts of the company's needs might not be covered with the selected safeguard. For example, if an encryption tool for Windows computers is selected by a company with many Linux computers, a high amount of computers that need protection cannot be covered. On the other hand, a high protection scope mostly leads to complex solutions and high costs. Therefore, a **limitation** of the scope is often the best way to handle cybersecurity efficiently. The saved effort in implementation, operation and maintenance can be tremendous. For example, if a company stores sensitive data everywhere, the scope will be much more difficult to cover than if the company uses exclusively a single dedicated file server for sensitive data. Knowing common limitation techniques, in particular network segmentation, point-to-point encryption, tokenization and outsourcing, can be very convenient for finding possibilities for an adequate scope limitation.

Powerful stakeholders might block crucial steps in a cybersecurity investment, e.g. the implementation of a safeguard or the completion of the decision making process. In contrast, they might support heavily criticized projects. Therefore, it would be negligent not to observe the **stakeholders** situation (see Fig. 7.4). An overview about common **cybersecurity stakeholders** facilitates an identification of

Fig. 7.4 Overview of stakeholders (with chapter references)

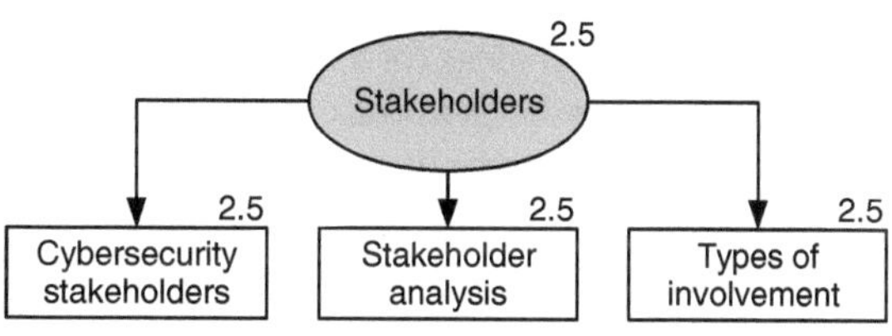

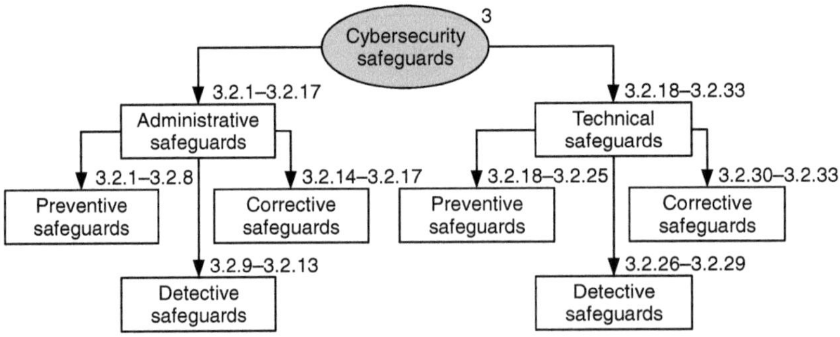

Fig. 7.5 Overview of cybersecurity safeguards (with chapter references)

company-specific stakeholders that can be relevant for cybersecurity investments. The stakeholder **analysis** is a systematic approach that shows powerful proponents and opponents. The types of **involvement** can be used to distinguish stakeholders and to influence them so that possible obstacles will be reduced.

Before the identification and selection of safeguards can be started, an understanding about the existing **safeguard types** (see Fig. 7.5) must be gathered.

- From the **functional** perspective, safeguards can be distinguished according to the integration of technical means. Safeguards that can be carried out without technical means are administrative, e.g. trainings, while safeguards that are supported or even enabled by technical means are technical, e.g. firewalls.
- Both types can further be distinguished from the **time** perspective. Preventive safeguards become effective before an event occurs, detective safeguards simultaneously to an event and corrective safeguards after an event.

If the decision maker is able to **distinguish** available safeguards according to these types, he will more easily find safeguards that really fit to the company and its needs. For example, a company that seeks full availability at all times would not be satisfied with detective and corrective safeguards because they only get active simultaneously or after the occurrence of a problem. Here, preventive safeguards would be the better choice because they get active before the occurrence of a problem.

Another strong reason for distinguishing safeguards is the huge amount of available solutions in the **market**. Only if the decision maker focuses on the type that is really needed, the huge amount of possibilities can be narrowed down to a more manageable number.

For all safeguard types, **common solutions** are described in the referenced chapters. Here, the decision maker can get a first impression of various options. Thereby, he can get ideas for a targeted search. For example, technically protecting sensitive data can be performed preventive (e.g. with encryption), detective (e.g. with intrusion detection) or corrective (e.g. with backups).

As mentioned before, the **economic aspects** (see Fig. 7.6) should be considered when selecting a safeguard. However, it is often unclear for the involved persons

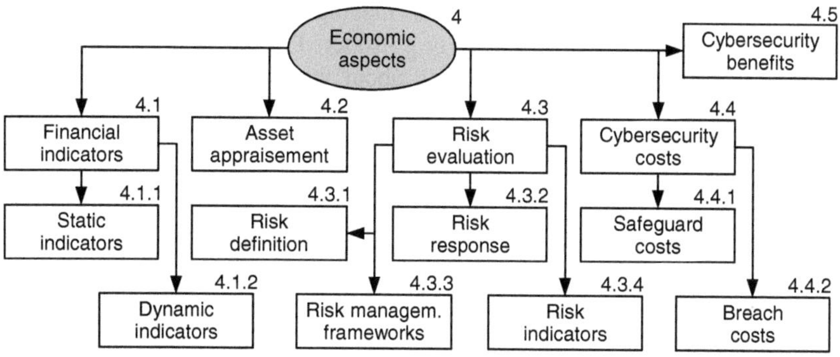

Fig. 7.6 Overview of economic aspects (with chapter references)

how this can be done exactly. Therefore, understanding various economic aspects is an important requirement for identifying reasonable attributes for the decision making. **Financial indicators** allow the calculation of values that represent different aspects in a monetary way, e.g. costs, benefits, and payment flows. The more sophisticated the calculation is, the more complex the indicators are. In particular, static indicators, like the return on investment, do not consider the time aspect. This is only covered by dynamic indicators, like the net present value. The measurement of **asset** values is needed for making a trade-off between the possible asset damages and safeguard costs. The **risk** that a breach occurs or an asset is damaged also has an economic relevance. In the risk evaluation, not only the damages but also the probabilities are considered. The risk definition provides the basic understanding around risks. Possible risk responses represent various approaches that a company can perform to handle the risks. These approaches are also part of multiple frameworks that provide systematic risk management approaches. The risk indicators help to express risks quantitatively or qualitatively. Besides, **cost** factors and collection methods are described with a focus on safeguard and breach costs. However, safeguards do not only incur costs. They also lead to **benefits** by reducing risks.

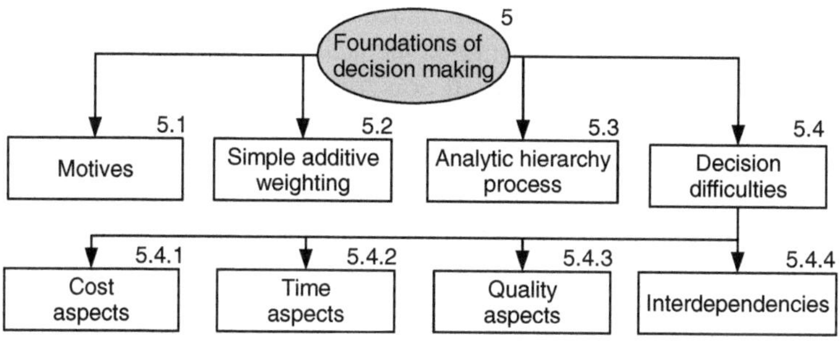

Fig. 7.7 Overview of foundations of decision making (with chapter references)

Before actually starting the decision making process, the **foundations of decision making** (see Fig. 7.7) should be considered. It can be a very helpful entry for the intended decision maker to think about the **motives** of a systematic and transparent decision making. Normally, only a proper and reasonable decision will be accepted by the stakeholders. In addition, knowing common techniques in decision making can reduce possible process flaws. Therefore, two common decision making techniques—the **simple additive weighting** and the **analytic hierarchy process**—are described in the referenced chapters. The first technique is easier to apply, but the second technique mostly delivers a higher quality. Considering possible **decision difficulties** can help to avoid problems or, at least, to reduce their impact. In particular, possible difficulties under cost, time and quality aspects as well as interdependencies should be taken into account.

7.2 Decision Making Knowledge

Sufficient knowledge about decision making shall enable the involved persons to perform the decision making process systematically, reasonable and flawlessly. With the **flowchart** in Fig. 7.8, the separate activities of the process are illustrated and combined with various outputs and different options.

In practical situations, the problem description is often too vague. For example, protecting sensitive data might seem to be a reasonable goal, but many open questions would occur in the process of achieving this goal. Among other things, it has to be determined which data are sensitive, how they should be protected and what kind of damages can possibly occur if the protection is not sufficient. It would be much better to answer these questions at the beginning so that back coupling and revision can be avoided. Therefore, the first step—the **decision problem identification**—aims at a thorough understanding of important preliminaries around the decision making. In particular, the strategy, scope, asset, risks, protection, technique and stakeholders are addressed. Thereby, a targeted process will be facilitated and the selected alternative will be best in matching the actual needs of the company.

The subsequent steps address the **decision making** in a narrower sense, i.e. identifications and evaluations that lead to a ranking of alternatives. Hereby, different techniques, standards and best practices can be considered in order to improve the outcome. How sophisticated the activities will be performed, strongly depends on the decision problem. If low risks shall be eliminated with less expensive safeguards, a complex and costly decision making process will not be reasonable. However, if the company's viability depends on a functional and reasonable safeguard, a more complex process will mostly lead to better outcomes, which can also improve the market situation of the company from the business perspective.

In the **attribute identification**, the decision maker must consider all relevant attributes that shall be used for evaluating the alternatives. Besides, he must specify precise value ranges and score assignments. The more sophisticated this step is

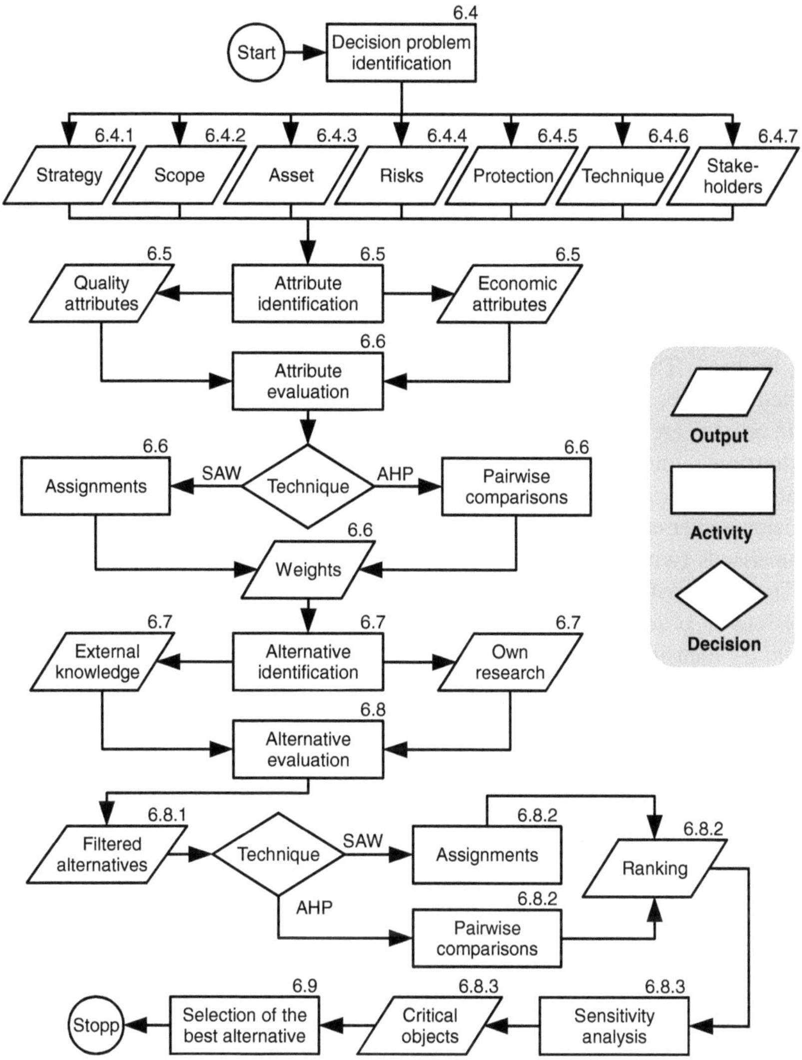

Fig. 7.8 Decision making flowchart (with chapter references)

performed, the more comprehensive and relevant the attributes are. Finding adequate attributes can be challenging. Generally, quality attributes and economic attributes should be considered. Starting points for the attribute identification can be relevant standards or best practices. In addition, the individual needs of the company should be represented sufficiently.

Identifying relevant attributes is still not sufficient for an evaluation of alternatives. Before this evaluation can be performed, the decision maker must also figure out how important the single attributes are. For this purpose, the **attribute**

evaluation is conducted. The outcomes are the weights that show how important each attribute is regarding the decision. Depending on the technique, weights can be determined with separate assignments or pairwise comparisons. Essential attributes can also be transformed into exclusion attributes, which will be used to filter all alternatives that do not meet the specified requirements for these attributes.

The **alternative identification** is a crucial step that would affect the decision quality strongly if it were not taken seriously. Briefly, the best alternative is just the best alternative from the pool of the previously identified alternatives. Therefore, excellent alternatives that were not identified before cannot be evaluated or selected. The outcome of the identification depends on the information that can be gathered about available alternatives. Hereby, external knowledge or own research results can be used. The more important the decision is, the more conscientiously the related activities should be performed.

In order to create a ranking that shows the best alternative on top, the **alternative evaluation** is needed. At first, the alternatives are filtered with the exclusion attributes. Then, the remaining alternatives get scores for the ranking. Again, the decision maker can choose between separate assignments (with SAW) and pairwise comparisons (with AHP).

The **sensitivity analysis** should always be performed in the case of complex decisions in order to identify and analyze the most critical evaluations and attributes. By focusing on these evaluations and attributes, a targeted quality check can be conducted. In addition, further analysis methods are available in some techniques, e.g. the consistency check that helps to assure reasonable evaluations in the AHP.

Finally, the best alternative—the alternative with the highest rank—can be **selected**. In particular, this is the alternative that meets the attribute requirements best from the group of all identified alternatives. Therefore, possible shortcomings in previous phases, e.g. missing alternatives in the alternative identification, can influence the final selection.

The decision making process must not be seen isolated. Moreover, it is an embedded part of an overall **lifecycle** of cybersecurity investments, as shown in Fig. 7.9.

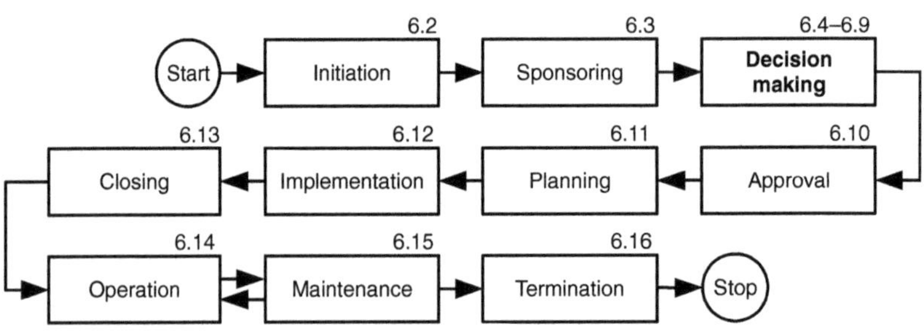

Fig. 7.9 Lifecycle flowchart (with chapter references)

If the preceding or following **steps** of the lifecycle are neglected, the decision making will not be effective:

- Without the **preceding** steps, the basis and support for the decision making will be missing. If the investment is not initiated and sponsored properly, the decision might not be accepted by essential stakeholders, e.g. the board of directors.
- Without the **following** steps, the decision making will be questionable or even pointless. Without an official approval, subsequent doubts and change requests from the stakeholders will be very likely. If the selected safeguard is not planned and implemented, the effort for the decision making will be in vain. The closing step helps to ensure the acceptance and transparency of the finalized implementation. A proper operation and maintenance are necessary to sustain the safeguard, which should be kept functional and effective continuously. Besides, the eventual termination should also be considered, e.g. if better alternatives are available.

7.3 Checklist

This checklist (Table 7.1) provides a concentrated guidance for professionals that prepare to walk through the whole lifecycle of a cybersecurity investment. Briefly, relevant questions for every step of the lifecycle are illustrated in order to ensure that nothing is overlooked in a practical application. Generally, all questions should be considered. However, very simple investments do not need to be covered by

Table 7.1 Checklist

No.	Question	Page	
Initiation			
1.1	The reason to initiate the cybersecurity investment has been found	164	☐
Sponsoring			
2.1	The sponsor for the cybersecurity investment has been confirmed	168	☐
2.2	The sponsor has been found suitable for the sponsorship	168	☐
Decision problem identification			
3.1	The strategy for the cybersecurity investment has been determined	173	☐
3.2	The asset to be protected has been identified	173	☐
3.3	The protection cause has been identified	174	☐
3.4	The protection goal has been specified	175	☐
3.5	The desired protection level has been found appropriate	175	☐
3.6	An adequate safeguard type has been chosen	176	☐
3.7	The number of desired safeguards has been determined	176	☐
3.8	The scope and its variability have been analyzed	177	☐

(continued)

Table 7.1 (continued)

No.	Question	Page	
3.9	The budget has been estimated	177	☐
3.10	The monetary goal of the cybersecurity investment has been defined	177	☐
3.11	The time-period for further analyses has been defined	178	☐
3.12	The scope for the cybersecurity investment has been determined	184	☐
3.13	The value of the assets that need protection has been calculated	192	☐
3.14	The risks have been analyzed	194	☐
3.15	The protection requirements for the assets have been specified	198	☐
3.16	An adequate decision making technique has been chosen	200	☐
3.17	Relevant stakeholders have been identified and involved	201	☐
Attribute identification			
4.1	Attributes that address company requirements have been identified	204	☐
Attribute evaluation			
5.1	The identified attributes have been evaluated	212	☐
Alternative identification			
6.1	Alternatives have been identified after collecting relevant knowledge	217	☐
Alternative evaluation			
7.1	The identified alternatives have been evaluated	223	☐
7.2	The identified alternatives have been evaluated with exclusion attributes	225	☐
7.3	The identified alternatives have been evaluated with comparison attributes	227	☐
7.4	The effects of changes in the evaluation have been analyzed	236	☐
Selection of the best alternative			
8.1	The strategy for the cybersecurity investment has been determined	238	☐
Approval			
9.1	The decision has been approved by senior management	240	☐
Planning			
10.1	The implementation of the selected safeguard has been planned	246	☐
Implementation			
11.1	The implementation of the safeguard has been performed and controlled	251	☐
Closing			
12.1	The successful implementation has been formally closed	256	☐
Operation			
13.1	The operation of the safeguard has been performed conscientiously	258	☐
Maintenance			
14.1	The safeguard has been maintained regularly	259	☐
Termination			
15.1	The safeguard has been terminated upon reasonable grounds	262	☐

every question, while very complex investments might lead to an expansion of these questions as needed.

References

AICPA (2002) AU Section 316—consideration of fraud in a financial statement audit. http://www.aicpa.org/Research/Standards/AuditAttest/DownloadableDocuments/AU-00316.pdf. Accessed 2 Jan 2016

Alberts CJ, Dorofee AJ (2001) OCTAVE criteria, version 2.0. http://resources.sei.cmu.edu/asset_files/TechnicalReport/2001_005_001_13871.pdf. Accessed 2 Jan 2016

Alberts CJ, Dorofee AJ, Stevens J, Woody C (2005) OCTAVE-S Implementation guide, version 1.0. https://resources.sei.cmu.edu/asset_files/Handbook/2005_002_001_14273.pdf. Accessed 2 Jan 2016

Barker EB, Barker WC, Burr WE, Polk WT, Smid ME (2012) Recommendation for key management—Part 1: general, NIST Special Publication 800-57, revision 3. http://csrc.nist.gov/publications/nistpubs/800-57/sp800-57_part1_rev3_general.pdf. Accessed 2 Jan 2016

Bleicher K (1991) Organisation: strategien—Strukturen—Kulturen, 2nd edn. Wiesbaden

Caralli RA, Stevens JF, Young LR, Wilson WR (2007) Introducing OCTAVE Allegro: improving the information security risk assessment process. http://resources.sei.cmu.edu/asset_files/TechnicalReport/2007_005_001_14885.pdf. Accessed 2 Jan 2016

Charnes A, Cooper WW, Rhodes E (1978) Measuring the efficiency of decision making units. European J Oper Res 2(6):429–444

CIS (2015) CIS Apple OSX 10.11 benchmark, v1.0.0. https://benchmarks.cisecurity.org/tools2/osx/CIS_Apple_OSX_10.11_Benchmark_v1.0.0.pdf. Accessed 2 Jan 2016

COSO (2004) Enterprise risk management—integrated framework, executive summary. http://www.coso.org/documents/COSO_ERM_ExecutiveSummary.pdf. Accessed 2 Jan 2016

Doran GT (1981) There's a S.M.A.R.T. way to write management's goals and objectives. Manage Rev 70(11):35–36

Federal Office for Information Security (2008) BSI-Standard 100-2—IT-Grundschutz methodology, version 2.0. https://www.bsi.bund.de/SharedDocs/Downloads/EN/BSI/Publications/BSIStandards/standard_100-2_e_pdf.pdf. Accessed 2 Jan 2016

Fishburn PC (1967) Additive utilities with incomplete product set: applications to priorities and assignments. Oper Res 15(3):537–542

Hwang C-L, Yoon K (1981) Multiple attribute decision making—methods and applications. A State-of-the-Art Survey, Berlin, Heidelberg, New York

Identity Theft Resource Center (2015) ITRC breach statistics 2005—2014. http://www.idtheftcenter.org/images/breach/MultiYearStatistics.pdf. Accessed 2 Jan 2016

Intel (2009) Prioritizing information security risks with threat agent risk assessment. http://www.intel.com/Assets/en_US/PDF/whitepaper/wp_IT_Security_RiskAssessment.pdf. Accessed 2 Jan 2016

ISACA (2012) COBIT 5—a business framework for the governance and management of enterprise IT. http://www.isaca.org/COBIT/Pages/COBIT-5-Framework-product-page.aspx. Accessed 2 Jan 2016

S. Beissel, *Cybersecurity Investments*, Progress in IS,
DOI 10.1007/978-3-319-30460-1

ISACA (2015) Risk management student book. http://www.isaca.org/restricted/Documents/Academic-Advocates/Risk-Management-Student-Book_res_Eng_0415.pdf. Accessed 2 Jan 2016

ISO (2006) ISO/IEC 14764, software engineering—software life cycle processes—maintenance, 2nd edn. http://www.iso.org/iso/iso_catalogue/catalogue_tc/catalogue_detail.htm?csnumber=39064. Accessed 2 Jan 2016

ISO (2011) ISO/IEC 25010, systems and software engineering—systems and Software Quality Requirements and Evaluation (SQuaRE)—system and software quality models. http://www.iso.org/iso/catalogue_detail.htm?csnumber=35733. Accessed 2 Jan 2016

Jones J (2005) An introduction of Factor Analysis of Information Risk (FAIR), Risk management insight. http://riskmanagementinsight.com/media/documents/FAIR_Introduction.pdf. Accessed 2 Jan 2016

Kaplan RS, Norton DP (1992) The balanced scorecard —measures that drive performance. Harvard Bus Rev 70(1):71–79

Marquis H (2008) 10 steps to do it yourself CRAMM. http://www.itsmsolutions.com/newsletters/DITYvol4iss50.htm. Accessed 2 Jan 2016

Nimwegen S (2009) Vermeidung und Aufdeckung von Fraud: Möglichkeiten der internen Corporate Governance-Elemente, Dissertation. Münster

NIST (2010) Guide for Applying the risk management framework to federal information systems —a security life cycle approach, NIST special publication 800-37, revision 1. http://nvlpubs.nist.gov/nistpubs/SpecialPublications/NIST.SP.800-37r1.pdf. Accessed 2 Jan 2016

OpenSAMM (2009) Software assurance maturity model—a guide to building security into software development, version 1.0. http://www.opensamm.org/downloads/SAMM-1.0.pdf. Accessed 2 Jan 2016

OWASP (2013) OWASP Top 10 2013—The Ten Most Critical Web Application security risks. http://owasptop10.googlecode.com/files/OWASP%20Top%2010%20-%202013.pdf. Accessed 2 Jan 2016

PCI SSC (2015) Payment Card Industry (PCI) data security standard—requirements and security assessment procedures, version 3.1. https://www.pcisecuritystandards.org/documents/PCI_DSS_v3-1.pdf. Accessed 2 Jan 2016

Peltier TR (2014) Risk Management: the facilitated risk analysis and assessment process. In: Peltier TR (ed) Information security fundamentals, 2nd edn. Boca Raton, pp 43–82

Resch O (2012) Stakeholdermanagement in IT-Projekten. In: Kammerer S, Amberg M, Lang M. (eds) Führung im IT-Projekt: Fachliche und soziale Kompetenzen für den Projekterfolg. Düsseldorf, pp 121–141

RIMS (2006) RIMS Risk Maturity Model (RMM) for enterprise risk management. http://rims.logicmanager.com/LogicERM/documents/rims_rmm_full_version.pdf. Accessed 2 Jan 2016

RIMS (2015) RIMS Risk Maturity Model. https://www.rims.org/resources/erm/pages/RiskMaturityModel.aspx. Accessed 2 Jan 2016

Roper C, Fischer L, Grau JA (2006) Security education, awareness, and training: from theory to practice. Burlington

Saaty TL (1994) How to make a decision: the analytic hierarchy process. Interfaces 24(6):19–43

Saaty TL (1996) decision making with dependence and feedback: the analytic network process. Pittsburgh

Saaty TL (2000) Fundamentals of Decision making and priority theory with the analytic hierarchy process. 2nd edn. Pittsburgh

Saaty TL (2001) Decision making with dependence and feedback—the analytic network process. 2nd edn. Pittsburgh

Symantec (2015) Internet security threat report, band 20. https://www4.symantec.com/mktginfo/whitepaper/ISTR/21347932_GA-internet-security-threat-report-volume-20-2015-social_v2.pdf . Accessed 2 Jan 2016

Westerman G, Hunter R (2007) IT risk: turning business threats into competitive advantage. Boston

Zelewski S, Peters ML (2002) Analytical Hierarchy Process (AHP)—dargestellt am Beispiel der Auswahl von Projektmanagement-Software zum Multiprojektmanagement, Arbeitsbericht Nr. 14. https://www.pim.wiwi.uni-due.de/uploads/tx_itochairt3/publications/bericht14.pdf. Accessed 2 Jan 2016

Index

S. Beissel, *Cybersecurity Investments*, Progress in IS,
DOI 10.1007/978-3-319-30460-1

MIX
Papier aus verantwortungsvollen Quellen
Paper from responsible sources
FSC® C105338
FSC
www.fsc.org

If you have any concerns about our products,
you can contact us on
ProductSafety@springernature.com

In case Publisher is established outside the EU,
the EU authorized representative is:
Springer Nature Customer Service Center GmbH
Europaplatz 3, 69115 Heidelberg, Germany

Printed by Libri Plureos GmbH
in Hamburg, Germany